"*Fresh expressions of church are multiplying at an extraordinary rate. Being Church, Doing Life is full of stories and lessons from this increasingly influential movement. This is a 'must read' for anyone serious about living out the Jesus Mission in everyday life.*"

– **Dave Ferguson, Lead Pastor, Community Christian Church, Chicago**

"*This book makes you think that anyone can do it, which of course is the whole point – you can!*"

– **Jonny Baker, Director of Mission Education, Church Mission Society**

"*Provokes us to search outside of the church walls, seizing opportunities for Christian witness. It will challenge your thinking and push you toward mission.*"

– **Ed Stetzer, President, LifeWay Research, US**

"*Wonderfully combines a depth of insight with a simplicity of practice which makes it a 'must read' for anyone wanting to start a witnessing community.*"

– **Dave Male, Director, Centre for Pioneer Learning, Ridley Hall, Cambridge**

"*Mike Moynagh is uniquely gifted as a visionary with a huge heart and intellect. The combination of his knowledge and enthusiasm will encourage and inspire you.*"

– **Revd Canon Phil Potter, Team Leader, Fresh Expressions UK and Archbishops' Missioner**

"*Shows how small witnessing communities, lovingly serving their neighbours, can offer a tantalizing 'taste of church' and intentionally plant signposts to Jesus. Read Being ̶C̶h̶u̶r̶c̶h̶, ̶D̶o̶i̶n̶g̶ Life for renewed vision!*"

– **Grace Sears, past president of ̶ ̶ of the King®**

"Mike Moynagh's lifetime work has been to assess the way the world is evolving and also how the church is evolving as a witnessing community. He shows how they can join up in practice in this book, which is peppered with stories. His characteristic skill is to pull together many strands, to distil wisdom from them and add that Moynagh dash of interpretative flavour. In a post-Christendom age, he shows how it is possible to put the church back in the public sphere through holistic service and Christ-centred witness. He longs to earth theory in practice and this book does just what the title says."

– **Canon Dr George Lings, Director, Church Army's Research Unit**

"This both sets a real challenge, and provides ample inspiration and encouragement to the church. A tremendously encouraging read."

– **Lesley Hamilton-Messer, Team Leader, Church Without Walls, Church of Scotland**

"Provides inspirational stories, practical insights and sound thinking to equip and encourage Christians to live out winsome and whole lives in the twenty-first century. Excellent stuff!"

– **Martyn Atkins, Chair of Fresh Expressions and General Secretary of the Methodist Church of Britain**

"Grounded in practical experience, this is a 'must read' for all who are passionate about seeing the church alive in the everyday."

– **Francis Brienen, Deputy General Secretary – Mission (designate) for the United Reformed Church**

"Explains simply how every Christian can be involved in effective mission. Let's read it together, apply it together, and see new dimensions of the life of Jesus transforming our networks and neighbourhoods with the yeast of the Kingdom!"

– **Bob and Mary Hopkins, Anglican Church Planting Initiatives**

"Offers both the whys and hows of developing 'witnessing communities', with many encouraging stories of people like you and me seeing gospel transformation as they step out on God's great adventure."

– Gareth Robinson, church planter and worship leader

"Mike Moynagh's insightful book extends our understanding of fresh expressions of church and puts the possibility of involvement within the reach of many Christians in their everyday lives."

– Rt Revd Graham Cray, Archbishops' Missioner and Leader of the Fresh Expressions Team 2009–2014

"Full of ideas to stir your imagination. Mike's wide knowledge of creative ideas for mission and evangelism helps the ordinary Christian to see their situation through new eyes."

– Revd Dr Martin Robinson, Together in Mission

"A thought-provoking, compelling argument as to how the church can expand its reach in an increasingly post-Christian society. Doing life in witnessing communities is what takes Jesus out of the sacred buildings. If the church desires to be a relevant force, we must learn to live as disciples who make disciples. This book is a true gift to the church."

– Rob Peabody, author, missional pioneer, and Director of Awaken Movement

Michael Moynagh has written the following for religious publishers:

Making Unemployment Work (Lion, 1986)
Home To Home: Understanding the Family (DLT, 1990)
Changing World, Changing Church (Monarch, 2001)
Liquid Worship (with Tim Lomax – Grove, 2004)
emergingchurch.intro (Monarch, 2004)
Church for Every Context (SCM, 2012)

In addition, Michael Moynagh is author or lead author of:
The State of the Countryside, 2020 (Report to the Countryside Agency, 2003)
Learning from the Future: Scenarios for Post-16 Learning (Learning & Skills Development Agency, 2003)
The Opportunity of a Lifetime: The Future of Retirement (Chartered Institute of Personnel & Development, 2004)
Working in the 21st Century (Economic and Social Research Council, 2005)
Going Global: Issues Facing the 21st Century (A&C Black/ Guardian Books, 2008)
Changing Lives, Changing Business: Seven Life Stages in the 21st Century (A&C Black, 2009)

BEING CHURCH, DOING LIFE

Creating gospel communities
where life happens

MICHAEL MOYNAGH

MONARCH
BOOKS
Oxford, UK & Grand Rapids, Michigan, USA

Text copyright © 2014 Michael Moynagh
This edition copyright © 2014 Lion Hudson

The right of Michael Moynagh to be identified as the author of this work
has been asserted by him in accordance with the Copyright, Designs and
Patents Act 1988.

All rights reserved. No part of this publication may be reproduced or
transmitted in any form or by any means, electronic or mechanical,
including photocopy, recording, or any information storage and retrieval
system, without permission in writing from the publisher.

Published by Monarch Books
an imprint of
Lion Hudson plc
Wilkinson House, Jordan Hill Road,
Oxford OX2 8DR, England
Email: monarch@lionhudson.com
www.lionhudson.com/monarch

ISBN 978 0 85721 493 5
e-ISBN 978 0 85721 494 2

First edition 2014

Acknowledgments
Scripture quotations are taken from The Holy Bible, New International
Version Anglicised Copyright © 1979, 1984, 2011 Biblica, formerly
International Bible Society. All rights reserved. Anglicised edition first
published in Great Britain 1979 by Hodder & Stoughton, an Hachette UK
company. This revised and updated edition published 2011.

The publisher has no responsibility for the persistence or accuracy of
URLs for external or third-party internet websites referred to in this
book, and does not guarantee that any content on such websites is, or will
remain, accurate or appropriate.

A catalogue record for this book is available from the British Library

Printed and bound in Great Britain by
Marston Book Services Ltd, Oxfordshire

To Liz

CONTENTS

ACKNOWLEDGMENTS

The heroes of this book are the thousands of people who form communities that actively witness to Jesus in everyday life. I have been inspired and educated by their stories, many of which appear in the pages that follow. Some of these stories have been told me in conversation, but most are documented, and in these cases I have provided a reference. The stories are, of course, snapshots in time and will have moved on since they were captured.

I am grateful to those who have commented on the emerging text and helped me to improve it: Emily Thrasher, Karen Carter, Vicky Cosstick, Dr Ed Stetzer, Bishop Graham Cray, Canon Phil Potter, and the Revds Andrew Roberts, Bob and Mary Hopkins, Dave Male and Norman Ivison. Any remaining shortcomings are mine.

I am grateful to the Commissioning Editor at Monarch, Tony Collins, for encouraging me to write the book, to Jenny Ward, who edited the text, and to the staff of Trinity School for Ministry, near Pittsburgh, who hosted a wonderful visit during which I met a number of exciting pioneers. I continue to learn a huge amount from the inter-denominational UK Fresh Expressions team, of which I am a member. I wrote the book at Wycliffe Hall, Oxford, where I have an enjoyable base. My biggest thanks, as ever, go to my wife, Liz, who has been an amazing support to me for over forty years.

Wycliffe Hall, Oxford, September 2013

FOREWORD

Something remarkable is happening in the Christianity of our times – the church is learning to innovate in new ways to express the love of God and people, and this is resulting in the creation of new forms of community. For instance, we are seeing gospel communities pop up in the context of the everyday life of people – in cafes, gyms, cafes, tattoo parlours, Laundromats, online gaming, and even in church buildings!

Freshly published research on the state of the church in the UK has now demonstrated for us how important this movement is becoming.[1] In it, the researchers have done a detailed study of nearly a quarter of the dioceses of the Church of England, Britain's largest denomination. What they have discovered is that "fresh expressions of church" now account for 15 per cent of the churches in these dioceses and represent approximately 10 per cent of the average weekly attendance. And what is especially remarkable is that most of these communities have only emerged over the past decade and are emerging now at an accelerating rate. This is very good news for a tired and outworn Christendom.

According to the leaders of these fresh expressions of ecclesia, only a quarter of those involved in the communities can be called regular churchgoing folk ("the churched"). A little over a third had stopped going to church ("the de-churched"), while an astonishing two fifths have little or no church background ("the un-churched"). Taken at face value, in terms of outreach and evangelism these new expressions of church must surely be

---

1 Church Growth Research Project, "Report on Strand 3b: An analysis of fresh expressions of Church and church plants begun in the period 1992–2012", October 2013, p. 6, available from Church Army Research Unit

considered our best chance for a renewed impact of the Gospel in the West.

This new wave of Christian mission is not unique to Britain. There are plenty of examples in North America, Australia and New Zealand, and growing interest in continental Europe. Three features, however, make the UK experience of particular significance and interest.

First, mainline denominations – initially the Church of England along with the Methodist Church – have taken the lead in encouraging these new Christian communities. Permission giving and some proactive leadership from the top have encouraged innovation at the grass roots, mainly by lay people – not insignificant given the clericalism associated with the mainline church. In the United States, by contrast, these new forms of church have tended to emerge outside the denominations. This is starting to change, however, as some North American denominations begin to welcome innovative approaches to church planting.

Secondly, extending the initial impulse by the two denominations, this new wave of mission in the UK has an increasingly trans-denominational flavour. More and more denominations are collaborating at a national level to encourage fresh expressions of church. Britain's Fresh Expressions team has members from not only the Church of England and the Methodists, but also – for example – the United Reformed Church, the Church of Scotland, and the Salvation Army. Some would say this collaboration is the most significant expression of practical ecumenism currently within the UK.

Thirdly, some of the observers of these fresh expressions have helpfully described the missional dynamics involved. After a process of listening to the context, the core team often begins by loving and serving the people it feels called to reach. A community gathers around this loving and serving, and within it people are signposted to Jesus. Individuals who want are offered opportunities to explore what it would mean to follow Christ, and church takes shape among those who come to faith. In some cases, this journey is repeated by the new Christians.

This turns the conventional approach to church planting on its head. Public worship comes near the end of the journey rather than the beginning. Indeed, the entire process is more organic, experimental, incarnational, local, and often smaller in scale than the more formulaic approaches of traditional church planting.

Despite these exciting developments, many in the UK would be quick to say that the garden remains far from rosy. Overall, the church continues to shrink at a faster rate than the numbers being added through these new Christian communities. Furthermore, how far will the historic, and more institutional, structures be able to contain this burst of Christian energy? Will the new wine of innovation burst the traditional wineskins of the denominations? Will the prevailing structures adapt fast and radically enough to embrace what is happening on the ground? Or will the pioneers of these new communities draw together for mutual support in networks that become increasingly detached from the mainline churches?

Whatever the answers, there is little doubt that we are witnessing a highly significant movement of God, not just in the UK but in North America and elsewhere. Is the Holy Spirit once more laying the foundations for a dramatic rebirth of the church in shapes that we have never seen before? I personally find myself feeling somewhat optimistic.

If you want to know more about this move of the Spirit, and in particular how you and your Christian sisters and brothers might get involved, then this really practical and well articulated book is for you. Its message is as simple as it is strong: find one or two other Christians in a segment of your life – a network of friends, a passion that you pursue, your workplace or neighbourhood. Ask

God to show you some simple ways to serve the people around you and in due course to share the gospel with them. Then see what God does.

Laced with over 120 real-life examples, Michael Moynagh adeptly sets out a new approach to mission in the local church, based directly on witnessing communities in everyday life. He joyfully describes easy ways for ordinary Christians to start these communities and turn them into hubs for making disciples. He shows how local church leaders, especially those called to a "pastoral" ministry, can encourage their congregations to get behind these communities and so join in with what God is doing in our time.

I am grateful that this very practical book has deep Biblical roots. Its theoretical and theological background lies in his rather weighty and complex previous book, *Church for Every Context*. I encourage leaders to study that book as well. Both help to change the missional conversation by shifting attention from how Christians can witness as individuals to how they can witness as small Christian communities. It is radical stuff. But it is not theory. It is based on what a growing number of Christians are doing right now.

So if you want to tear down the disconnect between church and life, if you want to find exciting and do-able ways to add kingdom value to your passion and if you want to witness to Jesus with other Christians rather than on your own, I warmly commend *Being Church, Doing Life*.

Alan Hirsch
Founder of Forge Mission Training Network and author of *Untamed*, *The Faith of Leap*, *The Forgotten Ways*, *The Permanent Revolution*, and many other award-winning books on missional Christianity.

INTRODUCTION –
WANTING TO MAKE A
DIFFERENCE

"Ministers are desperate to work out how to encourage their members to make an impact for God in the world," a colleague told me. "Most have little idea how to get started."

Maybe you are one of those leaders, or one of those members your minister feels desperate about! You love God. You have met Jesus in worship and through the ministries of other Christians. You have encountered the Holy Spirit and seen how God can change people's lives.

You are inspired by Scripture, and in particular by the kingdom's potential to transform life. You carry this hope with you as you seek to follow Jesus at home, at work, and in your networks.

But there is so much more to the biblical vision that you pray for. If only the blessings you have experienced could ripple out to others! You can't wait for the church to make more of a public difference – to enrich people and bring the gospel to them.

You realize that the church is surrounded by an ocean of social change. Yet you long for it to find new ways of connecting with the twenty-first century and to speak a language that reaches contemporary people.

Or perhaps your life stretches ahead. You are full of hope about making an impact. But you are also anxious – like the 22-year-old who had graduated with a good degree, landed a stellar job, and then imagined the treadmill ahead.

"Life isn't only about making money, is it?" she asked. She wanted to make a difference, but feared the tramlines of a conventional life.

Or are you worried about student debt, getting a job, having any sort of career, and climbing onto the housing ladder? The internet gives you a big platform to address the world, but will you do enough for anyone to listen?

Or maybe you can empathize with some of the readers described by the editor of a large Christian magazine. "If I could peep behind your readers' masks," I asked him, "what would be their top feeling about the Christian faith?"

Without hesitation he replied, "Disappointment."

Among their chief disappointments: a sadness that their lives are not making a bigger difference. They go through the same Christian routines. They go to church regularly. They try to live out their Christian faith. But, if they died tomorrow, there would not be much to fill an obituary. They would leave no mark on the trajectory of life. Rather than shaping the world, they suspect they have been shaped *by* it. They started life hoping to make a difference, but have seen the dream fade. Is it too late to dream once more?

Perhaps you have heard reports of a new movement that is engaging people beyond the church in the many settings of today's world – that is finding new ways of being church while doing life. Might this be what you have longed and prayed for? Could you become part of it?

Making a difference gives meaning to life, which is vital for human well-being. A 2013 study of nearly 600 Americans found that meaningful activity meets some of our core psychological needs.[1] Three are especially important:

- Competence – mastering an activity.

- Relatedness – being connected to others.

1 Aaron M. Eakman, "Relationships Between Meaningful Activity, Basic Psychological Needs, and Meaning in Life: Test of the Meaningful Activity and Life Meaning Model", *OTJR: Occupation, Participation and Health,* 33 (2), 2013, pp. 100–109.

- Autonomy – being in control of your life.

Making a difference to other people enables you to meet these needs. You show that you are competent, you enter into a relationship with others, and by acting out of choice you demonstrate that you are in control.

To suspect that you are not making a difference is to wonder "Am I effective?" "Do others value me?" "Am I powerless?" It is to stare into the abyss of "I don't matter."

A distinctive witness?

For a Christian, not making an impact can feel especially uncomfortable. You know you are called to live distinctively and bring good news to others.

You might describe this as being salt and light in the world, or being a loving presence, or witnessing to Jesus, or living out the kingdom of God, or seeing what the Spirit is doing and joining in.

Yet, when you review your life, you feel dissatisfied with the amount of difference you make. Perhaps feeling powerless is what holds you back. Problems in the news seem way beyond your ability to help. The achievements of celebrities leave you murmuring, "I could never do that." You feel like an insignificant brushstroke on a huge landscape. Your energy ebbs away.

Feeling powerless has many roots. One is our increasingly organized world. The number of organizations has leapt dramatically, whether it be registered companies in California (up fivefold between 1960 and 2001) or international non-governmental organizations, which grew from 176 worldwide in 1909 to over 44,000 almost a century later.[2]

---

2 Gili S. Dori, John W. Meyer & Hokyu Hwang, "Introduction" in Gili S. Dori, John W. Meyer & Hokyu Hwang (eds), *Globalization and Organization*, Oxford: OUP, 2006, pp. 2–7; Sara McLaughlin Mitchell, "Cooperation in World Politics: The Constraining and Constitutive Effects of International Organizations", paper prepared for presentation at the 2006 International Studies Association meeting in San Diego, California, p. 1.

Organizations are reaching into the informal parts of everyday life, even into childcare through pre-school nurseries. The voluntary sector is less informal. Nearly all the decisions that shape daily life are taken by organizations – by marketing companies, corporations, the media, governments, regulatory authorities, schools, hospitals, and many others. Though social media are empowering individuals in new ways, organizations still grip our lives.

Organizations themselves feel more organized – more regulations, more targets, and more accountability. British sociologists Paul Heelas and Linda Woodhead refer to the iron cage of "the targeted life". Individuals have become imprisoned by targets at work.[3]

At the same time, more organizations mean more choice and more opportunities – more activities, for example, for your family to choose from. Life becomes increasingly frenetic as you try to squeeze everything in. Whether it is ferrying children from one venue to another, killing yourself to meet a deadline at work, or burning out for your church, organizations drench you in a hailstorm of demands. You don't have the time or the stamina to make a big difference to your world.

Gathered for worship, scattered for life?

The way most Christians witness in ordinary life compounds this struggle to make an impact. Think about what happens now: as Christians, we come together for Sunday worship. Then we re-enter the world as individuals. Through the week at work, among families and friends, and in our leisure pursuits, we witness to Jesus mainly on our own.

Of course, we are sustained by the worship and prayers of the congregation, and by the fellowship of believing friends and

---

3 Paul Heelas & Linda Woodhead, *The Spiritual Revolution: Why Religion is Giving Way to Spirituality*, Oxford: Blackwell, 2005, p. 128.

relatives. We may also engage in the outreach programmes of our local church.

Despite this, the perceived experience of most churchgoers is that, having assembled for worship, we disperse as individuals – as Christians witnessing on our own – for the rest of the week.

Especially if we are in a part of the world where the church is strongly in retreat, we may look round our workplaces or apartment blocks and ask, "Is anyone else here a Christian?" Believers gather for support, but scatter to witness.

This gathering and scattering is so deeply ingrained that we seldom question it. Yet, alongside it, a different approach to making a difference is starting to emerge.

Usually in small groups, Christians are gathering in pubs, cafés, workplaces, friendship networks, and neighbourhoods to serve the people around them and to share the gospel.

Lunch by the gym

One group set up a monthly women's luncheon club in a centre for gym and other activities. The women have a good lunch and hear a talk on the theme of "fit lives". One woman described how she led a fit life while raising a child with a disability. The speakers are all Christians, so they include how Christ has helped them.

The lunch is held in an upstairs venue with large glass windows. Other people can see what is going on. The women are given a bunch of flowers. As they leave the centre, people arriving ask where the flowers came from. The response is an invitation to the next lunch!

Forty to fifty not-yet Christians attend regularly. The centre's manager tells his colleagues in other centres, "It's great for business!"

Catching on

Lubo and Dasa Badiar are lay members of the Lutheran Church in Slovakia. Decades of Communist rule had a destructive influence on families and contributed to a serious decline in church attendance, which is confined largely to Sundays.

Living in the second city of Košice, Lubo and Dasa caught a mission vision from the cell-church movement. But, as they listened to God and their context, they adapted it. They started a midweek "Family Fellowship" to rebuild family life around Jesus and the Bible.

It worked! Their community among family and friends outside church flourished. So they passed the concept on to other couples, who caught the model and took it to their family groups. It has proved remarkably successful. Over the next few years the idea has multiplied into a movement of literally scores of Family Fellowships across the nation.

Turning small groups inside out

In North America and the UK, a growing number of churches have launched mid-sized communities, sometimes known as missional communities.

Unlike typical small groups in church, each community exists to serve a specific neighbourhood or demographic outside the congregation's reach, such as children with disabilities, young adults at work, and people with an interest in justice or environmental issues.

In effect, the groups form small weekday congregations: they typically meet several times a month for mission and worship, while joining with their parent church on one or two Sundays in four.

St George's, Deal, England has found that these communities have released forty new lay leaders, a huge number for a UK

> *church.[4] The first community, Stepping Stones, focused on the families of pupils at the local school. They held parties in the school, beach outings, a weekend camp and an introduction-to-Christianity course for families. The community has been so fruitful that they have started a second one.*

By 2010, in just three years, 3DM – which encourages missional communities – had been involved in starting 725 new churches on both sides of the Atlantic. Most of these were mid-sized communities.[5]

These and other what I call "witnessing communities" enable followers of Christ to witness not on their own, but shoulder to shoulder. Faced by an organized world, Christians stand together for Jesus.

Three words encapsulate the nature of these groups:

- *Community.* Whatever the group's size, Christians make Jesus public in day-to-day life by sharing their lives in community. These communities normally have a core of believers, who draw others in by loving and serving them and sharing the gospel.

- *Visibility.* The groups meet not mainly for Bible study and prayer, but to serve people in the context and make Jesus known to them. Prayer and study occur in the slipstream of witness and energize it. Church is no longer something "over there". For people in the setting, church is right here, on their turf, intensely visible.

- *Activity.* These groups do more than support their members in personal witness. The community witnesses as a group. Members do things together to show others around them the love of Jesus.

---

4 www.freshexpressions.org.uk/stories/stgeorges (accessed 11 September 2013).

5 Mike Breen & Alex Absalom, *Launching Missional Communities A Field Guide*, 3DM, Kindle version, 2010.

Individuals are coming to faith and finding their lives changed. Luke, for example, started dealing in cannabis when he was fourteen, and by nineteen had a really bad cocaine habit:

I had a heart attack at the age of twenty, induced by an overdose, and then shortly after that I started taking heroin… I got to the stage where I feel that God actually brought me to such a level that I had no other option but to cry out to him and ask for his forgiveness. Being with… the rest of the people in the project: they actually helped me through my withdrawals as I'd started to come off methadone. They prayed me through it and I do know for a fact that it was nowhere near as bad as what it should have been. That was the power of God in my life: to help me through that struggle.[6]

Being Church, Doing Life is about how ordinary Christians and local churches can start and develop these witnessing communities. The next three chapters tackle the question "Why?", and include a galaxy of stories to whet your appetite. You will see that these communities are not an occasional phenomenon. They seem to be the vanguard of a new movement.

Chapters 4 to 7 offer some tools – not rules – for developing these communities. The two chapters that follow describe how local churches, denominations, and networks can encourage witnessing communities, while Chapter 10 unlocks the key to success.

All round the world Christians are bursting out of the local church, not to replace it but to start alongside it, in everyday settings, communities that touch the heart, lift life above the normal, and put Jesus on display. Whether you are a church leader or a churchgoer, you too can be involved.

---

6 www.freshexpressions.org.uk/stories/grafted/luke (accessed 16 December 2013).

PART ONE

Why communities in life?

Chapter 1

COMMUNITIES IN LIFE

> In Ajax, a Toronto suburb, Ryan Sim is working with others on "Redeem the Commute", a mobile app and website for nearby commuters.
>
> Busy young professionals often see the commute as wasted time. To help them redeem this time and make positive changes, Ryan plans to deliver good-quality content to their smartphones, starting with marriage and parenting courses. A Christian Basics course will introduce the Redeemer himself, followed by daily discipleship content for those walking with Jesus.
>
> The aim is not to start a virtual church, but to bring young professionals together in a dispersed form of cell church. Participants who start a course on their own will be encouraged to join a discussion group, meeting weekly in places such as trains, buses, workplaces, and homes.
>
> Churchgoers in the area will seed these new groups, which will be organic and self-organizing, centred on the gospel, and supported with coaching, oversight and regular visits from staff.[1]

This may be light years from your experience of outreach and church. But it is the tip of an iceberg, one example among thousands of how Christians are increasingly sowing the gospel in innovative ways.

---

1 www.freshexpressions.org.uk/stories/redeemerchurch (accessed 30 April 2013).

A new trend

To ignore what these Christians are doing would be to overlook signs of a new mega trend. It would be to bat away the Spirit's call for individuals and the local church to reach out through witnessing communities in daily life. It would play down how ordinary Christians can take the lead.

Across the world

Hold your breath! A remarkable transformation is sweeping across the church. In North America, Europe, Australia, New Zealand, and elsewhere, new expressions of Christian community are beginning to emerge.

In extraordinary research, Dr George Lings of the Church Army Research Unit has examined in detail ten Church of England dioceses. "Fresh expressions of church" – new types of Christian community – comprise as many as 15 per cent of the dioceses' churches and 10 per cent of their average weekly attendance. According to their leaders, roughly 25 per cent of those who come are Christians, 35 per cent are once-churched (people who had stopped going), and an amazing 40 per cent are never-churched. The numbers involved add the equivalent of one further average-sized diocese.[2]

Even more astonishing has been the pace of growth. The great majority of these churches have come to birth within just the last ten years.

Lings' research merely scratches the surface. The Methodists and other UK denominations have also seen an upsurge of these new communities. In addition there are Christians who are starting witnessing communities without using the fresh expressions label, such as North Americans who identify with

---

2 Church Growth Research Project, "Report on Strand 3b: An analysis of fresh expressions of Church and church plants begun in the period 1992–2012", October 2013, p. 6, available from Church Army Research Unit.

Forge International, 3DM or Church Multiplication Associates, founded by Neil Cole.

Cole, for instance, believes that church should happen where life happens. The movement of which he is part was launched in 2002. It planted ten churches in its first year and over 100 in the fourth, and has multiplied to thousands of churches "where life happens" today.[3]

On top of these are people who are starting communities without identifying with a denomination or network, such as the young couple who said to me, "We seem to be doing what you describe. We live in a poor neighbourhood, we've got to know some of the local teenagers, they now meet in our sitting room, and a kind of church is beginning to happen."

These new types of community are not confined to the "global North". They are beginning to emerge in Barbados, Chile, South Africa, and elsewhere. Through them, individuals are finding faith.

> One man was brought by his girlfriend's grandma to help out on one of the craft tables in an all-age example of these communities. He had no church background and was quite nonplussed by Christianity when he first came. He was not interested in church but was willing to get involved in this new expression of Christian community.
>
> He came along again and wanted to help. The leaders then started the Journeys course and he decided to attend. "He was a bit into space life and belief in other things out there... not sure what, but couldn't grasp Christianity. He is now wanting baptism."[4]

3 Ed Stetzer & Warren Bird, *Viral Churches: Helping Church Planters Become Movement Makers*, San Francisco: Jossey-Bass, 2010, p. 119.

4 www.messychurch.org.uk/messy-blog/discipleship-input (accessed 6 Sept. 2013).

We are at the frontier, it seems, of a new wave of Christian outreach and impact.

From church plants to intentional communities

This new work of the Spirit builds on a long tradition of church planting. In the global North, one planting model was for a local church to reach out for the kingdom by sending a sizable team to an area with little church presence.

The team made contact with people who were in limbo between churches or who used to attend church and were open to going again. (Reaching lapsed churchgoers was not always the intention, but was often the result.) When enough relationships had been built, a new congregation was launched based on these contacts.

Many of these plants were replicas of successful churches or upgrades of existing church for Christians who were dissatisfied with the offerings elsewhere. Yet, as populations in the global North have pulled away from the Christian faith, clones of existing church have had – with some exceptions – a diminishing impact on people outside.

Partly in response to the limitations of traditional church plants, recent years have seen the mushrooming of intentional Christian communities. These communities look rather different from conventional church. They are church, but not as we have known it. They serve people whom traditional churches and church plants do not reach.

Some are connected to an existing church. They work with homeless people, serve the residents of an apartment block, enable the "late middle-aged" to get to know each other, teach English as a second language, or equip young people for work. In the process, openings are created for individuals to explore Jesus.

St Paul's, Shadwell, in the East End of London, is a church plant from Holy Trinity, Brompton. Members of the congregation have now formed several new communities to serve demographic groups or geographical areas unreached by the new church.

One group has run a money management course for the local Bangladeshi population; another has facilitated a parenting support group, while a third has organized events on contemporary issues for young adults in a pub.

The church's leaders pray that some of these communities will grow and spawn further communities, which will multiply again. They seek to "plant pregnant churches".

Other communities are coming to birth beyond the orbit of the local church.

A young Brazilian man described his passion for surfing. The tussle between beach and church was a no-brainer. The beach won! But one day, as the evening was drawing in, one of his friends invited him to a group on the edge of the beach. It was a surfers' church, complete with surfboard as altar. He now attends regularly.

There are over 300 such churches in Brazil, and an international network. In 2013 one of the Brazilian churches launched an offshoot in Hawaii.

Accidental communities

Alongside these intentional communities is a further development – communities that have sprung up almost accidentally, without a great deal of forethought. These involve Christians who never planned to lead a gospel community in ordinary life but ended up doing precisely that.

Hot Chocolate, for instance, started in 2001, when a small group of volunteers went out to meet some of the young people in the heart of Dundee, Scotland. That was their only agenda. The volunteers took hot chocolate with them and the young people started calling the encounters "Hot Chocolate". The name stuck.

Within a few months, some significant relationships had developed. The volunteers began asking, "If you had a bit of space in the church building, what would you do with it?" The young people replied that they wanted rehearsal space and somewhere they could crash out and be themselves.

So it was that some thrash metal bands came to rehearse in the sanctuary of the church, and a space that the young people could call "home" was created within the building. Everyday life invaded the church.

Hot Chocolate has grown organically and sees itself as a community. It now has six paid staff (two full-time) and over a year works with about 300 young people, many from difficult backgrounds.

A number have found faith, often as they join the team and experience Christianity more explicitly. One young person started coming when he was thirteen or fourteen, found Jesus, and became a key volunteer.

Team members tend to describe their "church" as gathering round the dinner table three times a week. Worship, which includes a devotion, has evolved in response to the young people and the Spirit's promptings.

"In a way," says team member Charis Robertson, "everything that has happened so far in the way of church community is completely accidental."[5]

---

5 www.freshexpressions.org.uk/stories/hotchocolate (accessed 6 September 2013).

These intentional and "accidental" communities are what I call "witnessing communities". As I said in the Introduction, three words sum them up:

- *Community.* Christians prayerfully band together in small and sometimes larger groups.

- *Visibility.* These communities are present in everyday life, helping to make the kingdom tangible to ordinary people.

- *Activity.* They go beyond prayer support for their members. As groups, they launch initiatives to serve and share the gospel with others nearby.

Community

Witnessing communities have their roots in Scripture. God does not expect individuals to make a difference for him on their own. He wants them to work in teams. In Genesis 1 and 2, the creation mandate is given to the man and the woman together.

Adam and Eve were placed in a beautiful garden. They were to extend its boundaries till paradise stretched over the whole planet (Genesis 1:26). They were to do this as a team. "It is not good for the man to be alone," God said. "I will make a helper suitable for him" (Genesis 2:18).

When things went wrong, God did not adopt an individualistic approach to salvation. He called Abraham and Sarah's household and turned it into a nation. Through this community, God would bring salvation to the world.

The first thing Jesus did in his public ministry was to assemble a community of disciples. When he taught them how to "do mission", he sent them out not as individuals but in pairs. Karl Barth, the great Swiss theologian, said that Jesus would not be who he is if he lacked his community and if this community lacked a missionary character.[6]

Paul followed Jesus' example by travelling with a team on his missionary journeys. As the teams grew in size, members joined or left frequently in pairs – Silas and Timothy in Acts 18:5, Timothy and Erastus in Acts 19:22, and presumably Paul and Luke in Acts 20:6.[7] Central to Paul's approach were mini-communities.

God's process fits his purpose

God does mission through communities. This is hardly surprising, because God himself is community. He is three persons, Father, Son, and Holy Spirit, who are also one. God is the divine "communion-in-mission".[8] Channelling salvation through communities is an expression of his fundamental character.

Through Christ, God is bringing into being a new community, in which "all things" will be reconciled (Colossians 1:20). Church is a glorious outpost of this new community, "an embassy of heaven".[9]

When we become Christians we are given an identity in Jesus – we are in Christ. Being in Christ is not being in him alone, but being with all others who are in Christ. We belong to God's family. The loyalties of this new community supersede even the loyalties of biology (Matthew 10:34–37).

"Church is not another ball for me to juggle, but that which defines who I am and gives Christlike shape to my life."[10] Church

---

6 Quoted by John Flett, *The Witness of God: The Trinity, Missio Dei, Karl Barth, and the Nature of Christian Community*, Grand Rapids: Eerdmans, 2010, p. 218.

7 Bob Hopkins, *Church Planting 1. Models for Mission in the Church of England*, Bramcote: Grove Books, 1988, p. 12.

8 Stephen B. Bevans & Roger P. Schroeder, *Constants in Context: A Theology of Mission for Today*, Maryknoll: Orbis, 2004, p. 294.

9 Tim Chester & Steve Timmis, *Total Church. A Radical Reshaping Around Gospel and Community*, Nottingham: IVP, 2007, p. 48.

10 Ibid., p. 43.

is my destiny. Heaven will be church perfected.

God therefore uses missionary means, Jesus-led communities, to achieve his missionary end – a Jesus-filled community for ever. His choice of communities to bring about salvation reflects both his character and his goal.

As old as the church

Communities are God's strategy for individuals to make a difference. Believers are to link arms in small communities. These communities are to serve other people and lovingly share the gospel.

Christians have been doing this since Jesus. When the Celtic missionaries moved south from Scotland, for example, they formed highly mobile teams, which could pack up and move on like the nomadic people they sought to reach.

The Benedictine communities, which were schools for God's service, preached the gospel to unreached parts of Europe in the eleventh and twelfth centuries. In the high Middle Ages semi-monastic communities of lay women, known as the "Beguines", were the first known women's movement in the church. These communities were located just outside the walls of many northern European towns and served the local population.

In seventeenth-century England Nicholas Ferrar, a businessman, formed a semi-monastic community in a remote country house north-west of Cambridge. Little Gidding served many who sought physical healing and spiritual renewal, and rehabilitated the local church. A hundred years later, small groups were at the heart of the Wesleyan revival.

Christian Life Communities for lay people, founded by Ignatius of Loyola in the sixteenth century, still attract growing numbers of people worldwide who live out the exercises of St Ignatius in small communities of eight to ten members.

These local communities cluster into geographical areas and then regionally.

In the United States they serve others by providing mentoring in gaols, offering retreats for homeless people, campaigning for immigration reform, building houses in the global South and countless other ways. They do mission in community.[11]

Lesslie Newbigin, one of the last century's leading mission thinkers, described the congregation as "the hermeneutic of the gospel". What he meant was that the congregation is to interpret the gospel to the world. How can the church faithfully and credibly represent the gospel in society, he asked? "I am suggesting that the only answer… is a congregation of men and women who believe the gospel and live by it." Jesus did not write a book but formed a community.

Evangelistic campaigns and other efforts to bring the gospel to public life are all secondary to this, Newbigin argued. They are effective only "as they are rooted in and lead back to a believing community".[12]

Visibility

Yet how can the congregation represent the gospel to people if it is not present in their daily lives? How can outsiders understand what communal life with Jesus might mean if they cannot see what's involved?

How easily can evangelistic and other outreach events "lead back to the believing community" if the latter is some distance away? Church is often invisible to people through the week.

---

11 www.clc-usa.org/ (accessed 6 September 2013).

12 Lesslie Newbigin, *The Gospel in a Pluralistic Society,* London: SPCK, 1989, p. 227.

Witnessing to others in daily life and inviting them to church at the weekend frequently requires too big a jump. The style of Sunday worship, the language, and the assumptions ask too much. Visitors have a look. Sometimes they stay. But more often they think, "It's not for me", and don't return.

They would be more likely to remain if the gathering comprised people whom they met through the week, if it were located in the midst of ordinary life, if it addressed issues they were facing every day, if the style, language, and culture resonated with their day-to-day experiences, and if it met at a time that worked in relation to their busy existence.

This doesn't mean that there is no cost to following Jesus. Rather, the bulk of the population – in many places – does not get the chance to weigh that cost. For most people, church as a living community is invisible. Based mainly in residential areas, it is absent from swathes of life where people spend much of their time. It is not on the radar.

Jesus and his community in daily life

Yet when Jesus called his community of disciples, he not only went with them to the synagogue, he took them into everyday life. They were with him at the wedding at Cana. John 2:2 is explicit that Jesus was at this important event in ordinary life – with his community.

Being in life was so important that often Jesus instructed his disciples in public, with other people milling around – see Luke 12, for instance.

Likewise, when he taught them how to do mission in Luke 9, Jesus sent his disciples in pairs not to the synagogues, but to the villages. They were sent as micro communities into the midst of life.

Similarly, after Jesus returned to heaven, Christian communities multiplied at the heart of life – in people's homes where family, networks and occupations all intersected. In excavations of ancient Pompeii, over half the houses either incorporate shops or workshops or have horticultural plots attached.[13]

New Testament scholar Reta Finger describes the impact these home-based communities must have had on others nearby. City dwellings were packed together, with no glass windows to block the noise.

Many neighbours would have overheard activity around a communal meal in a small room or an open courtyard that was characterized by great joy (singing? laughter?). In the midst of the urban chaos and misery that characterized every ancient Mediterranean city, such a gathering must have sounded inviting indeed.[14]

Stitched into the fabric of life

Imagine that a trade union met in a community hall on Saturdays to change the workplace on Mondays. Would it be effective? Trade unions organize in the workplace because that is where they plan to have an impact.

Similarly, Christians must organize wherever people lead their lives if they want to love and serve them effectively. This will go beyond residential areas to being present in other slices of society as well.

Kahaila café began when Paul Unsworth gathered a group of Christians who shared his vision. Through prayer and hard work, they rented premises on London's Brick Lane and started a community "cafe with a conscience".

13 Eckhard J. Schnabel, *Paul the Missionary: Realities, Strategies and Methods*, Downers Grove: IVP, 2008, p. 298.

14 Reta Finger, *Of Widows and Meals: Communal Meals in the Book of Acts*, Grand Rapids: Eerdmans, 2007, p. 242.

> They run a variety of events from a Canadian Supper Night to an Origami workshop and host art exhibitions. Kahaila is now looking to set up a bakery to provide paid employment for women leaving prison or the sex trade. The idea came from one of Kahaila's young leaders working in the café.
>
> On Wednesday evenings they host worship, biblical teaching, and discussion groups. Anyone is welcome. Christians at the core see themselves as church, "but not church as you might understand it".[15] They are a community – in life.

Activity

Molly Marshall, President of Central Baptist Theological Seminary, Shawnee, Kansas, has asked whether calls for "Christian community" reflect a desire to escape the organized life we experience so often. Churchgoers want family-like communities in which they can be known in depth, be trusted by others, and trust in return. Yet idealizing this type of community may soften the church's call to work collectively to transform life. Comfortable intimacy can replace the hard grind of developing communities that minister to people in need.[16]

A growing number of Christians are gathering with small groups of friends – either within the institutional church or outside it – to hang out together, share their lives, and have fun.

> A Chicago couple, for example, emailed twenty of their friends, inviting them to form a small group. Ten showed up. They agreed to meet regularly to encourage each other in their growth towards Jesus. Their top goal was not, as

---

15 http://kahaila.com/church/

16 Molly Marshall, "Going Public: A Bold Church in a Changing Culture", *Christian Ethics Today*, 6 (5), 1996, available on www.christianethicstoday.com/Issue/006

> *a group, to serve other people, but to support one another through prayer, study, and fellowship. They hoped this would strengthen their Christian lives outside the group.*

But was this ambitious enough?

Of course, individuals should feel supported by fellow group members. Yet if that is all a group does, it will replicate the model of mission currently practised by the local church. Once more, members will return to the world to witness as individuals.

The power of organization

Today's world is highly organized. When Paul wrote that our struggle is "against the rulers, against the authorities, against the powers of this dark world..." (Ephesians 6:12), he was not referring to a struggle with disconnected individuals. He was talking about organized power.

In the face of these powers, witnessing just as an individual does not make sense. If the powers they wrestle against are organized, Christians should organize in response. They should not only form communities. These communities should not only be visible in ordinary life. These communities should be hubs of activity that telescope the kingdom into everyday life.

Although for much of the week Christians will inevitably love others and sometimes share the gospel as individuals, wherever possible they should band together to witness as a group.

Jesus' disciples acted as a group to make a difference. They shared in Jesus' ministry of exorcism and healing (Matthew 10:1). They served as gatekeepers, though without always understanding their brief (John 6:9; Mark 10:13–14). They assisted Jesus in feeding the five thousand and the four thousand (Matthew 14:13–21; Matthew 15:29–39).

Often it is only when you act as a group that you can make an impact. The influential British writer, journalist, and religious activist Margaret Hebblethwaite describes how Christians seeking to serve other people frequently talk of the need to organize.

Though "organization can almost smack of bureaucracy", alone we are vulnerable and powerless.

Strength lies in numbers. A people is organized when they have worked out how to convert a disorganized crowd into a coherent, coordinated body that can achieve goals. There must be order, not chaos; there must be communication, not ignorance; there must be accepted leaders, not manipulation by a few pushy entrepreneurs; and so on. Any community needs some organization... [17]

Groups make a difference

There is a huge difference between a collection of individuals competing on a football pitch and a team. Christians are more likely to make a difference to the world if they act in teams than if they act alone:

- *Groups pool resources.* You may have a wonderful idea, but to implement it you may need a colleague able to make things happen and someone else who knows the right people. Groups allow gifts to be shared. "Two are better than one... If either of them falls down, one can help the other up. But pity anyone who falls and has no one to help them up!" (Ecclesiastes 4:9–10).

- *They strengthen Christian motivation.* People often have more drive in group settings than on their own – think of the efforts individuals make for teammates, comrades in combat, or family members. Groups can provide encouragement and support.

---

17 Margaret Hebblethwaite, *Base Communities: An Introduction*, London: Geoffrey Chapman, 1993, p. 96.

- *They reinforce Christian identity.* One reason people join groups is to establish or maintain their sense of who they are. It is easier to see yourself as a rebel, for example, if you join a countercultural group such as a gang or an artistic clique. Likewise, it is easier to remember that you are a Christian, and to behave as such, if you belong to a group of fellow believers during the week.

> A Christians at Work group in the Wessex Water Company, UK ran a "Parenting Children" course on site during the week. The course was designed for those who did not belong to church as well as those who did. The last session included material with a Christian slant. The course attracted around fifteen people, of whom half were not churchgoers.[18]

Organizing this on your own would not have been easy. It required a small team. That is why groups must do more than support personal witness. Acting as a group to serve people nearby allows forms of witness that are impractical for individuals.

Making a difference by being different

At their best, witnessing communities that are visible in life and active in serving others have four characteristics. These communities are:

- *Missional* – they work mainly with people who do not attend church.

- *Contextual* – they find culturally appropriate ways of reaching people.

- *Formational* – they aim to form disciples.

- *Ecclesial* – they provide a taste of church for people involved.

---

18 www.transformworkuk.org (accessed 1 May 2013).

Frequently, they become church for those who attend.[19]

> A small group of Christians formed the core of a midweek luncheon club at the back of an English rural church. One week they invited diners to stay after lunch for fifteen minutes of Christian music, silent and read prayers, and a reading from Scripture.
>
> Individuals gathered round the holy table, which was brought down into the building and on which were placed a couple of lighted candles. For those involved, most of whom did not attend Sunday worship, this had the beginnings of "church".

Witnessing communities are not the same as conventional small groups in church, valuable though these are. Although the latter may pray for mission, their focus is on prayer, fellowship, or Bible study. In witnessing communities, on the other hand prayer, fellowship, and study serve the group's main purpose, which is to organize for mission, rather than being ends in themselves.

Witnessing communities also differ from many Christian groups at work. These groups may pray for the witness of their members, but don't organize to serve the workplace. By contrast, members of witnessing communities actively collaborate to love their colleagues in practical ways.

Witnessing communities do not exist in every part of an individual's life. Christians would die of exhaustion if they did! One segment of the week is enough. So start one of these communities among people who share a passion that you have, or where you spend the bulk of your time, or where the community is most likely to be effective.

Witnessing communities need not be an alternative to your local church. Some Christians make them their sole church, but for others they exist in parallel to church at the weekend.

---

19 www.freshexpressions.org.uk/guide/about/whatis (accessed 14 August 2013).

The New Testament never says you can have only one church experience in one setting during the week. So why shouldn't you be involved in two "churches"? They would both be part of the same body of Christ. Indeed, this possibility has been officially recognized by the Church of England. In a 2007 report, approved by the Church, the Church's Liturgical Commission acknowledged that sometimes people worship in two churches. In such cases, individuals should consistently belong to both churches rather than have a consumerist pick-and-choose attitude.[20]

You can be involved in a witnessing community:

- *spare-time*, on top of your other activities;

- *part-time*, maybe employed for some of the week and supporting a mission community for the rest of the time, like Paul with his tent-making. One lawyer works four days a week so that he has one day to start a Christian community in an area of poverty;

- *full-time*, possibly being paid by a denomination, a local church or a group of churches, or perhaps raising the funds yourself from friends and contacts who support your calling.

Anyone can do it – well, almost!

Churches, church plants and some intentional communities have frequently been led by people who seem to have a specialist calling. In the UK for example, founders of intentional communities are often called "pioneers".

Yet, as with the term "minister", "pioneers" can sound like a breed apart. The person has a particular calling – to be the spiritual equivalent of an entrepreneur.

---

20 Church of England Liturgical Commission, *Transforming Worship: Living the New Creation,* London: General Synod, GS 1651, 2007, pp. 25–26.

If that is your view, think again! Unplanned, almost spontaneous initiatives such as "Hot Chocolate" show that starting something new need not be an elite calling. Like the volunteers who went into the heart of Dundee, Christians who would never have thought of themselves as pioneers find they are the catalysts for something unexpected.

The experience of entrepreneurs may be suggestive. For years researchers have tried to distinguish the personal characteristics of an entrepreneur, but without much success. Entrepreneurs are so varied that it is almost impossible to find common traits, beyond perhaps the belief that they can do it.

Some researchers believe that entrepreneurial ability may be widespread, but remains hidden because circumstances do not draw it out. A nurse would have been entrepreneurial if he or she had had the opportunity.[21] In a similar way, many more Christians than we realize may be able to start witnessing communities if they are given the chance.

Coffee and chaos

In Souderton, Pennsylvania, for example, Jenifer Eriksen Morales invited her new neighbour for coffee. As two young mothers, they shared the joys and struggles of raising children.

Soon they met other mothers in the neighbourhood and had similar conversations. An impromptu Friday-morning coffee group developed. A few months later, the coffee group turned into a book club. Then something else happened. The women, most of whom didn't attend church, started having conversations about prayer.

The Souderton Mennonite Church, where Eriksen Morales worships, was in the neighbourhood but was not present in

21 David Rae, *Entrepreneurship: From Opportunity to Action*, Basingstoke: Palgrave, 2007, pp. 28–29.

the lives of Jenifer's neighbours. However, it embraced the coffee group as part of its ministry and provided childcare for some of the meetings, without expecting the mothers to visit a Sunday service in return.[22]

Build on what you've got

Maybe you are thinking, "I could never do that. For a start, I don't have the time!"

What helps to make witnessing communities feasible is that you don't have to follow someone else's blueprint. You just have to do prayerfully what comes naturally to you and build it into your everyday life. The secret is to develop what you've got – in particular:

- *Who are you?* Are you a teacher, for instance? Then think about what you could do among the parents, children or staff of your school.

- *What do you know?* You know about your school, of course. But perhaps you also have a passion for art history. Might there be children, staff or parents who would like to meet up, be introduced to some of the giants of painting and sculpture, discuss some of these artists' works, and go to the occasional exhibition?

- *Who do you know?* Can you think of a fellow Christian, preferably connected to the school, who would meet with you to pray about this? Is there anyone else who could help – someone who enjoys hospitality, perhaps, and could host the group in their home? Is there another person who would be great at inviting people?

---

22 http://freshexpressionsus.org/stories/coffee-and-chaos/ (accessed 30 April 2013).

Food and talk

In Paris, a woman and her husband stopped going to church
– "We were fed up with all the meetings that got nowhere."
But they still loved Jesus.

So they used what they had. The wife enjoyed welcoming
guests ("Who are you?") and her husband loved cooking
("What do you know?"). They invited four friends who
were in limbo from church ("Who do you know?"), and
between them they invited four others with little or no church
background.

They met regularly for food and discussion, on topics
ranging from politics to personal lives to God. She told a
conference that, over the previous six to seven years, during
which individuals had come and gone, four or five people
had become Christians each year.

New Creations

A Church of England bereavement coordinator in Merseyside,
Janet Cross, became aware of the need for some kind of
support group for the bereaved ("Who are you?"). She found
that one widow she was visiting had taken up crafts and it
was helping her ("What do you know?").

A keen card maker herself ("Who are you?"), she had the
idea of forming a craft group as "occupational therapy" for
the bereaved. She took the idea to her minister and asked
two friends – a member of the bereavement team and the
widow who had given her the idea – to help her to run it
("Who do you know?").

Having started with general crafts, they focused on Janet's
passion, card making. Each week had a theme. A monthly
"God slot" centred on the theme of the cards being made that
week, such as "leaves" and the idea of falling. Janet led the

slot, having been trained as a lay minister within the Church of England ("Who are you?" again).

New Creations has grown to about forty women. Two clusters, one for Christians and the other for people exploring the Christian faith, grew out of the group. They meet at 11.00 on Tuesday mornings, after which they join the rest of the card makers for lunch. After lunch, the serious business of making cards begins.[23]

If your local church wants to explore outreach through active, visible communities, it too should build on what it's got. Might the Christian core of a fringe group suggest a spiritual dimension, like the luncheon club described on p. 47 above?

If you run an evangelistic course among the never-churched, instead of allowing the group to disperse at the end and finding that many members do not make it to Sunday worship, might you keep the group together so that it becomes an expression of church for those involved?

Or maybe some members of your congregation would welcome an opportunity to serve their neighbours, or families with young children, or people who enjoy films, but are reluctant to do it on their own. Why not ask if there are others in the congregation who would like to help them? Churches have found that this releases new energy for service and outreach.

If you are busy or your church lacks resources, don't be put off. Starting a group to serve others need not leave a black hole in your time. It does not have to be a whole new activity, crammed into a hectic schedule. It can be part of what you already do and add value to it. You can be church while doing life.

If you do this, it will bring a rich dimension to your ordinary life – and to the life of others, such as Tracey, who came to faith

23 www.freshexpressions.org.uk/stories/newcreations (accessed 30 April 2013).

through a witnessing community among mothers and carers near Cambridge, England:

I've become a follower and lover of God because I was introduced to him like that by people who have God in them, and not the religious stuff. I'm being helped long-term. My circumstances haven't changed but I have. I've still got no money in my pocket and still sit in the dark 'cos we don't have the money for the electric meter, but... I'm being changed and my outlook on it is different.[24]

Too small?

Are these witnessing communities too small to make a difference? How can a little platoon of six to eight people stand against a global corporation, the all-surrounding media, or other social tanks that thunder through our lives?

The answer is that you do not have to be big to make an impact. In one organization, a number of people were being made redundant. A Christian workplace group paid for a consultant to give each person half an hour of free advice. Employees commented, "These Christians are better than our HR department!"

The Anglian Water Company's Christian Workplace Group in the UK has described how two of their members

were working late on a project when the cleaner came in upset and in tears. They spoke with her and discovered that her husband had just had a heart attack. Both Ian and Peter asked if they could pray for her, which they did. She was so thankful and they soon heard that the husband was much better.[25]

Just one family can make a difference:

---

24 Story told to member of UK Fresh Expressions team.

25 www.transformworkuk.org (accessed on 2 May 2013).

Breakfasts and parties

Ian and Ali, with their three sons, moved into a typical city neighbourhood in an English cathedral town. Two or three times a week they invite someone they have met to eat with them. Friendships form, and questions like, "What brought you here?" provide opportunities to talk about God's guidance and other Christian themes.

Soon after moving in, Ali met a couple of mums with young children. She invited them round the next week; the following week one of the mums invited another, and a "mums and tots" group was born. Ian invited the mothers and their partners to an evening meal, and suggested that the dads meet on Monday evenings. Six weeks later they formed a soccer team and entered the local league.

Later, one of the team, Darren, remarked over dinner, "I'm asking all these questions about Jesus, but I wouldn't be here if it wasn't for the football. I've discovered that you are ordinary people."

In time, Ian and Ali started a monthly Sunday breakfast in their home. Within a couple of years, around fifty people were crowding in, almost all from nearby streets. Alongside the breakfasts are other social events, such as an ice cream party in the summer and a chocolate party before Christmas.

One-to-one conversations point individuals to Jesus. So do simple introductory courses, which roll over into follow-up courses such as "The Big Story of the Bible" (in four weeks). As individuals move towards faith, they are invited to worship with the core team.

After three years, the team had grown from its initial three couples to about twenty people, and had multiplied into two groups. Lives are being changed as individuals find Christ.

Small beginnings

Any community of any size can make an impact – and sometimes small beginnings can have surprisingly large results.

> The Springfield Project in Birmingham, England now provides a professional nursery, family support work, after-school clubs, and facilities for dozens of families in its purpose-built children's centre. But a year after it began, as a stay-and-play group for parents in someone's home, numbers were so small that it was nearly closed![26]

Vitalise

In a different initiative, Richard Moy started by meeting with just two others to pray for his town in Britain's West Midlands. Others gradually joined, and after a year they began to meet in a café in the town centre.

Richard has moved on, but what is now known as Vitalise has successfully developed young and indigenous leaders to continue the work of worshipping fully, loving all, and serving the city.

Some people think that Vitalise is simply a youth church. While do they do work with a large number of young people, 47 per cent of the 135 people involved in the Vitalise community are aged nineteen or over. Activities include midweek groups, mentoring, a Sunday gathering, and other events.

Learning and worship opportunities vary. One group explores the use of contemplation in prayer. "Organic" – small – groups operate on a cell-church model and are geared towards food, worship, Bible study, and missional growth. Morning prayer and Bible study takes place in

---

26 www.freshexpressions.org.uk/stories/springfieldproject (accessed 23 May 2013).

Starbucks on weekday mornings at 9 a.m.

In the last two years Vitalise has released five people for ordained ministry, two for Methodist local preacher courses, and six for roles as lay workers. Others have been inspired to serve God overseas.

There have been ten baptisms in the last two years, one of which was actually at the Vitalise Sunday gathering. Three people have also been confirmed. Among those who have come to faith through Vitalise are staff at Starbucks and people in the homeless and homosexual communities.

Hannah, aged twenty-three, became part of Vitalise through working at Starbucks, where a group of them meets every weekday for morning prayer:

Through going to Vitalise, I was able to really grow into faith. Vitalise provided a stronghold for me, a group of people who welcome and do not judge, who accept and care, a place to feel safe and to completely escape into God's love and presence at the end of any kind of week, but also to start off every week.

I consider Vitalise a family, where I am always welcome, no matter what sins I have, what problems I'm going through, or if I'm feeling like the most blessed person in the world. They are there to support and simply be a part of everyone's life, mirroring the Father. I have a lot to thank Vitalise for. And I thank God every day that they are coffee drinkers![27]

You never know

Witnessing communities seem to be a new work of the Spirit. They are rooted in Scripture: wherever possible, God wants mission to be done prayerfully in community, which is visible

---

27 www.freshexpressions.org.uk/stories/wolverhamptonpioneerministries (accessed 1 May 2013).

in the midst of life and which engages in activities that put Jesus on display. This is not a task for elite Christians but for ordinary believers.

Time and again, stories about these new Christian communities start with straightforward people, taking small steps and being surprised by the results. So why not find a Christian friend in your neighbourhood, workplace or network, pray that the Spirit will show you how to love and serve the people you are in touch with, and try some ideas? You never know what the Holy Spirit will do!

The Order of the Daughters of the King® is an association of some 26,000 Anglican, Episcopal, Lutheran, and Roman Catholic women in the United States; there are also about 3,000 Daughters in eighteen other countries. Local churches sponsor chapters of women who take a vow to pray daily, serve, and evangelize.

Members regularly reach out as individuals to show God's love to others and draw them towards Christ and the church. Although their service may foster small communities outside the church (at a food bank, in a halfway house or among Alzheimer's patients), they currently aim to invite members to a church rather than introduce elements of worship into these communities.

Chapters often find opportunities to organize and serve as a group. For example in Washington, D.C., a Daughter noticed children who had nothing constructive to do while at the Laundromat with their parents.

With her chapter, she developed a team that reads with children at the Laundromat on the first Sunday of each month. Women of the church organized annual fundraisers so that chapter volunteers could give away the books they read to the children.

In this case, the Daughters could pray about adding some simple Christian stories or prayer cards to their reading sessions. If "Literature & Laundry" families welcomed that step, it could open the way for a small worshipping community to emerge in an unusual location.

The women have already blessed these families. Sharing a taste of church where they already meet could bring a new level of growth to everyone involved. The Daughters would have prayed, organized as a group, served, and evangelized.

Chapter 2

SEVEN REASONS WHY

I was homeless, on the streets, heroin addict,
everything... until I came here and found a way in God
and God found a way in me.[1]

Maybe you would love to be part of stories like this, helping individuals tread a path to Jesus. You are drawn to the idea of finding one or more Christians in a segment of your weekly life and gathering with them prayerfully to serve others, share the gospel, and make a difference.

But you are not convinced it would work for you. The outreach of your local church seems effective enough already. Or your other commitments seem more pressing.

As we explore these and other potential reservations, we shall uncover seven reasons why ordinary believers should get involved in witnessing groups – why community (joining with other Christians), visibility (being present where life happens), and activity (acting as a group) are so important.

#1. God wants communities on the edge

Perhaps you think that witnessing communities make sense in some situations, but not yours. Your local church runs effective social and evangelism programmes. You support some of them. Why do more?

---

1 www.freshexpressions.org.uk/stories/streetwise (accessed 16 December 2013).

Yet should you be so content? If you counted the regulars in your local church, how well would you be doing? Would those joining you in the past year exceed the number leaving (including people who left in a horizontal position)?

Of the new arrivals, how many came from other churches? How many used to belong to church and were returning? How many had little or no Christian background?

This latter group is ballooning rapidly in much of the global North. Can you be content if your church is not engaging with them?

Who are you not reaching?

Or ask another question: who is your church not reaching? Your neighbours? People you hang out with? Colleagues at work? People with whom you share an interest?

Tim Keller, founding pastor of Redeemer Presbyterian Church in New York, believes passionately that "the only way to change the culture in a city is to increase the number of churches engaged in it".[2]

These don't have to be big, complicated churches. They can be acorn communities that provide a taste of church. If we want to disciple the culture, we need Christian communities in every corner of society to serve people, share the gospel, and change life.

From "come" to "go"

The Spirit is preparing the ground for these communities. One sign of this is that many churches have abandoned their exclusive, "come-to-us" approach to mission.

Traditionally, Christians have asked what would work well for them and agreed the time, length, style, and place of their

2 Quoted by Ed Stetzer & Warren Bird, *Viral Churches: Helping Church Planters Become Movement Makers,* San Francisco: Jossey-Bass, 2010, p. 68.

Sunday worship on that basis. Then they have invited others. But the invitation has always been to "join us" on "our" terms. Evangelism occurs within this framework – "come to the church we've set up to suit us".

A growing number of churches have realized that this approach is too narrow. A renewed understanding of God's kingdom has helped them to understand that the church is not the be-all-and-end-all of mission.

The kingdom goes beyond drawing non-believers into church and God ruling in their lives. It encompasses the entire landscape of creation. As Christians serve the kingdom by pointing to this reign and being agents of it, mission becomes more than inviting people to church. It involves loving the world as God loves it.

This has encouraged a "Go" approach to mission, alongside "Come". Christians are to go into society and love it as God loves it. They are to collaborate with the Spirit in caring for other people and for the planet. Mission becomes seeing what the Spirit is doing in the world and joining in.

Church-planting guru Ed Stetzer writes of the United States:

In the country I live in, 70 per cent of the population is completely unchurched, meaning they have little or no connection or interest in Christianity. We have already reached most people who are open to the "come and see" approach. Churches that use this approach are "effectively reaching only 30 per cent of my local neighbourhood, and I live in Georgia".[3]

The Holy Spirit is calling the church to stretch out to the majority beyond its immediate circle.

---

3 Ed Stetzer, *Planting Missional Churches*, Nashville: B & H Publishing, 2006, p. 166.

From going-it-alone to going together

Till recently, "Go" has been expressed largely in terms of "Going-it-alone". As described in the last chapter, Christians leave Sunday worship and re-enter the world largely as individuals. During the week they practise mission mainly on their own.

Though better than relying on "Come" alone, this ignores how God does mission. The Spirit does not go into the world alone, but undertakes mission in community with the Father and the Son. They relate so closely together that they are one.

God wants us to do mission in community too. This intention is reflected in Adam and Eve working together, Israel's role in salvation, Jesus doing mission with a community of disciples, Jesus sending his disciples out in pairs, Paul's reliance on mission teams, and the subsequent history of the church.

It is much easier to serve people in your neighbourhood, network or workplace if you do it with others. As we saw in the last chapter, groups can reinforce Christian identity, strengthen Christian motivation, and pool resources.

> Members of St Philip's Church in a Toronto suburb said to themselves, "If people won't come to us, we'll go to them." So they started Pints of View, a bar-style gathering in their local Army and Navy club. The invitation is to share "a beer, some holy bull, and a blessing". The evenings weren't started by one person alone, but a team.

Witnessing communities kneaded through life:

- *Reveal the character of God.* If God is a divine community of three persons and Jesus chose to live his public life in community, Christian communities will show what God is like more effectively than individuals acting alone.

- *Display the nature of the kingdom.* When the kingdom arrives, it will have a corporate shape. As Jesus' stories about the heavenly banquet suggest, it will not be a collection of isolated individuals but a community gathered around its saviour.

- *Make church relevant.* When witnessing communities serve people in the cavities of life, others will be less likely to see church as "that irrelevant building over there". Church will be visibly touching their lives. A leading theologian, John Milbank, has called for the institutional church to focus less on writing reports telling the government what to do and more on getting radically involved in medicine, welfare, business, the arts, education, ecology, and more.[4] Christian communities in life can do this.

- *Help to draw in people from outside church* but who identify with the group's focus – whether it is serving single parents, promoting justice, safeguarding creation, or being a loving presence at work. A community organizing stress or conflict management, and other seminars for people in the workplace might welcome someone who catches the vision, explaining, "We always start by planning how to serve our colleagues. We usually discuss a story about Jesus (one of the world's greatest spiritual teachers) and we finish with some quiet music, during which those of us who believe in God offer silent prayers. You are welcome to join us." Social action and evangelism are clasped together.

- *Enable emerging Christians to experience the church where they are.* Through its warmth, prayers, and witness, a community may encourage someone to receive Jesus. At least at first, the person will not have to jump the hurdle of going to an unfamiliar church at the weekend. Imagine you organize a talk

---

4 *Church Times*, 16 December 2011.

by a Christian sporting celebrity for people interested in sport. How do you follow it up? Do you invite them to your local church, where they hardly know anyone and the worship feels uncomfortably strange? Or do you follow it up with another event for the same people, and then another and another, till the group gains momentum through the friendships that form? This can become the context in which individuals walk towards Jesus and have a deepening experience of church.

• *Disciple new Christians in a group with a mission focus.* Mission will be in the new believers' blood from the moment of their new birth. So they will have a head start in being formed into the likeness of the missionary God. The group's values will help to counter individualistic consumerism.

Pursuing Christ with others

These advantages are so strong that more and more Christians are doing mission together in the textures of life. Hugh Halter heads up training in church planting at Denver-based Church Resource Ministries.

CRM, famous for the standard-setting "Church Planter's Tool Kit", have scrapped their traditional church-plant training. Instead, they develop spiritual leaders who faithfully pursue Christ in their culture "with unwavering grace".

"The biggest assumption we had to get rid of is: If we build it, they will come to us if we just do it well enough," Halter said. "We had to start assuming they are not going to come. The only ones that are going to be drawn to our programs are Christians."

Being an effective personal evangelist is no longer enough. The community "is becoming the primary apologetic". Halter and others are learning how to form communities in everyday culture "where the saints go deeper with God and one another, and we want [non-Christians] along on the journey".[5]

---

5 Ed Stetzer, *Planting Missional Churches*, Nashville: B & H Publishing, 2006, pp. 166–168.

The next chapter will provide an amazing variety of examples of Christians doing what Halter describes – going deeper by serving others. To be content with your church's current programmes may be to miss out on this new move of the Spirit.

God is taking Christian communities into the micro settings of life. He wants communal forms of mission in those contexts. Are you being called to join in? Or are you avoiding the question, "Who are we *not* reaching?"

#2. A way of connecting church to the world

Perhaps you feel dissatisfied with your current church involvement. Neither your church nor you are having much impact on your friends. You think a witnessing community could be a better bet. But the thought makes you feel guilty. Should you not remain in your existing church and work to make its mission more effective?

Yet imagine that a company had mixed financial results. Some parts were doing well, but others not. You have the opportunity to move from your underperforming team to one with potential to put the company on a stronger footing. Would it make sense to stay in your existing role?

You may wince at the comparison, but an increasing number of Christians would recognize the parallel. Parts of the church are "doing well", such as some growing churches in London, but not all of it.[6]

A canyon between church and world

Using data from twenty-two nations in the European Social Survey, undertaken in 2002/2003, sociologist David Voas obtained startling results. He found that, in every country surveyed, each generation is less religious than the last. People

---

6 For examples of UK churches bucking the decline, see David Goodhew (ed.), *Church Growth in Britain: 1980 to the Present*, Farnham: Ashgate, 2012.

pray less, go to church less, and believe less in God.[7]

According to the Pew Forum on Religion and Public Life, the number of American adults with no religious affiliation – the so-called "nones" – surged from just over 15 per cent in 2007 to nearly 20 per cent in 2012.

A third of adults under thirty have no religious identity, compared to a mere tenth of sixty-fives and older. They are much less likely to be religious than older adults at the same stage of their lives.[8] Many commentators believe that the United States is on the same trajectory as Europe, where the church has been declining for decades, but one or two generations behind.

For much of Australia, Canada, Europe, New Zealand, and America's North-east and West coasts, an ocean has come between the church and the world. If individuals are in trouble they turn to doctors, counsellors, coaches or mentors, but never think of seeing a minister.

This is largely because of the church's retreat from the pivotal points of life, in stark contrast to the New Testament. There Jesus took the embryo church, his community of disciples, into everyday settings, and taught them to do mission by going in pairs into ordinary villages.

After he returned to heaven, churches mushroomed at the epicentre of life – in people's homes, where family, networks, and occupations all intersected.

The same pattern continued into the Middle Ages. The medieval church was integral to the village, where all aspects of life – work, home, friendships, and festivals – took place. Church was local court, social service, and meeting place for the whole community.

---

7 David Voas, "The Rise and Fall of Fuzzy Fidelity in Europe", *European Sociological Review,* 25 (2), 2009, p. 167.

8 *"Nones" on the Rise: One-in-Five Adults Have No Religious Affiliation,* Pew Research Center's Forum on Religion and Public Life, October 2012, www.pewforum.org

The church's presence in the midst of life was ruptured by the Industrial Revolution. Work and then important dimensions of leisure moved some distance from home, but the church remained in its residential setting.

Church, as a community presence, became increasingly remote from the office, the café, the bowling alley, and other centres of people's lives. Physically remote, it became culturally remote too. It seemed less and less relevant.

The death of church?

Some commentators have concluded that the church has had its day, much as many people in Britain wrote off the cinema in the 1980s: they pointed to falling attendance and the competition provided by television and videos.

But cinema owners took a different view. They believed there was still a market. So they spruced up the buildings, installed more (and smaller) cinemas to give people a wider choice of films and times, made the seating more comfortable, and sold better popcorn. It worked. Attendance rose.

Despite its differences, there is still a "market" for church. People remain interested in issues of meaning, life and death, and spirituality. Community, which of course is vital to church, has never been more popular – look at all the social networking sites! Like cinemas, if slowly, the church too is adapting to social changes.

Helen Shannon works for St Barnabas, a middle-class church in North London. Nearby is Strawberry Vale, a neighbourhood that is far from middle-class:

I realized that it wasn't the case that people didn't believe in God [on this estate]: it was because they hadn't been introduced to him... At the start I would have said that the gap was geographically too wide for people to come to church at St Barnabas. Now I would say that for some the cultural gap is an issue too.

So she gathered a team from St Barnabas, started some youth and community activities, got involved in the community centre, and built relationships.

It took about two years before "church@five" was launched on a Sunday afternoon at the community centre.

We have lots of cups of tea, an informal service around tables with sung worship, share community news, someone prays for our church and the community, and then we have the offering because we wanted to build in the value of giving back to God right from the start. We read together from the Bibles... have a short interactive talk and prayer ministry time, and drink more tea and then eat together.[9]

New connections to the world

Churches are emerging not just in community centres, but in pubs, schools, gyms, workplaces, sports clubs, and other settings. The idea that faithful communities can reveal God in the hubs of daily existence is once more coming to the fore.

George Lings' research, mentioned in the last chapter, shows not just that "fresh expressions" represent 15 per cent of the churches and 10 per cent of the attendance in the ten Church of England dioceses surveyed, but also that in seven of the dioceses the number attending these new communities is roughly the same as the dioceses' overall fall in attendance between 2006 and 2011.

In other words, the dioceses' drop in attendance would have been twice as great without these communities. New communities are beginning to stem the hemorrhage from church. Start more of them, and the decline could go into reverse!

---

9 www.freshexpressions.org.uk/stories/churchatfive (accessed 9 May 2013).

According to their leaders, over a third of those who come to these fresh expressions had fallen away from church, and even more – two-fifths – have little or no church background. No conventional church has figures like that!

These new communities are typically started by teams of three to twelve people. For every member of these teams, two and a half others now attend the main meeting. This is a growth of 250 per cent, mostly within ten years. Other churches would die for a similar record![10]

All of this means that, if you prayerfully contribute to one of these communities, if these communities are visible in daily life, and if they actively engage in mission, you will help to reconnect church and society and to reverse church decline.

You will witness to a future when God will be "all in all" (1 Corinthians 15:28) and Christ will fill – or complete – everything in every way (Ephesians 1:23). No fraction of life will be beyond the presence of Jesus. Every segment will be completed, made perfect, by him.

As extensions of Christ's body, Christian communities in life point to, and begin to make a reality of, this future – of the time when Jesus will fill all the places where we lead our lives.

Too many churches?

Some people in the United States, especially where every residential street has a church, think that there are too many churches already. But this misses the point.

We need more Christian groups in more niches of society. The more numerous the groups, the more they will fill up society with tangible signs of God's family, and point to the time when Christ will fill all the networks and settings of life.

10 Church Growth Research Project, "Report on Strand 3b: An analysis of fresh expressions of Church and church plants begun in the period 1992–2012", October 2013, p. 6, available from Church Army Research Unit.

God's call often comes through a holy discontent with the status quo – think of the Old Testament prophets! So if you feel dissatisfied with your current church involvement, don't feel guilty. The Spirit may be prompting you to start a community in life – an expression of church that is connected to the world and points to the time when God will be fully present in all human existence.

#3. Brings new life to the church

Perhaps you realize that the church's mission needs a revamp, but you are still holding back. You are not sure witnessing communities are "proper church". If you had to drop some of your church commitments to free time for one of these communities, might you be turning your back on church in favour of something less than church?

On the other hand, if these communities are real church, would it be acceptable to do both? Could you belong to two local churches – a witnessing community and your current church? Might this dilute your involvement in existing church and weaken the congregation?

The answer depends on how you understand "church". The New Testament has a relational view. Its metaphors for church – such as the body of Christ, the household of God, and the vine and the branches – are strongly relational.

The church began with people encountering the risen Lord, encountering each other, and telling others about their encounters with Jesus. As the church spread, relationships were established between local churches.

Holy Communion, a channel for Christ to kiss the church, was instituted within a community that had been on the road with Jesus for three years. As regards sequence, the community came first.

Four sets of relationships

Four sets of relationships are at the heart of church – with the Trinity, with the wider church, with the world, and within the fellowship. These entwined sets of relationships, centred on Jesus, are the essence of the church. They can be shorthanded as relationships:

UP towards God
OUT towards the world
IN towards fellow members of the individual church
OF in the sense of being part of the whole body of Christ.

The four relationships of church

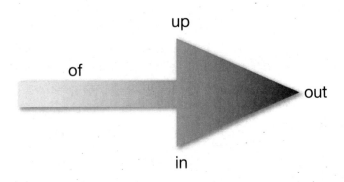

Preaching the word, sacraments, care for the poor, and other practices that the wider church values still matter. If a gathering is committed to its relationship with the whole church, it will take with utmost seriousness activities that the universal church thinks are important.

But implementing these practices will be tested against the four sets of interlocking relationships that comprise the church. For example, "Does how we celebrate Communion help us grow in our relationship with God, and express our praise and thanks to him? Does it strengthen our fellowship and our outreach to others? Would the church at large recognize it as Holy Communion?"

If a gathering in a home, pub, school, restaurant or workplace begins to grow in these four sets of relationships, it can be considered church. So to get involved would not mean that you were turning away from the church. You would be turning towards a different kind of church.

Two churches rather than one

"Does this mean I would have to choose between churches? If I experienced a different type of church during the week, would I have to stop going to my Sunday church?"

The answer is that there is nothing in the New Testament to say you must belong to only one expression of church. Rather, the first disciples had two centres of worship: the temple and churches in their homes (Acts 2:46).

Belonging to more than one expression of church will often make sense.

- *It is warranted by Scripture.* The New Testament Christians worshipped in two "local" churches – their home church and the town or city-wide gathering of all these home churches. 1 Corinthians 14:23 refers to the "whole church" coming together. There is a similar reference in Romans 16:23. New Testament scholar Roger Gehring writes:

  In recent research scholars tend to agree that the early Christian movement was characterized by the existence of two church forms: the house church and the whole church at any given location.[11]

11 Roger Gehring, *House Church and Mission: The Importance of Household Structures in Early Christianity*, Peabody: Hendrickson, 2004, p. 157.

- *The two expressions of church are part of the one body of Christ.* Just as you might belong to two teams in the workplace but be employed by the same organization, there need be no split loyalty when you belong to two churches. Your ultimate loyalty is to Jesus. He holds the two together in the one church.

- *You can have a richer experience of church.* Someone who meets two branches of the same family will have a greater knowledge of the extended family than if they meet just one branch. If the same grandparents are present in both branches, the person will form a more rounded view of the grandparents by seeing them in different settings. So it is with Jesus. When we encounter him in more than one expression of church, we have a richer experience of him.

- *Belonging to more than one type of church encourages connectivity.* As life fragments into more compartments, to be present in all of life the church must fragment too. So how do we hold these fragments together? Belonging to more than one "local" church can be part of the answer. You will provide a bridge between two fragments. For example, you will be able to invite a new Christian in your midweek church to your Sunday one. The person will get a fuller taste of church than in their midweek community alone.

- *It creates stability.* Some witnessing communities may last only for a season. A key person involved may change jobs or move away. The community loses momentum and draws to a close. If that happens, having roots also in a more durable weekend church will lessen the disruption. To maintain continuity, emerging and new believers can attend the Sunday churches of others in the group.

- *It is nothing new.* There have always been some people who have worshipped in two different congregations – perhaps a midweek Communion (with others who do not attend on Sundays) and a Sunday service.

- *It can solve a practical problem.* You can be involved in a different expression of church during the week while continuing to worship with your family on Sundays.

So belonging to two types of church is not to be frowned on. Nor should it be merely tolerated as a necessity. It should be positively welcomed. Existing church can be a base from which to bring a flavour of church into another section of life.

Dual church involvement is not to be undertaken lightly, however. You will want to consider prayerfully the personal and family implications, and how you will express your commitment to each of the communities concerned. Rather than a consumerist, pick-and-choose approach, there should be deep commitment to both kinds of church.

To allow time for a second expression of church, you might have to shed some of your existing commitments. Would this weaken your church? Or would you not be joining a grass-roots movement that promises to revitalize the church?

In Warrington, Cheshire, UK, for example, New Song Café meets monthly, attracting up to 130 worshippers. About a third sees this as their church. Between meetings, discipleship evenings attract eighteen to twenty-five people. A network of churches is emerging – with a pub church and New Song Breakfast – known as New Song Network.

New Song Breakfast links to Latchford Methodist Church's traditional Holy Communion, and strengthens it. The network has so far deliberately chosen to stay under the authority of Bold Street Methodist Church, who see their own future as being more secure as a result.[12]

---

12 www.freshexpressions.org.uk/stories/newsongscafe (accessed 3 May 2013).

Tas Valley

Again in the UK, Tas Valley Cell Church in rural Norfolk has cells containing fifty adults. About half also attend a Sunday congregation. The leaders have encouraged a growing crossover between the cells and the longer-established congregations, with the two getting together three times a year.[13]

Someone came up to me after a meeting and said, "I suppose we must be doing what you described. We are a heavy metal congregation in London, and have started meeting each month with an Anglo-Catholic church across the road. We can't believe that there has been a church there for 1,000 years!"

The mixed economy

Witnessing communities woven through life can strengthen the local church:

- *New and old can work together,* as in the examples just described. Emerging believers can be introduced to the riches of the Christian heritage, while long-standing believers are energized by the new blood.

- *New Christians may find their way into existing church.* If a church's attendance is declining, an influx of new members – as Bold Street Methodist Church found – may make the future more secure.

- *Mission communities can revitalize small groups.* As has begun to happen, a local church can encourage members to move from small groups with an inward bias (prayer, Bible study, and fellowship) to communities that serve specific demographics outside the church. Fellowship, study, and prayer can occur in the slipstream of active mission.

---

13 www.freshexpressions.org.uk/stories/tasvalley (accessed 3 May 2013).

- *The local church may find a new role.* If members join witnessing communities, some of the church's existing ministries – such as small groups – may become less important. But a new role will emerge: to train and support members in being effective in their communities. Chapter 7 describes how "Sunday church" can bless and back "midweek church" as part of its mission.

In the UK, many people use the phrase "mixed-economy church" to describe this vision of new and existing expressions of church working together in mutual encouragement and support. One type of church is not better than another: they have different ministries.

So, if you were to join a witnessing community, you would not only be doing mission in God's preferred way (through communities), you would not only be helping the church to connect with the world, but you would be helping to re-energize local churches. Far from letting the local church down, through the Spirit you would be contributing to a movement with huge potential to strengthen the local church.

#4. Aids discipleship

Over the last half century, many Christians have rediscovered the concept of vocation. They have realized that they are called to collaborate with the Holy Spirit in taking forward God's work of creation, particularly in their jobs. They are to help the entire living world achieve its glorious potential.

Some Christians have concluded that their jobs per se are a form of discipleship. Being a good lawyer, hospital porter, teacher or supermarket shelf-stacker is central to following Jesus. Doing jobs well contributes to the health of creation. If this becomes the focus of your daily mission, you might think there is no need for witnessing communities. It is enough for you to work hard and effectively.

But the New Testament makes vocation more demanding. Christians are called to more than just doing their jobs well: they are to do them distinctively. Zacchaeus for instance breaks with convention, and becomes a more honest and generous tax collector after his encounter with Jesus (Luke 19:1–10).

Individuals are to put Jesus first in their lives (Matthew 6:24), including at work. This will mean exceeding others' expectations in patience, kindness, self-control, and other fruits of the Spirit. It will involve standing against all forms of evil (Ephesians 6:11–12).

It will include looking for ways to transform the workplace. Paul expected the gospel to change the nature of the master–slave relationship radically: masters and slaves were to respect each other, which was far from the contemporary norm (Ephesians 6:5–9). Vocation goes beyond working conscientiously to promoting kingdom values while doing the job.

This is hard without the support of other believers. So local churches have increasingly sought to provide help by equipping believers to be faithful to their vocations during the week.

Yet in doing this churches face a hurdle: often members are too distant from each other's lives to provide adequate support.

In my local church, a number of us decided to meet over a meal on several Friday evenings to describe our jobs, discuss some of the problems we face in the light of Scripture, and prayerfully support each other.

We've had a great time. We have got to know each other better. We have offered a listening ear to people who have described their work and been able to pray for them. The groups have been popular.

But it has been difficult for us to give one another practical support. We're not present in each other's workplaces. We don't know the other personalities involved and have often struggled to understand the intricacies of the matters described.

Frequently, to find common ground, the discussion has been at a high level of generality. This has made it difficult to conclude with practical steps for the individual to take. To allow time for others to share their stories, there is no opportunity in subsequent meetings for each person to feed back to the group how they are coping with the issue they raised.

Groups in context

These problems are greatly reduced when you belong to a witnessing community connected with a passion of your life – whether it is among friends, people who share one of your interests, or at work.

These groups can better support your Christian discipleship.

- *Members know the situation,* so they can offer practical advice – "I know what he is like. This is how I would deal with him." Their prayers can be more specific. They can relate Scripture to the details of the setting.

- *They can hold you to account and provide support.* When you leave church on Sunday, usually no one in the congregation will see you at work on Monday. But if you belong to a Christian group in situ, fellow members will notice whether your behaviour matches your beliefs. They can encourage you when they bump into you.

- *You can work together* to serve and witness to people round you. You don't have to do it on your own. KBRS, a railway engineering company in south-west England, applied for an award in 2010. The application, written by someone who was not a Christian, noted that the Christians at Work

Group "provides an alternative spiritual support within the organization, which would be missing without it".[14]

Witnessing communities are not inward-looking with a focus on prayer, Bible study, and the problems their members face. They look out to serve and share the gospel with others in the context.

To achieve this, a group might have a simple agenda each time it meets: purpose (to serve and share the gospel), problems (faced by individuals), and presence (coming into God's presence through Bible study and prayer). Starting with purpose will keep the group focused on mission.

"Purpose-driven" communities in ordinary life do wonders for discipleship. They provide the framework, accountability, and support for Christians to take up their cross, serve people near them, and make Jesus public. They help individuals to live out their vocations – and expand the very concept of vocation.

#5. A great means of service

A conference on communicating the gospel concentrated on how to get the Christian message across. But every so often someone would ask, "How do we prepare people to hear the message?" Delegates began to realize that, with the church and world sliding further apart, this was perhaps *the* question.

Like many Christians, you may think that mission mainly involves evangelism. You can't see yourself forming a witnessing community because you doubt that the people you know would be interested in the gospel. They would not be ready to receive it. Perhaps you sense the need for a prior step.

If this is your instinct, it is a godly one. Jesus did not only proclaim the good news. He served people through acts of compassion. He healed them, fed them, provided enough wine at

---

14 www.transformworkuk.org (accessed 3 May 2013).

a wedding, and accepted hospitality from social outcasts.

These acts were ends in themselves, essential aspects of the kingdom, but they also opened individuals' hearts to him. People fell in love with Jesus because he loved them first.

Like Jesus, witnessing communities include evangelism but go beyond it. Christians come together to serve people outside the church, and to share the gospel in the context of service.

Spreading care

Witnessing communities are especially good at serving people because their focus is very specific. Imagine that a small-town church is known for its community concern, such as its food bank for families in extreme poverty and its volunteers who drive the housebound to hospital, dental, and other appointments. Each activity concentrates on a group of people with a need.

To multiply that caring, the church encourages witnessing communities, which find simple ways to address the longings of an identifiable group – to discuss a film or a book, to learn how to cook, to clean up the environment, or to go on informational walks through nature.

As individuals are signposted sensitively to Jesus and come to faith, they journey into an increasingly full experience of church. They begin to serve other people they know, perhaps giving birth to further micro communities.

By serving specific groups in varied ways, the caring life of the church seeps into the nooks and crannies of its small town.

The more a witnessing community focuses on a particular demographic, the better it will be able to serve others. It will meet at a time and place that best fit the people concerned. Its activities will be tailored to their preferences. It will adopt a style that makes them comfortable.

The interests of one grouping will not be buried by the competing claims of others – the concerns of the able-bodied swamping the needs of individuals with disabilities, or the better-educated running the show but leaving less-educated people with fewer opportunities to exercise their gifts.

One church in a poor neighbourhood gained a reputation for being "successful". Middle-class people began to arrive. As their numbers swelled, old-timers complained that the atmosphere had changed. The original working-class members started to drift away. "It's no longer our church," they said.

You can picture how the scene might look today. Betty has been taking the minutes for years – in a tatty exercise book. A retired headmaster arrives, iPad in hand, and offers to do it more efficiently. Betty feels mortified. "There's no room for me here," she thinks.

The New Testament ideal

Some Christians recoil at this focus on specific groups. They harbour the ideal of gatherings that are thoroughly mixed and diverse. "Isn't that the New Testament picture," they ask, "neither Greek nor Jew, man nor woman, but everyone coming together whatever their age or background?"

Actually, the New Testament picture is more complicated. First-century cities were much like today's. Different ethnic and income groups lived in different areas. So when Christians formed home-based churches, these little communities would have drawn people from different neighbourhoods and networks. Each gathering would have served a particular group of people.

However, as we have seen, these churches came together from time to time. In Jerusalem, the first believers broke bread in their homes but also met together in the temple courts (Acts 2: 46–47). In Antioch, Paul confronted Peter "in front of them all" – presumably during a meeting of the whole church (Galatians 2:14).

In 1 Corinthians 14:23, Paul writes of the "whole church"

coming together. In Acts 20:17 he summons the elders of the Ephesian church, referred to in the singular: clearly, these leaders had a sense of being one church in the city, no doubt because their home-based churches met together from time to time.

It was in these wider meetings that people of different ages, backgrounds, and ethnic groups intermingled. Social divides were blasted away.

So it is not an either-or – either expressions of church designed for specific groups or an experience of church in which everyone is mixed up. The New Testament suggests it is both. Socially specific home churches also met as the whole church.

This means that Betty's notepad culture and the headmaster's iPad one can retain their own identities, yet also enrich each other by coming together in a larger whole.

To do this, witnessing communities must prioritize connections with the wider body. These links can take many forms, such as:

- *Joining a parent church* for a social event, a weekend away, a series of teaching evenings, Easter and other church festivals, or an outreach initiative.

- *Joining in events organized jointly by local churches* in the area, or going to a Christian conference or festival.

- *Accessing resources of the wider church* (books, podcasts, videos, blogs, and much else), or connecting with Christians online.

In a society that wrestles with diversity, witnessing communities not only drill into the social stratum to lovingly serve specific groups, they also model God's strategy for combining unity with difference. As well as enabling us to do mission in God's communal way, to connect people with the church, to energize it, and to be faithful disciples in everyday life, they are a brilliant means of serving today's world.

#6. Ordinary people can do it

Perhaps you can see the rationale for these witnessing communities, but you lack the confidence to get involved. "What happens if it doesn't work? Might I look stupid among my friends? Could I do it?"

Ask yourself: would God have made communities central to mission if he thought they were beyond ordinary people? Jesus founded the church by calling disciples from ordinary backgrounds. New Testament churches were led by everyday people in typical homes.

One reason the church grew so rapidly was that it was "doable" by normal people. It was not complicated like many of today's churches – with their expensive buildings, programmes through the week, and complex Sunday services (complete with worship band, children's groups, and much else).

The New Testament church was simple. It met round a meal in someone's home. Leadership was shared among people with different gifts – the burden did not fall on one person. It was tailor-made to be led by "Mr Average".

In the church's history, outpourings of the Spirit have regularly released lay people for ministry and mission. In eighteenth-century Britain, for example, part of John Wesley's genius was to release thousands of ordinary people to become local preachers and class leaders. Today's new types of church are mostly led by lay people.

Be realistic

Some people shrink from starting one of these communities because they imagine they have to do what others have done. Perhaps, for example, you have a mental image of a church planter leading twenty people to form a new church – "That's way beyond me."

Yet a witnessing community does not have to be like that. You can begin by finding one other Christian, meeting together for coffee, chat, and prayer, and asking, "What small things could we do to serve the people we know?"

Or maybe you have heard about a workplace Christian community and think you ought to try the same in your office, but are feeling nervous because you can't see how it would work. Before plunging in, ask whether the two situations are similar.

Possibly the workplace community was in a stable, quite cohesive setting, whereas your workplace is fragmented, colleagues travel a lot, and staff turnover occurs every three years. It would be difficult to meet with others on a regular basis. What was practical for someone else may not be practical for you. No wonder you feel daunted! Might the Spirit be calling you to form a witnessing community in another part of your life?

Start with what you've been given

New Testament churches grew from what people had. Individuals had their homes, networks, and families. Through the Spirit, they used these to form churches-at-home, which spread through their networks.

> "Talking Point" emerged because Charlotte started with what she had. She was a health visitor in an English medical practice. She noticed that a number of young mothers nearby suffered from post-natal depression.
>
> She approached the local minister and his wife, who agreed to open their home once a week to young mums who wanted to meet others and consult the health visitor. Twelve to eighteen women started coming on a Thursday morning. Following this contact with church, a few asked for their children to be baptized.
>
> After much prayer, Charlotte sensed God was asking

her to do two things: set up pizza social nights for the Talking Point women, and consult one of the graduates of a local Alpha course (a British-based introduction to the Christian faith). She asked the person how she might share Jesus more overtly.

Following these discussions, Stepping Stones – an informal monthly session for children and their mums – was launched on Tuesday mornings. An interactive Bible story ends with quiet reflection.

After a while, Charlotte and her team asked the women at Stepping Stones to complete a questionnaire and comment on how to take it further.

The result was the arrival of sixteen women at the minister's home for a "pizza and pud" evening, followed by discussion. Once the group gelled, Charlotte offered the women a choice of purely social events, a course on family, a course to explore Christianity, or a course called Journeys (five sessions of Christian testimonies).

The women chose Journeys. By the end, all the women had owned a move towards Jesus. They took another course, Life Stories, after which their group became a permanent cell within Grange Park church.[15]

Charlotte would never have got going if she had fretted about what she had not got. She started with what she had – she was a health visitor, she knew the mums, she knew the local minister, and she knew others who could help her. Once the initial group had formed, each step was based on prayer and on asking the group what it wanted to do next.

"It is vital that the group owns how they want the group to be run," Charlotte said, "rather than have an unwanted choice

---

15 www.freshexpressions.org.uk/guide/develop/becoming/grangepark (accessed 5 September 2013).

imposed."[16] The leader does not have to strive and push. The group and the Spirit power growth and development.

#7. Mission is a first step for God

Perhaps, finally, you are not sure how important this all is. You may be like many Christians who believe in mission – in working for the redemption of the world by caring for creation, loving and serving others, challenging injustice, helping individuals find Jesus, and supporting them in their lifelong journey with the Holy Spirit. But other priorities take over.

Your church life revolves around Sunday worship and belonging to a small group for prayer, study, and fellowship. Though you support mission financially and help with the occasional outreach event, Sundays and the small group take up most of your church time.

Through the week you try to live by Christian values, but active mission – going the second mile in loving service and in sharing the gospel – gets pushed to the margins. Mission is a second thought in your life, not the first.

Mission as a second step for God?

This reflects a mistaken view of God – one that I held for years. Till recently, my story of God went something like this:

From all eternity Father, Son and Holy Spirit have been in intimate relationships of love. These bonds are so close that the three persons of the Trinity are one. Then "one day", light years ago, Father, Son and Spirit came up with a plan. They would create a universe, which they would love, and it would include human beings. If things went wrong, they would take the initiative to put them right. The three divine persons devised a mission – to create

---

16 www.freshexpressions.org.uk/guide/develop/becoming/grangepark (accessed on 7 May 2013).

and then to save. Creating and saving have a sense of going out. God moves out towards the universe in creation and he moves out to save. When theologians talk about the mission of God, they use the Latin term "Missio Dei", the core idea of which is sending, or going, out.

In short, my story contained a "before" and "after" in God. There was a time before he engaged in mission and a time afterwards. There was a time prior to God moving out and a time later. Mission, if you like, was a second step for God. And if mission can be a second step for God, it can be a second step for us.

I now realize that this story is flawed. It is not plausible that members of the Trinity suddenly switch from not doing mission to doing mission.

If mission – reaching out – is fundamental to how God relates to human beings, a characteristic so basic to God cannot be absent one "moment" and present the next. It would mean that God had changed in his essential nature.

Yet we know that God's character does not change. God is the same yesterday, today, and for ever. Mission has always been at the heart of God, not least because going out – the nature of mission – is how the Father, Son, and Spirit relate to each other. They go out to one another in love.

Love involves moving out. It is more, of course – I could go out to another person in hatred. But among the ingredients of love, moving out is vital. When I love another person I go out to them. So when members of the Trinity love each other, they engage in the dynamic of mission.

Mission is in the heart of God. It is reflected in God's relationship to the world in creation and redemption. It should be echoed by men and women as they go out to each other and to the natural order.

Old Testament scholar Chris Wright describes the big story

of the Bible as God going out in mission, calling the community of Israel to do the same, sending his Son to make mission possible, and then bringing to birth the church to continue this mission, through the Spirit.[17]

Mission continues even in heaven, where God will still go out to us in love and we too shall keep going out in love to him and to one another. Mission is not just for this world, it is for ever.

Mission should be a first step for us

If mission is a "first step" for God, it must be a first step for us. We were made in God's image, and through salvation the Spirit restores that likeness. Our lives must therefore reflect God's mission heart. We must pray that the Spirit helps us to become more like God in placing mission at the kernel of our lives.

This will mean prayerfully looking for the best ways to go out to people in love. Just as God has not settled for a second-best means of salvation, we must not be content with carrying salvation to others in a second-best way. Like God, we must search for the best means of engaging in mission. If forming small groups in everyday life is one of these means, we cannot let it slip down our priorities. Mission is a priority for God: it must be top of the agenda for us. It cannot be outsourced to a church sub-committee!

> *Levi Santana sees mission as a priority. He leads a small witnessing community on the edge of London, called The Valley Network. By late 2012 forty Christians, lapsed Christians and not-yet Christians were meeting in local coffee shops for discussion and Bible study, and in a nearby church for worship.*
>
> *In their coffee-shop discussions, Levi says:*

---

17 Christopher J. H. Wright, *The Mission of God: Unlocking the Bible's Grand Narrative*, Nottingham: InterVarsity Press, 2006.

> I always make it clear that I'm a Christian, though people have to be free to share their opinion – whatever it is. We always start with people talking about the lowlight and the highlight of the past week.
>
> One of the girls who comes to the groups is going through a sex-change process. So she came in and said, 'The highlight of my week is that I'm going to be a boy.' She had a letter for an appointment in London to see a specialist, and what struck me was that she was confident she could share that letter with us.
>
> I realized then that this community was effective... As a result we have seen that group develop into a little family.[18]

Witnessing communities are transforming people's lives:

"Zac's Place has personally helped me to find my way, my faith and my belief and... to find peace and move on from the past."

"About eight years ago I moved into the YMCA, then I heard two people speaking about this church and they thought it would be nice for me to come along. So I did. I got baptized five and a half years ago and that's when I changed."

"I think that when I came along to re:gen I wasn't expecting at all to be accepted because I had been in hospital for nearly two years and I'd kind of gone back a year in school and I had suffered quite a lot with self-harm behaviours and stuff like that. You can come along and you've still got people here who like you, despite what you've been through, despite all these things, and they're willing to give time and support you along the way as well."

"I used to be a violent man; you can't change yourself – only God

---

18 www.freshexpressions.org.uk/stories/valleynetwork (accessed 9 May 2013).

can do it. He's given me love for other people that I wouldn't have had love for before."[19]

Seven reasons why

- God does mission through community.

- Witnessing communities connect the church to people.

- They re-energize the local church.

- They support everyday discipleship.

- They serve other people.

- They are practical for ordinary Christians.

- Mission is a first step for God and should be for us.

Conclusion

Of course, witnessing communities raise questions about accountability, how they foster spiritual depth, and many other issues, which we shall explore in later chapters. Assuming these questions have answers, witnessing communities are the best place for not-yet Christians to experience gospel life and learning. They plant seeds in daily life – seeds of loving service and of the gospel. As the seeds take root and grow, they begin to change the terrain.

Diana is assembling a team to hold "Grown-up Sunday school" for people with dementia, whose memory loss starts with recent events and progresses back in time.

In her local care home, residents sing Christian hymns and songs that they remember from their childhood Sunday schools, say the Lord's Prayer in the version they originally learned, and hear Bible stories that they once knew as children.

---

19 Stories reported to members of the UK Fresh Expressions team.

The impact is not high-profile, but for the people involved it makes a difference. Individuals who are passive for most of the week take part actively. Others who are agitated become calm. People who dropped out of church as adults reconnect to the Christian faith. An expression of church grows.

Chapter 3

IDEAS TO STIR THE IMAGINATION

The past exercises a muscular grip on many believers' imaginations. Maybe you are steeped in church as it is now, and struggle to imagine how Christian community could be expressed in different ways. Held back by the drag of mental habit, you find it hard to picture a small expression of church in a gym, a skateboard park or online.

To break free, it helps to look at real-life examples. So this chapter provides a banquet of stories about witnessing communities in everyday life.

The aim is not for you to click and drag one of the stories to your situation. What suits one setting may not fit another. Rather than replication, these examples are for inspiration – "That wouldn't work here, but it makes me wonder if we could do…"

If the way to have one good idea is to have lots of ideas, I trust these stories will spur you on to envisage prayerfully a tale that the Holy Spirit could write through you.

Growing communities at school

In countries like the UK, where a strong church–school divide does not exist, a growing variety of church outposts are being established among children, parents, and staff within schools.

Prayer spaces

In five years, "prayer spaces" in schools have welcomed nearly 300,000 people into simple, transformed classrooms where students and staff can explore their hopes, dreams and prayers in creative ways. Teachers and pupils report that prayer spaces impact the educational, behavioural, spiritual and pastoral aspects of school life. Some have the potential, in time, to become expressions of church.

In Gloucester, England, Joe Knight and a chaplain friend at a Church of England secondary school set up their first prayer space.

"On the final day," Joe records, "my friend confessed he thought we'd have ten people, but half the school had voluntarily come, with very meaningful encounters, including expressions of thanks, sorry and please prayers, and prayers wrestling with big questions. We've hosted fifteen prayer spaces in the school since then. Trust has grown as we've responded to people's needs through counselling, hosting Christmas concerts and even gardening courses. But it's the individual encounters of rekindled hope and faith that continue to amaze and far surpass our original dream."

Elsewhere, Christian communities are forming around lunchtime and after-school clubs, among pupils or among parents. They are overseen by school chaplains, Christian members of staff, youth workers, parents or members of the local church.

By 2013, over 275 schools had seen "prayer spaces" established under the umbrella of the 24/7 international prayer movement. (See www.prayerspacesinschools.com.) At least some of these had the potential to grow into something akin to an expression of church.

Nooma and coffee

Thirst Café Church emerged among parents at a primary school near Cambridge. It grew out of eleven years of relationships and prayer. Parents would meet outside the classroom at "pick-up" time. About ten of them, including some who did not profess a faith, began to chat about spiritual matters.

Arising from these close encounters of a "school-gate" kind, in 2006 these friends stepped out in faith. They served good coffee, food, fruit, and juice in the school lounge, and invited others they knew.

Thirty people, most of whom did not attend church, gathered to watch a Rob Bell Nooma DVD, after which a discussion began spontaneously. The group continues to meet regularly.

A few months later, a weekly prayer time was offered, including a spiritual activity of some kind, and a five-minute talk and discussion. By early 2012, a weekly Bible study had also been introduced, incorporating a simple Holy Communion.[1]

If you see the mission potential of your local school, you may find it best not to leap in with ideas for evangelism. Why not prayerfully ask how you can best serve the school? For example, Eagles Wings, which is supported by two local churches, runs a school breakfast club, where it makes contact with parents.[2]

---

1 www.freshexpressions.org.uk/stories/thirst (accessed 8 May 2013).

2 www.freshexpressions.org.uk/stories/eagleswings (accessed 9 May 2013).

Growing communities at work

Janet (not her real name) used to have lunch every day with the same group in her work canteen. One day they were discussing a story in the news, and Janet described how she responded as a Christian.

This provoked a lively discussion, at the end of which one person said, "We ought to do this more often." So they did, once a week. The group grew in size, with the management offering them an adjacent room at no cost – "It's good for staff relationships."

Several years on, around fifteen people were still meeting weekly for discussion with a little Christian input. Had Janet not left her job, the group would probably have evolved more intentionally in a Christian direction.

Very different is the request from a café in Birmingham, England. As one of its community offerings, the café has asked some local Christians to provide a weekly meditation (from within the Christian tradition) for people leaving work at the end of the day.

The meditation allows busy people to clear their heads, and will be supplemented at other times of the month by a discussion group on life issues, a spirituality and art group, a group for Christian meditation, and one for worship. The Christians involved hope the initiative will eventually evolve into an expression of church.

The workplace is a challenging arena in which to form witnessing communities. People are busy; they are not always there at the same time, while rules about what you can and cannot do may impose severe constraints. Various ideas have been tried or mooted – for example:

- A couple of Christians might start a spirituality-at-work group or a justice-at-work group, and encourage members to travel towards Jesus.

- Two Christians might offer to pray for colleagues in confidence, and then start a group for people who would like to explore prayer further. The group might use a book of Ignatian meditations, based on Scripture, and see what the Spirit does.

- Christian doctors or community nurses might start a weekly after-hours prayer and support group. Some general practitioners have done this in Dorset, England. They formed a Monday-evening group for patients who wanted prayer support. The group now has a settled core, with individuals regularly coming to faith.

- In a large town, a group of Christian lawyers or accountants might organize regular workshops and seminars for continuing professional development. At the end of a day on, say, "Improving business conversations", they might offer a free, optional half hour on "Spiritual resources for lawyers (or accountants)". These half hours could become springboards to discussion groups, reflective prayer sessions, and other opportunities for individuals to get to know Jesus.

- As a variation, a city-centre church might encourage some of its members to start a cell to serve colleagues at work. The cell might organize seminars on themes such as "Using spiritual resources to overcome stress", "Mindfulness", "Becoming a better leader", and "Managing office politics". Groups to explore the Christian faith might arise out of these events. The hope could be that other church members would form similar cells. Might the church's home groups eventually morph into mission cells at work?

- Some town-centre churches are developing an explicit ministry to the workplace. For example, St Margaret's in Uxbridge, West London, has a fourfold strategy:
  - to develop relationships through coffee-bar work, a confidential listening service and chaplaincy;
  - to meet needs and sow seeds through regular business events that address work topics (breakfasts and lunches with a speaker and seminars);
  - to provide opportunities for spiritual exploration;
  - discipling.[3]

- The Christian owner of a company might organize optional lunchtime or after-hours events for staff on a variety of spiritual themes. As interest grows, these events might include an apologetics course, which would evolve into a worshipping cell as members grow into the faith.

- Christians might use a workplace carol service to advertise monthly seeker events (perhaps in a pub after work), and then extend personal invitations to their colleagues.

- In a refocusing of "post-industrial" chaplaincy, chaplains might form mission groups in the workplace as one of their responsibilities.[4]

Growing communities at "play"

Experiences of church can be found in a skateboard park, in pubs and bars, in sports centres, and in tattoo parlours. In one such parlour, a Bible-study group met regularly in the basement. The owner would talk about his faith while doing his artwork, and invite clients to the group.

3 George Lings, *OASIS – Work in Progress*, Encounters on the Edge, 24, Sheffield: Church Army, 2004.

4 www.freshexpressions.org.uk/guide/examples/workplace (accessed 8 May 2013).

Virtual community

One person in Pittsburgh, PA described how he had stopped going to church. But he loved computer games.

In one game he had to gain weight to cross a bridge. Normally he would have had to buy the extra weight. But, in this case, a group of players offered to get him across free if he watched their video.

The video was all about grace. At the end he was invited to an online Bible study, which he enjoyed and attended regularly. After a while, he decided to reconnect with church in physical life. Here was a group of Christians furthering God's mission on the web.

Church in a Laundromat

An initiative with a different spin was described by a woman with a vision for a Christian community in a Laundromat. She had found that people came at regular times to do their laundry, which took about ninety minutes. This is plenty of time to chat.

She had begun to sit with a group at the same time each month, pay for their laundry, and get to know them. She was building a team of Christians to help her and be present more often.

Her prayerful hope was that the Christians would form caring relationships with the people present. In time, perhaps the conversations would include spiritual themes. Possibly members of the group would welcome prayer and eventually a Bible study. "Who knows!" she said. "We might end up with church in a Laundromat!"

Biscuits and Bible

By contrast, "Biscuits and Bible" happens in Weston's Store, Red Oak, South Virginia. The store is a good place to meet people. On Sunday mornings the women are at church and the men in the store. Baptist pastor Mike Lyon got to know the men and kept inviting them to church.

One day, in frustration, he said, "Tell me the truth, guys. You have no intention of coming to church, do you?" One of the men exclaimed, "No! Why don't we just have church right here?" So they did.

Mike brings his Bible and a bag of ham biscuits. The owner of the store puts on some coffee. Mike shares a thought from Scripture. The men talk about life. Then they pray. Anyone milling about or standing in line for gas or cigarettes is invited to join them. Mike then goes on to the women, meeting as a more conventional church.[5]

Third Place Communities in Tasmania, Australia are not so different. They involve Christians who refuse to gather in sacred, isolated spaces. In the mid-noughties they were meeting in such places as pubs, bars, playgrounds, and cafés.

Remarkably, and harking back to Christian gatherings in Jerusalem's temple courts (Acts 2:46), they worshipped publicly in these venues, but not in ways that put others off. On average, curious non-churchgoers comprised about 60 per cent of each meeting.[6]

5 http://freshexpressionsus.org/stories/biscuits-and-bible-a-fresh-expression-in-a-country-store/ (accessed 8 May 2013).

6 Alan Hirsch, *The Forgotten Ways: Reactivating the Missional Church*, Grand Rapids: Brazos, 2006, pp. 239–240.

Café church

"Church meets café" is no longer news. Recently, café church has spread like wildfire. But there are many types. One way of thinking about the differences has been suggested by Bob and Mary Hopkins, who are at the heart of Britain's "fresh expressions of church" scene.[7] The mission dynamics vary for each type.

"We'll do a café-style event in our church building." Some Christians literally reorder the church building with chairs and tables, serve refreshments, and put on an event with some Christian input, such as a testimony or reflective prayer.

"We'll do an event in a commercial café." A Christian group rents a commercial café and puts on an event when the café isn't normally open. The café gets another use for its facilities, while Christians can use state-of-the-art premises near where people gather. Costa Coffee, a major British chain, is encouraging its venues to be used after hours for this purpose.

Like café church in a church building, the approach is "attractional" – Christians put on an event (in the café) and attract others through invitations and publicity. The events can be seen as the "Willow Creek" of café church – seeker-sensitive, but in a café rather than a church.

"We'll do an event in a community centre." Christians lay on a café-style event in a community centre at the heart of a village, town or neighbourhood. All sorts of people, many with little or no church contact, will be using the centre for a range of activities.

Christians among them may spot an opportunity for some kind of café-based initiative alongside the other activities. Word spreads through the centre's networks. As the café becomes established, a spiritual dimension is added with the support of those who come. Instead of attractional, "come-to-us" mission, this is "we'll go to them".

---

7 www.freshexpressions.org.uk/guide/examples/cafe (accessed 8 May 2013).

> One example emerged from a partnership between St Mark's, Haydock in Merseyside, England and the neighbouring church of St David's, Carr Mill. Members of both churches are involved in the Moss Bank community centre – the photo club, art group, craft group and so on. Some of them built on their existing relationships to develop a thriving café church, which has drawn in folk from other groups in the centre.

"*We'll set up a café ourselves.*" Taste & See is a Christian café in Kidsgrove in Staffordshire, England. Local Methodists acquired a café in the town centre and opened it six days a week as a profit-making venture. It has a back room converted for quiet, meditation, and prayer, and also for spiritual conversation and events that support individuals on their journeys of faith.

Whereas the first three types of café church provide an event for non-churchgoers, Taste & See is more than an event: it represents a Christian presence within café culture. People looking for a good café experience are made welcome.

"*We'll set up a café with non-churchgoers*" takes this Christian presence a step further.

> A group of Lutherans have set up Café Retro in the heart of Copenhagen. The café is run as a commercial venture and is open at normal café times. The difference is that the cafe is run not just by Christians. All the leadership team of five are churchgoers, but the other six teams – bartenders, renovation, events, design, PR, international concern, and mission trips – are roughly 50 per cent churchgoers and 50 per cent not-yet-Christians.
>
> By partnering with people they feel called to serve, the leaders intend the initiative to be more deeply immersed in café culture and that church will emerge within this context.

"We'll go into a café that already exists." This is, perhaps, the ultimate step into café culture. A good example is described by Neil Cole in *Organic Church* (Jossey Bass, 2005). His evangelistic team was thinking about reaching people in the coffee-bar culture. They were discussing how to set up a coffee bar when someone asked, "Why don't we just go into a coffee bar that already exists?"

It made sense. They didn't have to learn about a business they knew nothing about. They could focus on their call to evangelism. Unlike the "Costa Coffee" approach, they did not have to advertise or invite people. The coffee bar was already full!

So they went into a local coffee bar, played pool with other people, got to know the regulars, chatted about girls, life, and the rest, and in time found opportunities to share their Christian faith. When someone asked to know more, they suggested that the person invite their friends to their apartment, where they shared the gospel. When those interested continued to meet in the apartment, a small church was born.

Communities of interest

Communities for mission can form round films, crafts, books, walking, sport, and other interests.

> *A couple of Christian women in South Wales have formed a photography group – fun, photos, and friendship. Members exchange advice, organize competitions, and hold exhibitions. The two Christians hope that their relationships will enable them to put Jesus on the agenda.*

> *Peter Homden set up a bike project, where he and young people mend bikes together and talk about "life issues". In 2009, this was one way in which he was serving a settled Gypsy Traveller community on England's south coast.*

Might "Share your passion, share your life, share your faith, and share their journey" become your vision? Providing a platform for people to pursue their interests will be an act of Christian love. It will create opportunities for them to chat about things that matter, during which you can share naturally how Jesus affects your life. Once individuals show an interest, you can accompany them patiently on their spiritual journeys.

Cooking up prayer

Inspired by celebrity chefs, many young British people are interested in cooking. So Katharine Crowsley decided to start a cookery club in her Methodist chapel. She gathered a team, sought the advice of a community food worker, and ran a pilot.

Cook@Chapel was launched in 2009, attracting between seven and nine twelve-to-sixteen-year-olds. Most were not involved in church. They prepared a meal, ate, and talked. It was all very informal. By 2013 numbers had grown, a core of regulars had emerged, and a sense of community had developed.

Prayer grew quickly out of taking it in turns to say grace using a grace dice. The young people were invited to drop written prayers into a kitchen bowl, the bowl was passed round, and individuals picked up a prayer to read out loud. This "Mixing Bowl of Prayer" has become popular and is now the cornerstone of the evening.

Discipleship occurs through conversations and supporting outside projects, such as cooking a safari supper to raise funds for an education project in Ghana. Plans include offering a taught course to deepen the young people's Christian understanding, and an allotment to grow vegetables for their meals and to care for creation.[8]

8 www.freshexpressions.org.uk/stories/cookatchapel/apr13 (accessed on 10 May 2013).

Different demographics

Christian communities are springing up in groups of every age.

> One couple invited children from their local school to their nearby church on Wednesday afternoons. After school the children were given a drink and played some games, while their adult carers had a good chat. Then there was story time and simple worship.
>
> Within two years, some thirty people were attending Worship on Wednesday (WOW!). Most did not attend church, but some were calling WOW! "my church".

> ### The wheels on the bus
>
> More elaborate is the after-school club run by Captain Louise Weller of Church Army New Zealand. With a small team of Anglicans and Baptists, she started by taking a bus into a suburb of Christchurch.
>
> From this emerged X-site, which attracts about thirty children and nine adults. Visits to the families involved are an important element.
>
> Like WOW!, the children arrive from a local school and are given a drink and games to play, after which there is singing, prayer, and a simple Bible reading. Next, one of the puppets introduces the theme for the day. Pre-school children then leave for their special time, while the others learn through mime, drama, crafts or games with a purpose.[9]

Churches with few teenagers are increasingly working together to connect with this age group. In Sussex, England, for example, the Eden project developed a pattern of monthly regional youth

9 www.freshexpressions.org.uk/stories/x-site/may12 (accessed 9 May 2013).

gatherings, with separate groups on the other Sundays.[10]

The North Rice Lake Youth Ministry Project, north of Toronto, involves five churches within four rural communities in close proximity. Recognizing that hardly anyone came to their traditional youth groups, the churches employed a youth worker, who has launched events that rotate round the different communities.[11]

> LegacyXS has achieved fame for allowing an expression of church to emerge on a skateboard park. One teenager commented, "I never knew that God could be interested in my skateboarding."[12]
>
> This initiative in Essex, England has inspired a church in Perth, Ontario to work with the owner of a skate shop and open its doors to skateboarders. It is the only place in town where the young people can skateboard in winter. It is a bold move and an act of reconciliation: in 2009 skateboarders broke into the church and did considerable damage.
>
> The church hopes that the Christian music and videos included in the programme, the Christian literature lying around, and the relationships that form will open the door to conversations about Christ.[13]

The Spirit is full of surprises

Many communities develop in unexpected ways, as these two examples show:

10 George Lings, *Leading Fresh Expressions: Lessons from Hindsight,* The Sheffield Centre: Encounters on the Edge, 36, 2007.

11 Diocese of Toronto, "A Missional Road Trip", YouTube.

12 "Expressions: the dvd-1: stories of church for a changing culture", www.freshexpressions. org.uk/resources/dvd1

13 www.freshexpressions.org.uk/stories/skateboardsperth (accessed 9 May 2013).

A student worker attached to the chaplaincy at Britain's Leeds University joined a student knitting group in a café. The students were not connected to the chaplaincy in any way, but they asked her to lead a Bible study in the café where they knit.

Matt Ward, Lead Chaplain, comments:

To be honest I have mixed feelings because part of me wonders how this is sustainable because she's only with us for a year, but, on the other hand, I'm thinking, "How can I support this group and help it develop...?" The bottom line is that the whole thing is a risky enterprise which requires you to trust God all the time![14]

In Swansea, Wales, "Under the Canopy" for eighteen-to-thirty-year-olds has grown organically. It started when youth worker Dan Evans and his team launched music nights on the last Sunday of the month.

To develop the faith side of things, they came up with Headspace nights on the second Sunday of the month, involving panel discussions on topics such as "Does Love Win?"

They then introduced Sustenance, a meal on the third Sunday, inspired by how the early church ate together. "Transmission Sundays" on the fourth Sunday focus on prayer and meditation – "We have tried all sorts of things..."[15]

This prayerful step-by-step, trial-and-error approach is typical of how experiences of church are gradually being slotted into every section of contemporary life.

---

14 www.freshexpressions.org.uk/stories/emmanuel/jan13 (accessed 9 May 2013).

15 www.freshexpressions.org.uk/stories/underthecanopy (accessed 9 May 2013).

Messy Church

Messy Church seeks to bring together people with little or no church background in all-age activities that are fun, include a meal, and introduce participants to Christian themes in a relaxed and accessible way.

A core value is enabling family members to take part in the activities together. Since the first one in Portsmouth, England in 2004, Messy Churches have mushroomed not just in the UK but around the world. One very rough estimate reckons that by 2013 half a million people worldwide had attended a Messy Church at some stage.[16]

These communities normally meet monthly and require quite a bit of work to prepare the activities and the food. The big challenge, recognized from an early stage, is how to disciple individuals who get a taste of Jesus at a monthly event.

Here are some ideas, inspired by Bob and Mary Hopkins:[17]

- *Provide resources for families* to nurture their faith at home, such as family prayer, Bible readings with helpful discussion questions, family rituals or "traditions", and suggestions for activities and social outreach.

- *Encourage families to organize social concern activities,* from supporting mums having babies, to providing clothes for Romanian orphans, to supporting the bullied.

- *Start additional social meetings* during the month, such as a simple "Messy Meet-up" after school – a purely social gathering without the pressure to offer a full programme of activities.

- *Organize a parenting course or support group.* If babysitting is

---

16 Bob Jackson, "Church Growth Conference", Durham, 12–13 December 2013.

17 www.acpi.org.uk

a problem, you could do one for mums and one for dads on different evenings.

- *Introduce baby massage and prayer.* Mums love their baby being pampered and blessed. Baby massage can be turned into active prayer for the little one, and Mum will often be touched by God at the same time.

- *Offer "adoptive grandparents".* Encourage older Christians to volunteer as friends, supporters, and mentors. The gospel will spread through natural conversations.

- *Introduce an all-age prayer school.* In a mixed-age setting, adults can learn informal prayer and break "the sound barrier".

- *Introduce cells for different ages.* In Norfolk, England Sally Gaze has birthed five adult cell groups and two cells for teens from a Messy Church-type event.[18]

- *Invite individuals to discuss the stories Jesus told.* One person did this with young mums. She invited them to some evenings on "spirituality". When asked what would be the content, she replied, "Jesus is known as one of the world's greatest spiritual teachers. Why don't we look at some of the stories he told and see if we agree with him?"

- *Use published courses such as Alpha*, a British course introducing Jesus. But you may need to adapt the course or put in something before Alpha if people are not ready for Alpha. "Puzzling Questions", a pre-Alpha course published by Lion Hudson, might be a possibility.

- *Start a Sunday church with direct links to Messy Church.* At least one midweek Messy Church is planting a similar style but "deeper" Sunday gathering alongside it.

---

18 http://www.freshexpressions.org.uk/stories/tasvalley

- *Develop an online presence,* so that individuals can keep in touch during the month, praying for each other and perhaps doing online Bible study.

Older People

"You've given me an idea," she said. "I lead a sewing group in 'sheltered accommodation'" – an apartment block for older people who are less mobile. "If they agree, I'll suggest that we have a prayer at the end. This could take them a first step towards Jesus."

Sometimes referred to as Molly's Church, the seeds of a very different expression of church were planted when Molly and Graham Bell focused on the needs of the large proportion of older people on their English housing estate.

The Bells have helped to inspire a good-neighbour scheme, a discipleship cell group, a lunch club, a day centre, and a monthly afternoon tea, "Molly's Church".

Minibuses bring elderly housebound people to the tea. When they arrive, they have excellent refreshments, discuss a topic at their tables, watch a drama on the theme of the day, have a short meditation, and sing a couple of well-known hymns.[19]

If you want to serve older people, why don't you run a "holiday at home" event for frail elderly people in your area, or start a friendship group of those recently bereaved? Or perhaps run a "Questions of Life" course for seniors, or introduce a midweek Holy Communion followed by tea and scones?

If you want to reach the late middle-aged, you could advertise an evening for people old enough to be grandparents, see who

---

19 www.freshexpressions.org.uk/guide/examples/older (accessed 9 May 2013).

comes, and ask them how often they would like to meet and what they would like to do.

Or you could follow this example:

> A church that had provided an occasional worship service for the elderly in an old people's residential home shared a vision for witnessing communities. Folk from one of their cell groups were inspired to start visiting. They got to know elderly Christians in the home and worked with them to start church there. Soon staff were coming to the meeting on their day off. Relatives began to time their visits so that they could attend too.

Different "geographics"

New neighbourhoods are common as the population expands in many parts of the "global North". Imagine that your denomination employed you to launch a church that would fit the culture of one of these neighbourhoods. How would you start?

> Heather Cracknell began by holding a get-to-know-you party. On the walls she put up lists of possible activities that individuals might like to join or lead. She hoped the activities would help the recently arrived residents get to know each other.

Discovery Days

> Under the banner of "Discovery Days", Penny Joyce sparked a mixture of social events and those with a Christian flavour in a new neighbourhood near Oxford.
>
> Families met for Sunday tea and Christian-based activities. Men met for football. Readers met in a book group. Home-based workers met for lunch. Mums with young children met weekly.

Christians on the estate met in one of two weekly small groups, Discovery 1 and 2, while a second kind of Discovery group served seekers. Her vision was for Christian cells to multiply round the neighbourhood, meeting weekly and then jointly once a month.

Residents who were not yet seekers could attend Breathe, a social evening with wine, chat, and the possibility of moving through a series of stations that provoked thought about a life issue.

Penny sees evangelism in terms of a line from 10 to 1 (the Engel scale), on which individuals may be at the uninterested end (10) or the Christian end. She placed events along that line so that people could choose.

Christians were involved in all the activities. Penny's prayer was that, as these Christians became friends with the others, not-yet Christians would be nudged along the line.

"If you're journeying at 7 or 8 you won't want to come straight into a church situation," she explained, "but you might be interested in something that makes you aware of Jesus and whets your appetite for more. We journey spiritually with someone and don't expect them to travel from a 9 to a 1 in a giant leap."

One lesson from Penny's experience is that it is important to stay in the neighbourhood the initiatives have taken root and strong local Christian leadership has emerged. If the pioneer leaves too early, the initiatives may be too fragile to endure – denominations and funders, please note!

From tea to café church in a suburb

A group of churches in a West London suburb jointly supported a Sunday afternoon tea for homeless people and *others on the edge of society. After a number of years they paid for a full-time person to work with this demographic.*

After the tea, which was held in the basement of a flourishing church, the newly appointed worker invited the guests to attend the evening worship upstairs. A few came and sat on the back row, very much spectators.

One Sunday, as an experiment, the worship was held café-style. The congregation sat at tables, sipping coffee and nibbling refreshments. The minister noticed that for the first time guests from the tea downstairs were involved. "We should do this every week," he said.

They did. Gradually, the numbers from downstairs increased, while many of the original worshippers found their home in the Sunday-morning congregation. What has emerged is café church for homeless people and others on the social margins. Fifty to sixty of them regularly attend.

Christian commuters in the suburbs often say that evangelism is difficult because they don't know their neighbours. But there are vast opportunities for suburban Christians to serve people with specific needs and longings. Volunteers from the church can get to know local people through loving service.

Take the church that hosts the café-style worship. It also runs "Snips", a meeting place for parents and carers of babies, toddlers, and pre-school children, with a café as well. The team has recently launched "Family church" as part of the Snips offering.

Early bird in a rural area

When in 1997 Victor Howlett became an assistant minister in a rural town in Wiltshire, England, he found that families were not coming to church. So he gathered a small team from the congregation and suggested that they launch a monthly half-hour Early Bird service at 9 am on Sundays.

None of the team was quite sure what the service would comprise, but they visited local children's groups with an invitation. In the event, forty to fifty people started to come. Two-thirds were new to church. Unusually, dads outnumbered mums – and they sat at the front!

The service is "very unchurchy". Songs have no more than two verses. They are sung from a book of six coloured sheets and announced according to colour. If one proves unpopular, it is replaced. The service is always based on a Bible story. "If it goes well, we tell it again."

Coffee is served afterwards, and as people leave they are given an invitation to the next month's Early Bird. Children are texted or emailed between services to keep in touch.

Victor is now in his third church and still repeats the Early Bird recipe, albeit under the name "Jump Start Sunday". At least a dozen Early Bird services have started in other churches.[20] People with an interest in God can explore the faith in a short, family-friendly event that leaves the rest of Sunday free.

The Wesley Playhouse

A Methodist chapel in a commuter village near Leeds, England was facing closure when church steward Caroline Holt visited a commercially-run activity zone with her goddaughter. "Why can't we do something like this in our church?" she wondered.

After much consultation and fundraising, The Wesley Playhouse – with its children's soft-play area, climbing frames and ball pool – was launched inside the church building.

There is a monthly Playhouse Praise and other events, such as a Mother's Day four-course meal for mums and their

---

20 www.freshexpressions.org.uk/stories/earlybird (accessed 15 July 2013).

families – "a chance for people to relax while we wait on them. It should always be about service."[21]

Between its launch in 2007 and April 2013, over 24,000 people had come through the project's doors – a long way from when the church had just ten members attending regularly. Caroline reports:

We now have 3,000 sq. ft. of play area, a café that operates alongside it and a supportive local community, who have taken it to their hearts and now use The Wesley Playhouse as the venue for birthday parties and celebrations. We've even had several christenings there as a result of people feeling so much part of what has very much become their own fresh expression of church.[22]

Uncommon Grounds in an ex-mining town

You can find the Uncommon Grounds Café in a small Pennsylvanian town. It was started by a Christian worker and his wife for people who were struggling financially or emotionally.

They sell coffee for 50 cents, people can hang out for as long as they like, and there is space where individuals can talk and be listened to.

Open Mic nights allow individuals to share poetry, music or dance. Art shows give opportunities to local painters, photographers, and potters. Other people learn how to cook. As they receive appreciative feedback, individuals who have had little affirmation start to feel valued. On Saturdays, a free meal is followed by informal worship.

Mark was an angry, disruptive, and horribly broken

21 http://www.freshexpressions.org.uk/news/a-fresh-expression-of-church-is-not-a-cheap-and-cheerful-option-by-caroline-holt (accessed 15 July 2013).

22 www.freshexpressions.org.uk/stories/playhouse (accessed 15 July 2013).

alcoholic. The café's leaders found him almost uncontrollable, but with much prayer and spiritual help continued to love him.

One day, completely out of character, Mark came to Saturday dinner quietly, joined in the discussion peacefully, stayed for prayer, prayed publicly himself, and received prayer.

From that day on he was transformed, more under control, and confident that God was working in his life. After several months, on his own initiative he entered rehab.

Outreach in socially deprived neighbourhoods (as elsewhere) is often based on hospitality. A Christian family moves into the area and keeps inviting people to their home. Relationships slowly deepen, individuals start eating together regularly, mealtime conversations touch on matters of life and create opportunities to share the gospel, simple Bible study and prayer eventually become part of the meal (or occur at a different time), and slowly people enter the kingdom.

A church in Bristol, England extended hospitality to a marginalized section of society nearby. It opened a Sunday "Drop In" on its premises with a cup of tea, some food, pool and table tennis, newspapers, and a prayer board. Towards the end of the session, someone invites requests for prayer and a short prayer time follows.

In 2010 numbers varied from fifteen to twenty-five each week. Some had asked to be baptized. The leaders see Drop In not as a staging post to the existing congregation, but as:

an experiment in a new way of being church, at a time when regular church has lost its draw. We do not know where it is leading, or whether it will last...We think we have created something – small and fragile, certainly – where healing and transformation can take place, and a new kind of community can grow.[23]

Crossing ethnic boundaries

In a multicultural area, Barry and Camilla Johnston have gathered a small community, called Sidewalk. Every Saturday during spring, summer, and autumn, the team take their yellow van to the same local park where children, many from Muslim families, gather to play.

They run an hour of activities that include songs, games, a memory verse, a drama based on a Bible story, three object lessons, and a life lesson – a cartoon story tying it all together.

Though it's aimed at children, parents and older siblings watch from the back. Some are increasingly taking on small responsibilities and suggesting ideas.

Members of the Sidewalk community visit the families of children who attend. The community itself meets regularly for fun and food. Individuals start in the park to build relationships with whomever is there, and then gather in a team member's home.

The community includes seasoned Christians, new Christians, and not-yet Christians. In 2012 members were asking what kind of deeper spiritual input would sustain such a diverse bunch.[24]

Shaped for the context

A thread through all these stories is that witnessing communities take different shapes in different settings. They seek to express the life of the church in ways that both fit their context and remain faithful to Jesus.

---

23 *Church Times,* 16 December 2011.

24 www.freshexpressions.org.uk/stories/sidewalk (accessed 9 May 2013).

Some Christians are nervous about this. They worry that, in trying to connect with the surrounding culture, Christian communities risk selling out to that culture and soft-pedalling the costly demands of the gospel. Church could lose its distinctiveness.

Yet some degree of accommodation to culture is part of normal life. In conversation, we adjust ourselves to the other person out of respect. When we go abroad we adapt to the local customs. Public speakers tailor themselves to their audiences. They address themes that are important to their hearers and use illustrations that resonate with them.

God himself adapts to culture when he speaks to us. Scripture is not an abstract, otherworldly book, dropped out of heaven. The books of the Bible were connected to the ancient cultures in which they were written, and so spoke to them. The Bible was written in the languages of the day – Hebrew, Greek and a little Aramaic. Temples, priests, and sacrifices, which were woven into the ancient world, were very much part of the Old Testament too. The New Testament books address different issues and use similar material in different ways because they were written initially for different audiences.

As biblical scholar Peter Enns puts it: "When God reveals himself, he always does so to people, which means that he must speak and act in ways that they will understand."[25] God respects human beings so much that he adjusts his level and method of communication to suit them.

Following Jesus

Jesus is the supreme example of adapting to others. He did not hover above culture to avoid being contaminated. He thoroughly immersed himself in the Jewish way of life.

---

25 Peter Enns, *Inspiration and Incarnation: Evangelicals and the Problem of the Old Testament*, Grand Rapids: Baker, 2005, p. 20.

He spoke Aramaic with a Galilean accent. He took part in his society's celebrations and traditions. His parables drew on the Jewish patterns of thought and the rhetorical traditions of his day.[26] He spoke in different ways to the crowds and to the Pharisees, to Nicodemus and to Peter.

When he rose from the dead and ascended to heaven, he did not leave his Jewishness behind. He ascended as a Jew. Jesus retains his Jewish flesh while sitting next to the Father.[27]

This is important. Christian communities do not abandon their cultures when the Spirit draws them closer to God. Your cuisine, music, clothes, social habits, and general patterns of life are not embarrassments, to be jettisoned as you become more like Christ.

Rather, when Jesus welcomes a Christian community, he welcomes it with its ordinary life. As members of the community live out their faith individually and corporately, they become exhibitors – though imperfect – of what "the way we do things round here" would be like if it was under Christ. They witness to the transformation of culture within the kingdom.

So in taking varied shapes to fit the context, witnessing communities follow the examples of Scripture and of Jesus. It is only by looking different in different cultures that they can tell the full story of Jesus, which transcends culture.

Four boundaries

Does this mean that anything goes? Clearly not. To live out the *distinctive* story of Jesus, the church cannot be the same as every other organization and social group. It must be different – like Jesus, who lived an everyday life but in a singular way.

---

26 Dean Flemming, *Contextualization in the New Testament. Patterns for Theology and Mission*, Leicester: Apollos, 2005, p. 21.

27 Markus Bockmehl, "God's Life as a Jew: Remembering the Son of God as Son of David", in Beverly Roberts Gaventa & Richard B. Hays (eds), *Seeking the Identity of Jesus: A Pilgrimage*, Grand Rapids: Eerdmans, 2008, p. 76.

Christian communities can do the same if they put four boundaries round adapting to context – boundaries that allow them to say, "It seems good to the Holy Spirit and to us" (Acts 15:28).

- The first is to remain faithful to Scripture.

- The second is to consult the wider church when interpreting Scripture. Individuals do this, for example, when they use Bible-reading aids and commentaries in their devotions.

- The third is the mission context. Does an application of Scripture aid or hinder God's mission?

- The fourth is shared discernment. When the interpretation and application of the Bible is shared prayerfully within the Christian community, as it was at Corinth (1 Corinthians 12 – 14), one person is less likely to lead the community astray.

For some fifteen years I have been speaking to audiences about new types of church, many of which meet on a weekday. Yet, surprisingly, on only three occasions has someone asked me about Sunday observance. "Is it right for these groups not to worship on the first day of the week?"

Imagine that a witnessing community sees itself as church and worships during the week. How might it address Sunday worship, working within these four boundaries?

First, as it seeks to remain faithful to Scripture, it would not simply ignore what happened in the New Testament. The first Christians deliberately met on the first day of the week, the day Jesus rose from the dead. This should raise a question for the community about worshipping on a weekday and not a Sunday.

As the group wrestles with this, it would also need to reference the church at large. Many Christians have interpreted Sunday worship flexibly. The Roman Catholic Church, for example, often celebrates Mass on Saturday evenings for those who don't come on Sundays. Many evangelical churches, too, have weekday services for people who don't attend at the weekend.

In addition, the community would have to think about its mission context. If it serves people who work shifts or have family commitments on Sunday, would inviting them to a Sunday-morning event be realistic?

Finally, through a process of shared discernment, members of the group would need to pull together Sunday worship in Scripture, the flexibility allowed by the wider church, and the requirements of their mission context. "What makes sense in our situation?"

Members might conclude that when they worship during the week, they would make a special point of praying for Christians meeting on the coming Sunday. They might decide that whoever was available would worship together on Easter Sunday. Or they might come up with another solution.

Whatever they resolved, their conclusion would be within the four boundaries of Scripture, the wider church, the mission context, and shared discernment within the community.

Conclusion

Many people hold back from starting a witnessing community because they are stuck in the train tracks of traditional thought. Yet growing numbers of Christians have broken out of their inherited mindsets. They are spotting new opportunities for small or larger groups of Christians to make a difference to others in their day-to-day lives.

At their best, as described in Chapter 1, these groups are missional – they work mainly with people from outside the church. They are contextual – they fit the culture and circumstances of those involved. They are formational – forming disciples is central to their thinking. They are ecclesial – rather than being stepping stones to church, they encourage an experience of church in situ.

Some of the examples in this chapter look so different from "normal" church that you may wonder if they are church at all. Some probably aren't, but they all offer at least a taste of church. The more they grow in the four relationships of church – with Jesus, with his wider body, with the world, and within the fellowship – the more fully church they become.

Charles Darwin, the British naturalist, said, "It is not the strongest of the species that survive, nor the most intelligent, but the most responsive to change."

These touches of church, which are to be found in more and more fragments of society, provide signs that the Christian faith is not dying, as many sociologists have predicted. It is responding to change. It is coming alive in fresh ways. Fired by the Spirit, Christians are prayerfully joining together to find innovative means of serving people, revealing Jesus, and seeing lives transformed.

PART TWO

Tools for developing witnessing communities

Chapter 4

ONE SECRET YOU SHOULD KNOW

St Laurence, Reading, UK focuses on young people. Now a church, it started when a small team hung out with young people at local schools, listening to their concerns and ideas. Nine years later, nearly fifty young people were growing in the Christian faith. Few had any previous church experience.

St Laurence was far from an overnight success. After a few years, Chris Russell and his fellow leaders felt frustrated. They were making contact with young people in all sorts of ways. They had formed some good relationships. But hardly any teenagers had come to faith.

The breakthrough came when a senior church leader suggested a framework for thinking about their work, illustrated below:

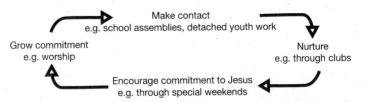

"Make contact" involves building relationships with young people and engaging in simple acts of service. "Nurture" centres on community. A variety of clubs attract teenagers not mainly through activities, but by encouraging a sense of belonging.

Special weekends "encourage commitment to Jesus". As individuals come to faith, they join a worshipping community in which they "grow commitment" to Jesus.

This framework has encouraged the leaders to ask of any activity, "What happens next?" "Is the step from one stage to the next too big?" For example, in 2010 they were planning a "Nurture 2". The leap from "Nurture" to "Encourage commitment" would become two shorter steps.

Being intentional about a journey

Some people cannot envisage how a witnessing community might develop. They can imagine joining with a couple of friends to serve others in their neighbourhood, at work or through a shared passion or a network, but they cannot see how this might take others on a path to Jesus. They stare at the canvas without knowing how to create a picture on it.

The one secret you should know is how to prayerfully paint this picture. It involves being intentional: creating a journey for people that combines loving service with evangelism, putting up signposts to Jesus, and placing these signposts at appropriate milestones on individuals' pathways to faith. You must be purposeful about a journey, signposts, and pathways.

A framework, not a plan

The starting point is not to travel blind, but – like St Laurence – to have a framework that will enable you:

- to recognize the road you are on and be encouraged;

- to chart your progress and understand what to expect;

- to be strategic. Their framework encouraged the leaders of St Laurence to home in on activities that would help the young people move from one stage to the next. They could avoid squandering time and effort on initiatives that would lead nowhere.

A framework is not the same as a straitjacket. You need not feel boxed in, enslaved to an imposed plan. Rigid plans do not usually work. Members of the group may come and go. Circumstances may change. New opportunities may take you by surprise.

Witnessing communities tend to travel on journeys that are fluid, haphazard, and take an unexpected turn. This is hardly surprising. We live in an unpredictable world.

So you can't rely on plans, because events will often blow you off course. But planning is vital because you need to think through the next step. Rather than a plan, therefore, it is better to have a framework – a satnav that charts your course but leaves you free to adjust your route.

A worship-first journey

Many Christians belong to, or know of congregations that have encouraged church planting, where the emphasis is on the public launch of a new worshipping community.

Sometimes a church will send out a large team of around fifty people, with two or three paid staff. Once the ground has been prepared, a congregation is planted in vacant premises or perhaps in a church building threatened with closure.

The plant offers worship and/or preaching as a shop window, and members invite their friends. Through presentations, discussions on life issues, and other events, these friends are invited to attend a course to explore the faith further. If they make a commitment, they join a small group and get more involved in the church's life.

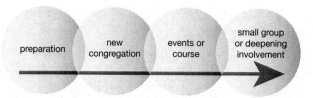

preparation · new congregation · events or course · small group or deepening involvement

Often these church plants scale up quickly. As the new congregation grows, it rapidly takes financial responsibility for its staff and adds more. The mission of the new church expands on a self-sustaining basis.

Planting at scale can be highly fruitful, especially among people who are dissatisfied with their existing church, have moved into a new area and are looking for a church, or who attended church in the past and are ready to return. But it is impossible for many churches, and can put ordinary Christians off – "I could never lead something that big." If you think this is the only model for taking Christian community to society, you will be likely to stay in your pew. But it is not.

Alongside these large church plants a growing number of Christians are getting together with a few friends, forming small witnessing groups in their everyday lives, and as a group loving and blessing the people they know.

Planting in depth is complementing planting at scale. Though they reach many people, large church plants cannot reach everyone. Their networks embrace only a section of the population. This is where small witnessing communities come into their own. They can burrow into parts of society untouched by the new church.

For example, a new congregation of (mainly) professionals may have few, if any, links into a low-income apartment block. Two or three members of the congregation may decide to live in the block. As they get to know their fellow residents, they may host social events in their home and start a weekly discussion, which evolves into a Bible study and eventually a small worshipping community.

For the residents, meeting with others from the block is a more manageable step than attending the much larger church plant, full of confident and articulate professionals.

So, if you start a new congregation using this worship-first approach, why don't you combine planting at scale with planting in depth? Why don't you encourage members of your new congregation to start witnessing communities among people you are not currently reaching?

A relationships-first journey

In much of the global North something interesting has happened. The preparation stage of traditional church planting – hanging out with people and putting on events to prepare for the public launch – has been getting longer. More time is spent listening to the context and building relationships before inviting people to a Christian event.

For most people, starting quite quickly with public worship is too big an initial step. That was the experience of one pioneer who used the traditional church-planting approach among young people in north-west London. He described his emotions after the public launch of their congregation.

I remember feeling deflated on the first Sunday we hired a community centre for Sunday-night worship. As I looked at the twenty people gathered there, I said to myself, "Why aren't there more people here?" A more appropriate question would have been, "Why should they come?"[1]

Where people are not ready to accept an invitation to something explicitly Christian, the journey may look more like this:

---

1 Quoted by George Lings, *Leading Fresh Expressions: Lessons from Hindsight*, The Sheffield Centre: Encounters on the Edge, 36, 2007, pp. 8–9.

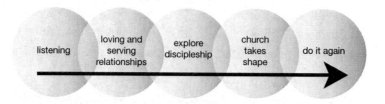

Listening and building relationships lasts considerably longer than with traditional church planting, and may include a variety of social activities. On the basis of loving and serving relationships, the witnessing community invites individuals to a Christian event where they can explore becoming disciples of Jesus. Church takes shape around those who come to faith. At its best, the new believers are encouraged to repeat the process and start a small Christian gathering themselves.

The Christian event may be meetings of the core team.

For example in Nashville, Tennessee a married couple joined up with another couple. They hung out with friends who had left church or were in limbo between churches, and made contact with their friends' friends.

They met them in cigar lounges and in other public places, where they could also bump into others and widen their circle of acquaintances.

People would inevitably ask them what they did. They replied that they were church planters, which often led to interesting conversations. If someone showed interest, they would be invited to a team meeting, where they could take part in the worship if they chose and explore following Jesus.

As these guests attended regularly, the team ballooned in size. Once it was large enough, the new church was launched publicly. Eighteen months later, seventy to eighty people, including children, were attending regularly.

Or people may be invited to a "discovery Bible study", a group for quiet Christian reflection, a discussion group on spirituality based on the life of Jesus, or to some other explicitly Christian activity.

> In Cincinnati, Ohio Moveable Feast comprises informal gatherings to discuss God, spirituality, religion, life, work, and culture. Gatherings can take place in people's homes, bars, coffee shops, parks, studios, or other locations. Moveable Feast conversations are an opportunity to ask questions and explore faith in a community setting.
>
> Revd Jane Gerdsen, the catalyst behind them, was clear that these groups needed to focus first on conversations, not worship. A worship-based group would self-select around people who were drawn to creative worship, omitting those at an earlier stage in their spiritual journeys.[2]

In cases like this, the worship-first method of church planting has morphed into *A relationships-first journey*. This second type of journey is well suited to people who feel some connection with the Christian faith, but need a deep experience of Christian love before they are ready to attend an event with Christian content.

In immigrant and some traditional working-class communities, where family and network ties are strong, "persons of peace" may play a key role in the journey by inviting others. "Persons of peace" (Luke 10:6) are individuals who are open to the gospel. They are well connected to other people and able to draw them together. They are natural gatherers of people.

Through "listening" and "loving and serving relationships", the witnessing community gets to know people, identifies one or more persons of peace, whets their appetite for the gospel, and then encourages them to invite their friends to their home or another suitable venue.

---

2 www.freshexpressions.org.uk/stories/moveablefeast (accessed 14 May 2013).

The Christian friend comes too and leads the gathering in a series of discovery Bible studies, based on stories from the gospels, during which individuals find Jesus and something of church takes shape round them.[3]

The Bible studies are based on a simple framework, such as these four questions which are adapted to the context:

What is the story about?
What does it mean to you?
What will you do in response?
Who will you share this with?

This approach is easy to use for emerging and new Christians, who are encouraged to repeat the approach with their friends.

Australian Steve Addison, who is a strong advocate of this approach, describes how he

was meeting with some Christian workers in Bangalore, India. They told me how they trained existing Christian believers to share their story, to share Jesus' story and to disciple new believers. They train with the expectation that people will immediately put into practice what they are learning. Recently they had trained 120 people. After the first week, the trainees were encouraged to share their story with five people before they returned for the next session. Every week they put into practice what they were learning. Every week the class size got smaller. After six weeks there were just fifteen participants.

Before I could ask the workers why they thought this approach was a good idea, they told me that the fifteen remaining participants had already started nine new churches. They pointed across the road and said, "There's a church meeting in that garage for taxi drivers and their families."[4]

---

3 For helpful resources, go to www.cmaresources.org; www.movements.net; www. newformsresources.co.uk

4 Steve Addison, *What Jesus Started,* Downers Grove: IVP, 2012, p. 178.

A serving-first journey

Maybe you are thinking, "That approach would never work with the people I know. They would never come to something explicitly Christian." In these situations, which are increasingly common in the global North, *A serving-first journey* will often be more appropriate.

This third type of journey does not start with worship, nor does it rely only on loving and serving relationships. Instead, after "listening", the witnessing community develops some kind of "loving and serving activity".

Around the activity, attention is given to "forming community", which emerges out of the relationships that are established naturally. Within the community relationships deepen, there are signposts to Jesus, and individuals are invited, where appropriate, to "explore discipleship".

As people come to faith, an experience of church takes shape round them and ideally they learn to "do it again" – to start a witnessing community in an area of their lives.

The journey differs from *A relationships-first journey* in that loving and serving take more organized forms. In both journeys, Christians start small <u>communities</u> that are <u>visible</u> in daily life and are <u>active</u> in loving and serving others. In *A serving-first journey*, however, the organization of loving and serving is more pronounced.

A serving-first journey is well suited to people who would not respond immediately to an invitation to an explicitly Christian activity, such as a Bible study or a discussion of Christian spirituality. "Loving and serving activities" provide a context in which people can be drawn together, relationships can form and grow, individuals can experience Christian love, and opportunities to explore Jesus can be introduced.

The journey also has the great merit of being an holistic form of mission. Loving and serving activities – "works of mercy" – are combined with evangelism and making disciples.

A good example of *A serving-first journey* has been described by Barbara Glasson, a Methodist minister.

> She walked the streets of central Liverpool, England for a year, watching and listening. With a group of friends she began to bake bread, giving the loaves away. Others joined this loving and serving core. As they made bread together, a community began to form.
>
> They started a period of quiet reflection in the side room in the middle of the day. Participants were invited to comment on a Bible passage but not interrupt each other. Silent prayer and reflection followed. As individuals explored the Christian faith, "church" gradually took shape.[5]

Another example is TANGO on Merseyside, UK – Together As Neighbours Giving Out.

> TANGO began in 2000 and has grown into a café and recycling centre, in which Christians witness through action and conversation.
>
> Expanding from one day a week to three, Wednesdays evolved into a craft day for "Golden Oldies", who developed a sense of belonging.
>
> The latter were then offered, as part of Wednesdays, an

---

5 Barbara Glasson, *Mixed-up Blessing: A New Encounter with Being Church,* Peterborough: Inspire, 2006.

opportunity to pray for half an hour. Twenty to thirty Golden Oldies attend; some are churchgoers and others not. An evening cell held at the home of one of the leaders provides an opportunity to pursue faith further.[6]

Listening

It may be helpful to look more closely at the circles in *A serving-first journey*, recognizing that many of them will also be found in *A relationships-first journey*.

Prayerful listening is vital. This is what Jesus did. As part of preparing for his ministry, the twelve-year-old Jesus stayed behind in Jerusalem and listened to the temple authorities. He established a relationship as he sat respectfully among them. He asked questions, engaged in dialogue, took time (he was there for three days), and presumably took a risk: would he incur his parents' anger?

The purpose of listening is to discover what God wants you to do. It involves listening to the people you feel called to serve: what are their longings and concerns? How might you best serve them with the resources you've got? What do they think of the ideas you're starting to hatch? Who else serves them? What has been their experience?

Listening also involves, crucially, paying attention directly to God through prayer and Bible study, and listening to Christian friends and prayer partners: what is their advice?

You might also listen to the wider church – by reading books and blogs, talking to people, and much else. In particular, have other Christians done something similar to what you have in mind? What have they learned? Go to www.freshexpressions. org.uk/stories. You will find hundreds of stories of witnessing communities. Why not email someone who is doing the sort

---

6 www.freshexpressions.org.uk/stories/tango (accessed 14 May 2013).

of thing you are thinking about, and ask for a phone or Skype conversation?

You can think of listening as taking your bearings from four points of the compass.

"360-degree listening"

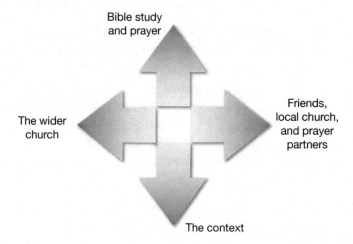

Bible study and prayer

The wider church

Friends, local church, and prayer partners

The context

Sometimes this listening can take a while. Perhaps you feel that you and your Christian friends are getting nowhere. Despite lots of praying and talking together, you cannot see a way forward. You are getting impatient.

Do not despair! Cambridge University psychologist Sara Savage has written, "The experience of being listened to is so close to the experience of being loved as to be indistinguishable."[7]

So don't short-change the listening process! Use the time to get to know your friends better, keep exploring ideas, and remember: listening is not wasted time; it's an investment of time – in love.

---

7 Beta Course, Session 2, www.beta-course.org

Loving and serving activities

As part of this "360-degree listening", members of your witnessing community will strengthen their relationships with the people they plan to serve, and perhaps establish some new ones. (The circles are overlapping because the stages are not discrete.) In the process, they will be led to some practical ways to serve them.

> An example is the Earlybird Café for parents and carers who are dropping off children at the St Paul's Church nursery in Dorking, England. The Café started with the simple offer of a weekday place in church to chat. This loving service then evolved into a first-Sunday-in-the-month café church, which in 2011 was attracting eighty children and 175 adults.[8]

Reverb

Reverb is a Methodist initiative in Inverness, Scotland, which seeks to serve the community in four ways:

• *dig your heart out.* Local businesses and churches sponsor garden makeovers for deserving local people. This creates opportunities for young people connected to Reverb;

• *wash your heart out.* This is a means of getting to know people based on Jesus' washing of the disciples' feet. Members of Reverb's core group say, "If you tell us who you are, we'll wash your car";

• *sing your heart out.* This took the form of a carol service on a football field;

• *path people.* During winter, any disadvantaged person can ring a number to ask Reverb to clear their path of snow and ice.

---

8 www.freshexpressions.org.uk/stories/stpaulscafechurch (accessed 15 May 2013).

Forming community

Community develops around the relationships and activities the core Christians establish. Individuals get to know each other, trust one another, and develop a sense of belonging. Often this occurs naturally, but being intentional can inch the process along.

> *Breakfast@9 is a café-style church on Sunday mornings. Forty to fifty parents and children attend each week. At first, people sat round separate tables. But the leaders noticed that people were not talking to each other. "By putting two tables side by side, the families began to chat a lot more."[9] Little things can strengthen the experience of community.*

Forming community is valuable in its own right. Jesus did this when he ate meals with his followers, travelled with them, and devoted periods of special time to them. But a loving community is also important for mission. It:

- reveals something of Christ;

- gives people a partial, though important, experience of church;

- creates trusting relationships within which to share the gospel;

- spurs people to come back. Some of Britain's secular Recovery Groups have discovered the secret of encouraging drug and alcohol addicts to return to the group: ask other members to send them a card saying they're missed.

Exploring discipleship

Low-key evangelism may occur during the "listening", "loving and serving", and "building community" stages. But, when the need arises, you may have to create more explicit opportunities

---

9 www.freshexpressions.org.uk/stories/breakfastat9 (accessed 14 May 2013).

to explore following Jesus.

You can start by mentoring individuals on a one-to-one basis, for example. One person may be followed by another, till there are enough to form an explorers' group.

Once you have sufficient people to start a group, you can use or adapt a published course, write your own material, or simply discuss the stories Jesus told. When the group is hooked, you might work through Mark's Gospel.

Church takes shape

As individuals come closer to Jesus, you can introduce them to a progressively fuller experience of church – for example, by inviting them to worship with your core group.

Your worship will change, of course, as you adapt to people who are new to faith (and you may have to create an additional opportunity for long-standing Christians on the team to study and worship in greater depth).

Alternatively, you could encourage an explorers' group to stay together and become a worshipping cell. If the cell multiplies, two or more cells might cluster together in monthly or occasional meetings to provide a larger experience of church.

It is important that a new cell grows in its connection to the wider church. Believers are baptized into the whole body of Christ. They must be involved with the wider body if they are to identify with it, give to it, and receive from it. So where the initiative is under the umbrella of a local church, emerging Christians should be invited to social events and other activities of the parent church.

If the initiative is beyond the local church, new believers can:

- be encouraged to explore the resources of the wider church online;

- be invited to prayer retreats, conferences, and other events organized by your denomination, or by one or more churches in your locality;

- be invited to your "weekend church" if you have a second church involvement. If they find a home there, like you they may end up attending two local churches. As discussed in earlier chapters, nowhere does the New Testament say that you must attend only one local church.

Christian cells will strengthen the spiritual life of the wider group from which they emerged, so that the whole group has a stronger flavour of church. Occasionally a luncheon club, influenced by the new Christians, might include an optional Holy Communion or "a remembrance of the Last Supper".

Remember, as I said in Chapter 2, the essence of church is four interlocking sets of relationships centred on Jesus: with God, the world, the wider church, and within the fellowship. As your community grows in these relationships, it will experience something of what it means to be church.

Do it again

In 2002, Methodists in a former mining town in Nottinghamshire, England held an Alpha course. At the end three-quarters of the group, all with very little church experience, wanted to carry on.

They continued to meet fortnightly on Thursday evenings at a local teashop, known as Grannies, for coffee, cake, prayer, worship, and discussion. They used material such as Nicky Gumbel's book A Life Worth Living.

When a new Alpha course was proposed, this follow-up group supported it by praying at the same time as the Alpha evenings, serving food or sitting at tables to aid discussion.

After four Alpha courses (and follow-up groups) over

> *two years, the next follow-up group developed into a new*
> *church in its own right, known as Fellowsihp@Grannies. It*
> *too planned to resource future Alpha groups.*[10]

Fellowship@Grannies illustrates the principle of "Do it again" – graduates from each Alpha course supported the next. New Christians learned how to repeat the pattern of making disciples that the Spirit had used to bring them to faith.

The same has been true of Sorted, which began among early teens who enjoyed skateboarding. Eight years on, while retaining links to the original group (Sorted 1) Andy Milne, the founder of Sorted, started a second initiative – Sorted 2 – in a different school.

A year later, older members in Sorted 1 were talking about doing it again themselves – this time among younger teenagers in the original school: "We want to give something back."

Echoes of Jesus

This pattern of listening, loving and serving, building community, exploring discipleship, experiencing something of church, and doing it again echoes Luke's account of Jesus' public ministry.

Having met Jesus in listening mode in chapter 2, in his early years we see him teaching, healing, and performing exorcisms. He is loving and serving.

Then in chapters 5:1–11 and 6:12–16, there is a new focus on calling disciples. Jesus forms his community, describing it as his family (8:19–21).

Building community persists alongside his public ministry, but attention shifts to making disciples – for example, sending out the Twelve and the Seventy-two in chapters 9 and 10, teaching specifically directed at the disciples (as in chapter 17) and the Last Supper in chapter 22.

---

10 www.freshexpressions.org.uk/guide/develop/becoming/grannies (accessed 14 May 2013).

Luke describes how church takes shape in Acts, his second volume, where "doing it again" is a strong theme. The apostles do what Jesus had done – they heal the sick, cast out demons, and pass on Jesus's teaching. Paul's church planting was a continuous movement of reproduction.

Not a means to an end

Each stage in *A serving-first journey* (as with *A relationships-first journey*) has its own integrity. "Listening" is valuable in its own right. Even if you never proceeded further, your time would have been well spent. The same is true of "loving and serving activities". If your journey stopped there, you would still have done something wonderful for the kingdom. Likewise with the other circles.

This makes the *journey* quite liberating. You need not feel pressured to get to the end. Each stage is not *merely* a stepping stone to the next.

You can enjoy each stage as you inhabit it. If the Spirit builds momentum from listening, you can try out some expressions of practical service. If these create Spirit-filled energy and attract people, you can help community to form and deepen. If this creates a context in which individuals awaken to Jesus, you can work with the Spirit to help them explore further.

Don't bash down doors between one stage and the next. Just prayerfully open a door if the Spirit beckons.

Be flexible!

A worship-first journey, A relationships-first journey and *A serving-first journey* are models. They are generalizations. What each model looks like in practice varies immensely. Sometimes differences between the models become blurred.

The methods used in one model can often be used in the

others. This is particularly true of the "discovery Bible studies" favoured by some proponents of *A relationships-first journey*. The simplicity of these studies enables new Christians to learn how to do something similar with their friends. The approach is well suited to *A serving-first journey*, for example.

The stages in each model overlap and not infrequently occur at the same time. In *A serving-first journey*, for instance, "community" may form almost immediately the "loving and serving activity" gets under way.

You may think you are on one journey, only to find that you are on a different one. You started on *A worship-first journey*, found the "preparation" involved "listening" and forming "loving and serving relationships", and then discovered that it was too big a step to invite people to an explicitly Christian event. So you put in a "loving and serving activity" and now find that you are travelling on *A serving-first journey*.

Or the Spirit calls you to do something entirely different and you create your own journey! Stay flexible. Keep listening to the Spirit. These are the keys.

Being intentional about signposts

On *A serving-first journey*, you may wonder how individuals can be invited to move through the circles – through "loving and serving activity" and "forming community" to the point where they want to explore Jesus. How can they be encouraged to open their hearts to him?

This is, of course, the work of the Holy Spirit. So there is no substitute for the prayers of the Christians involved. At the same time, as you "pray continually" (1 Thessalonians 5:17) for the people you lovingly serve, you can put in signposts that point them to Jesus.

These signposts are vital if "loving and serving activities" are not to be just another piece of charity. Acts of mercy are an important part of the kingdom. But they become even more worthwhile when accompanied by pointers to Jesus.

What might these signposts look like? They can range from acts of kingdom kindness to missional worship.

Acts of kingdom kindness

Being kind reveals Jesus' heart of love. People with little or no faith can catch a glimpse of him. Of course Christians in the core group will want to be kind to those whom they love and serve. But being kind can be more than that. It can be an attitude of the initiative as a whole. Believers and non-believers alike can engage in acts of the kingdom that show Christian love to people outside the initiative.

Inviting not-yet-Christians to join with you in kingdom kindness can open them to the Holy Spirit. Many of those who don't yet know Jesus will share your kingdom concerns. As they join you in serving others, they will be drawn to the One who is the source of their loving and serving values.

A "fathers-and-sons" soccer team might support a nearby family with a disabled son. A book club with a spiritual dimension might support a school library in Uganda. A gathering around food might encourage regular donations to fight hunger in the global South.

Most people long to be good, but struggle to achieve this on their own. Belonging to a group with an altruistic dimension will help them:

- to do some of the good they aspire to;

- to be more committed to the group – "It feels so worthwhile! We have this link with Uganda";

- to be open to Jesus, as they discover that their acts of kindness faintly mirror his acts of grace.

Being kind to people outside the group is especially important when the group gathers around a hobby or shared interest. This type of group can easily become inward-looking – "We meet together and discuss issues that matter." But what about serving others? Acts of kingdom kindness insert outward-loving DNA into the community.

Imagine that two or three Christians invite their friends to a fortnightly discussion over a meal. Supporting a water project in rural India will help the gathering to be more than a means of consumerist self-fulfilment.

If some of these friends seek Jesus, they will do so in the context of a *serving* community. They will be walking in the way of the kingdom before their conversion, and their hearts will be warmed.

Stories about Jesus

Telling stories about Jesus puts Jesus on the agenda more explicitly. In natural conversations, Christians can share with others what Jesus has done in their lives.

"Did you have a good weekend?" "Yes, thanks. My church had a successful fun day..." The other person learns that you belong to a church.

As the person gets to know you better, he or she may ask what the day involved. In time, the conversation may extend to questions about what "going to church" entails, and perhaps even why you attend. Slowly the Spirit opens the door for you to share Jesus in response to the other person.

"Why did God allow that earthquake, then?" the person asks. You might reply, "I wish I could answer that! But what I can tell you is that when I lost my job last year – a tiny disaster compared to the earthquake, but real to me – Jesus was a lifeline."

Stories about Jesus may include events that provoke questions about him.

> *Penny Joyce, whose work in a new neighbourhood was described in the last chapter, held pre-Christmas events for fathers and sons to wrap Christmas presents, with mulled wine, juice, and mince pies.*
>
> *She included a short talk about what Christmas meant to her. If someone expressed an interest, she invited them to another event in which, for example, a speaker might share how Jesus made a difference to them.*

Some café churches have a "God slot". Publicized in advance, someone gives a testimony or a short Christian reflection, which can open up fruitful conversations.

> *When she started "New Creations" for people making cards, Janet Cross suggested that each week had a theme, such as spring time, holidays, and Mothering Sunday. Gift cards were made on the theme. Janet would introduce the theme and briefly describe what it meant to her as a Christian. Gradually, Jesus was put onto the agenda.*

Prayer and healing

Answered prayer goes beyond someone else's story about Jesus. The not-yet-Christian becomes a direct witness of God at work. He or she has a story about Jesus too.

A twenty-year-old commented, "My friend had no interest in God till she knew that I was praying for her grandmother. When her grandmother unexpectedly got better, her interest jumped a mile."

> *In north-west London, a language café hosted afternoon tea for ethnic women with poor English. The women sat at small tables and were invited to discuss a topic over tea.*
>
> *The leaders were frustrated because they did not know how to combine their act of service with evangelism. Then*

> *they were given an idea. They put up a prayer board and invited the women to pin prayer requests on it. The team promised to pray for these requests, as well as for requests made confidentially to the team.*
>
> *Six months later, the women were all talking about their prayer requests, enabling Christian themes to be included in the topics for table discussion. A course introducing Christianity became the next step.*

Healing, as one form of answered prayer, can provide an especially powerful experience of God. Healing may come through the love of Christian friends, prayer in personal devotions or corporate worship, healing services, or other types of prayer ministry. Some people have called it power evangelism, while for others it is lower-key.

Miraculous healing is not given mainly for personal blessing – it is important not to collude with the contemporary illusion that we can cheat death. "God wants everyone to be healed" is true of the next life but not this one. Miraculous healing witnesses to God's coming kingdom. It points to and is a foretaste of the world's destiny – to be refashioned by Jesus.[11]

When the purpose of healing is explained to the non-believer (the miraculous must be accompanied by the word), it becomes a dramatic signpost. The drama of the kingdom is enacted in front of the person who has yet to find faith.

Missional worship[12]

This is "halfway-house" worship designed for people who have little faith or are confused about God. It goes beyond warming

---

11 Luke Bretherton, "Pneumatology, Healing and Political Power: Sketching a Pentecostal Political Theology", in Jane Williams (ed.), *The Holy Spirit in the World Today*, London: Alpha International, 2011, pp. 138–139.

12 This is based on Ann Morisy's concept of "apt liturgy". Ann Morisy, *Journeying Out: A New Approach to Christian Mission*, London: Morehouse, 2004, pp. 156-167.

people's hearts. It does more than enable the not-yet-Christian to hear about Jesus or see him at work. It creates opportunities for the person to actually encounter God. These encounters can heighten spiritual awareness and encourage individuals to explore more.

> One example is baby massage and prayer, which is exceptionally well suited to today's young families. Mothers can be invited to massage their babies and pray for them at the same time. They often get an experience of God they never expected.
>
> Very different is the retired persons' luncheon club that put lighted candles on the table after the meal, played some Christian music, invited someone to read a few verses from Scripture, allowed time for silent prayer, and included some spoken prayers – all in about twenty minutes. Guests could leave after lunch or stay on.

Some church-run cafés have adjacent quiet rooms, perhaps with lighted candles, where individuals can pray and reflect silently.

Leaders running the UK-based Alpha course among people with little church background often testify to the key role of worship as part of the course. Worship can be quite "full-on" if sensitively led.

As individuals come to faith, missional worship can evolve into a richer expression of Christian worship. Holy Communion can be introduced and more time can be given to unfolding the word.

Being intentional about pathways to faith

Your witnessing community will not necessarily put in all these signposts of kingdom kindness, creative spirituality, stories about Jesus, prayer and healing, and missional worship. Nor will you necessarily introduce them in this order. Several will exist at the same time.

They should emerge naturally as your initiative develops, and should be sensitive to individuals' pathways to faith. You should take time to pray intentionally about these pathways and understand them.

From point to pathway

How people become Christians has changed dramatically. When I was a teenager, I used to attend Billy Graham rallies where people were encouraged to make a commitment. Local churches put on guest services with a similar emphasis.

It was assumed that there was a *point* at which conversion occurred – "a crisis moment, in which an emotionally charged sinner was brought to release and sudden insight by the power of the Spirit."[13]

During the 1990s, perceptions in much of the West changed. The evangelistic appeal shifted from "Get up out of your seats and come forward now…" to "Join a group that will be exploring the Christian faith over the coming weeks at…"[14]

The idea of conversion at a point in time was not lost, but greater emphasis was placed on the *process* of conversion. Courses such as Alpha, Christianity Explored, and Emmaus, to take three British examples, led people through a movement to faith.

More recently there has been a further shift. Writing about contemporary spirituality, the philosopher and intellectual historian Charles Taylor notes that when spirituality is pursued intentionally today, it takes the form of the quest.[15]

People prefer to be on a journey than to reach a destination.

---

13 Graham Tomlin, *The Provocative Church,* London: SPCK, 2002, p. 89.

14 Robert Warren, *Signs of Life: How Goes the Decade of Evangelism?,* London: Church House Publishing, 1995, p. 65.

15 Charles Taylor, *A Secular Age,* Cambridge, MA: Belknap Press, 2007, pp. 507–508.

Destination speaks of closure, whereas a journey keeps options open. Possibilities must not be shut down by presuming a person's starting point or ruling something out of court. Individuals must travel their own paths and respect the paths of others. In seeking support, people would rather have resources than ready-made answers.

In this climate, while some people will come to a point of conversion and many will follow the process of a structured course, an individual's *pathway* to faith is of special importance. There is a greater emphasis on the personal nature of the pathway an individual is on.

It is important to remember that these are not alternatives – someone's pathway may involve a process of study at some stage, and during that process the person may come to a point of commitment. Rather, the emphasis has changed.

Pathways speak of :

- *variety* – your journey to faith may be different from mine. A signpost to Jesus that works for one person may not work for others;

- *duration* – journeys to faith can be prolonged, especially among the growing number of people with little or no Christian background. You will need patience as you wait for someone to come to faith;

- *companionship* – it is comforting and helpful to have someone with you on a longish journey. To be a companion, respect and trust are the bottom lines.

Milestones to faith

In the group that gathers round your "loving and serving activity", individuals will be at different stages on their pathway. Being aware of these milestones will help you to signpost them to Jesus appropriately.

A post-modern path to faith

- From distrust to trust – "Christians are OK".

- From complacent to curious – "Jesus is interesting".

- From curious to open – "Jesus could be for me".

- From meandering to seeking – "Jesus is worth taking seriously".

- From seeking to joining – "I'll turn to Jesus".

- From joining to growing – "Help me to live like Jesus".

Source: Don Everts and Doug Shaupp, *Pathway to Jesus: Crossing the Thresholds of Faith*, Nottingham: IVP, 2009 (slightly adapted).

Through the Holy Spirit, some people may need encouragement to cross from *distrust to trust* – from being suspicious of Christians to seeing that "Christians are OK". Being generous of heart, laid-back in speaking about your faith, and a reliable friend will help to win their trust.

For those who have paused at this milestone, loving reliability is vital. "Acts of kingdom kindness" by the community may be sufficient signposts to Jesus.

Individuals may stand on the stepping stone of trust, but remain complacent about the Christian faith – "It's irrelevant to me." So a possible next step is from *being complacent to being curious*. The person starts thinking, "Jesus is interesting."

Alongside "acts of kingdom kindness", "stories about Jesus", "prayer and healing", and "missional worship" may be helpful nudges along the way.

A further step may be from *being curious to being open* – from

"Jesus is interesting" to "Jesus could be for me". All the previous signposts may still play a part, but slightly more challenging conversations may be important.

In some cases, an additional step may be from *meandering to seeking* – from "Jesus could be for me" to "Jesus is worth taking seriously". Some people find it easier to stand on the edge than to commit to exploring Jesus purposefully.

So, invitations stressing the limited commitment involved in the next step can be helpful. "Why don't the two of us look at a story Jesus told, as a one-off?" If the discussion goes well, you can suggest meeting again. Taster evenings for a brief course could be another approach. Keeping an explorers' course short – to a few evenings – may be crucial, too.

A fifth step may be from *seeking to joining* – from exploring Jesus to "I'll turn to Jesus". Some people may find the opportunity to make a commitment helpful. But in our low-commitment culture, others may find this too big a step. They may prefer to journey gradually and cross the line, as it were, imperceptibly.

Carol (not her real name) came regularly to one of my enquirers' courses. She then moved away. A couple of years later I met her at a Christian conference. She told me how she had been drawn into a discussion with a Jehovah's Witness. The person asked, "Are you a Christian?" Carol replied, "Yes" – and then thought, "I've never said that before."

If you are unsure what to do, remember the golden rule: ask the people concerned. So ask the person if it would help them to make a commitment or whether they would prefer to inch along step by step.

Once someone has turned to Jesus, the journey of course does not stop. There is a further step from *joining to growing* – from "I'll turn to Jesus" to "Help me to live like Jesus".

Helpful conversations

Often Christians are reluctant to share their faith, fearing they will embarrass themselves. Behind this lurks the correct instinct that you should say the right thing at the right time. But individuals lack a framework to think more deeply about this.

"A post-modern path to faith" offers a map on which to prayerfully locate where the other person is on their journey. If the person is hovering round mistrust or complacency, being a kind friend may be the best form of personal evangelism.

If they are further along the path, nearer the curious or meandering milestones, inviting them to a one-off outreach event or taster evening may be a suitable act of evangelism. In a subsequent conversation, it may be enough to describe what Jesus means to you. When personal evangelism is sensitive to the milestones individuals have reached, it becomes much less intimidating. It becomes something that any Christian can do.

At the same time, Christians who are tempted to rush things can be encouraged to slow down by asking, "What milestone has the other person reached?" They cannot expect someone to jump from being suspicious of Christians to "Jesus is worth taking seriously" in one leap! It is enough to help the person to their next milestone.

Different stages, different signposts

"A post-modern path to faith" will also help your witnessing community to discern when to put up a signpost and what type of signpost is appropriate for whom. For example, you may be able to provide a series of signposts, such as:

- cleaning up the environment, as a witness to the kingdom;

- opportunities to request prayer;

- a series of discussion evenings on life issues;

- events in which Christians describe the difference Jesus makes to their lives;

- a simple course introducing Jesus.

Being aware of the different milestones individuals have reached will help you to point them to the most appropriate signposts. You might invite one person to a life-issues evening and someone else to the course about Jesus. You won't start the latter till enough people have reached the "seeking" milestone.

Pointing to Jesus

If you are starting a witnessing community, what is the one secret that you should know? It is how to combine serving others in the midst of life with evangelism. You can do this by travelling *A worship-first journey*, *A relationships-first journey* or *A serving-first journey*. The latter – a journey through listening, loving and serving activities, forming community, exploring Jesus, a deepening experience of church, and doing it again – is likely to prove most fruitful among people who have little church background and are not yet ready to attend an explicitly Christian event.

Since this is the fastest-growing demographic in the global North, *A serving-first journey* is likely to become the missional method of choice for witnessing communities in the twenty-first century.

As you prayerfully walk the journey, you can put up signposts to Jesus involving kingdom kindness, stories about Jesus, prayer and healing, and missional worship.

These signposts will be most effective when they take account of the milestones individuals have reached on their own personal spiritual pathways.

Signposts are not a device to force individuals down a route to Jesus. They give individuals a choice. They tell people what they will find if they continue along the path. The person can either head in that direction, stay where they are, or turn back.

Signposts are a gift – of knowing what lies ahead if you wish to travel that far. The person may receive the gift by journeying further, or not.

A decision not to travel could be a response to the Spirit. The Holy Spirit may be telling the person it is not the right time. Your task is to erect the signpost, pray for those who see it, and leave the rest to the Spirit.

Ending the great divorce

As an evangelical, for most of my life I have been influenced by writers such as John Stott and Lesslie Newbigin, who emphasized that social action and evangelism are not alternatives. Both have a central place in God's kingdom. They belong together.

The trouble was that I could never see this in practice. Local churches and Christian initiatives practised either evangelism or social action. Where a church did both, they tended to be done by different people in different programmes. Rarely did I see the two combined.

This is now changing. As witnessing communities follow myriad versions of *A serving-first journey* in particular, as they put in signposts to Jesus, and as they tailor these signposts to the pathways of individuals, social concern through "loving and serving activity" is being clapped together with evangelism. Mission is becoming more holistic.

> The Springfield Project in Birmingham, UK provides a professional nursery, family support work, after-school clubs, and other forms of loving service to its predominantly Muslim neighbourhood.
>
> At the same time there are regular prayer meetings, information is given about Christian festivals and beliefs, and

staff – even if they are not Christians – discuss how Christian values should drive the project's services.

The church's determination to see the Christian faith distinctively shape its outreach in a multi-faith context has not led to inter-religious tension and suspicion. Rather Muslims, Sikhs and Hindus have respected the church all the more. We have been seen to be serious about our spirituality.[16]

Evangelism and social action have clasped hands.

---

16 www.freshexpressions.org.uk/stories/springfieldproject (accessed 23 May 2013).

Chapter 5

GETTING STARTED

> Just west of Richmond, Virginia, USA, Greg asked a few people from his Baptist congregation to start meeting in coffee shops. They were to invite friends whom they would typically meet for coffee but not for church.
>
> Each small gathering starts with participants catching up with each other's news. A short spiritual input sparks a conversation. The meeting closes with prayers for those present and other people in the area.[1]
>
> The Christians involved recognize that the gap between today's culture and the church is too wide for their friends to jump. So, instead of inviting their friends to church, they are taking church to their friends.
>
> Individuals form a tiny community, which has visibility in daily life and engages in the corporate activity of witnessing to Jesus.

You may sense a call to start this type of community in part of your life, but are unclear how to begin. Not able to picture yourself in the role, you wonder whether this is a real call from God or a fantasy. Or you may be excited by the possibility and be keen to forge ahead. The risk is that you rush in too fast and make unnecessary mistakes.

---

1 www.freshexpressions.org.uk/stories/upstart (accessed 27 May 2013).

Whether you are hesitant or enthusiastic, you would be wise to take stock, pray, seek the advice of Christian friends, and get God's perspective. How might you check out whether you are called to help set up one of these communities?

The first thing is to remember that witnessing communities often follow a route akin to one of the journeys described in the last chapter. Among people with little church background, listening often leads to loving and serving activity, around which community forms. Signposts to Jesus encourage individuals to explore Jesus, after which new believers have a deepening experience of church. All being well, some will start their own little communities.

Communities tend to travel this journey not mechanically step by step, but spontaneously and opportunistically. The stages of the journey overlap, are fluid, and look different in every context. Trial and error is the order of the day. An opportunity arises unexpectedly. The core group tries one response and then another. Finally, the community heads off in a direction no one had planned.

What might help you to make such a journey? The following are culled from the numerous experiences of others. They are not rules, but tools – pieces of wisdom intended to help you clarify your call and spark prayerful thought: "Is that something I should think about?"

Pray for a mission heart

Starting a witnessing community – or what some call a fresh expression of church – may excite you, but you have enough self-awareness to know that your enthusiasm can trip you up.

Or you may find the idea rather daunting. You wonder whether you have the ability, what others will think, how you will cope if it doesn't work, and much else. These fears wrap your call in doubt. "Is the Spirit really asking me to do this, or are my doubts warning me that it is not feasible?"

A helpful response is to pray for a mission heart. When the Holy Spirit gives a mission shape to your thoughts, your anxieties are not always taken away. (After all, anxiety can be a good thing. It can be an antidote to foolhardiness.) But a mission heart gives you the strength to punch through your fears, sifts your motives, and tunes you in to God's rhythm of work.

It is the crux of your mission call. When you desire passionately to serve other people, all your other priorities will fall into place. Your life focus will shift from what works best for you to what is best for the people you feel led to serve. Time, money, and friendships become "re-engineered" around your call.

Remember you are loved

The beginning of a mission heart is to remember that Jesus loves you passionately – enough to die for you. You were in his mind when he went to the cross.

Maybe you see the cross as a route to your salvation. But it is more than that. Jesus died so that you can contribute to the salvation of others. He loves you so much that he wants *you* on the stage of his cosmic drama, the coming kingdom. There would be a hole if you were not.

Like Paul and others in his team, you are to be a spiritual ambassador (2 Corinthians 5:20). You are to represent Jesus and his kingdom to the world. Christ's death gives you the credentials to stand for him in your networks, your neighbourhood, your workplace, and wherever you lead your life.

This is the big story of your salvation. Jesus died not merely to bring the kingdom to you, but so that you can join the Spirit in bringing the kingdom to others. Christ died because his kingdom needs you. If that is one of the purposes of his death, he will not leave you stranded when you seek to play your part. The Holy

Spirit will be up close guiding you, supporting you, and providing comfort when things get tough.

Dying to live

When God gives you a mission heart, he starts to fill you with a desire to serve others. He taps you gently on your shoulder. As you turn to see his welcoming face, you turn away from any self-doubt or excessive self-confidence to trust in him.

You are captivated by all the people around Jesus who are beckoning to you, "You are just the person we need. Come, and be there for us!" As you respond, the focus moves from you to what the Spirit will do through you.

Central to a mission heart is being willing to die so that others can live. Just as dying for others was pivotal to Jesus' mission, so crucified egos – through the Spirit – are vital to sharing in his mission.

Dying to live may include dying to your preconception of what personal witness involves. You may need to allow your individualistic view – you witness on your own – to die, so that the Spirit can bring to life a more collaborative approach.

Instead of being held back by the question "What difference can I make on my own?", you will be open to the encouragement and support that comes from working with fellow Christians. Not in all parts of your life, of course, but in one or two aspects, witnessing will become a relational adventure in which joys and struggles are shared with others.

Dying to live may also mean that existing priorities die so that different ones can come alive. You may have to prune some of your commitments to create space for a witnessing community. Spending less time with your current friends could leave more time for the people you feel led to serve.

One person told me that he was involved in a men's group. "The problem is that I just don't have time." Perhaps the answer was to withdraw for a season from his separate Bible-study group, meet fortnightly with others in the initiative to plan, pray, and read Scripture, and make this planning meeting his study group and a mission priority.

A gift to nourish

If God is beginning to give you a mission heart – if you feel a willingness to change direction to serve others – this could be a sign that he is calling you to start a witnessing community. In which case, thank God for this wonderful gift and nourish it. It will be easy for other concerns to distract you.

When he was leader of the Net in Huddersfield, England, Dave Male found that every month he had to remind his fellow leaders, "Remember why we are here. Remember the majority in our town who have never had any church connection."

Find a focus

Your life will have several compartments – your neighbourhood, your children's school perhaps, your work, friendship networks, and others. You won't have time for a witnessing community in each of these. So pray that the Holy Spirit will show you where to witness in a communal way.

Be specific

When you focus on a specific group of people, you echo the manner in which God works. Through the dynamics of election, God chooses the particular to reach the universal. God chose Abraham so that through his descendants "all peoples on earth" would be blessed (Genesis 12:2). He chose the nation of Israel to reach other nations. With the incarnation of Jesus, election was narrowed down to one person. Jesus in turn did not go to everyone, but chose a small group of followers to take his salvation to the ends of the earth.

God selects a specific group so that through its relationships with other groups the story of the kingdom can be passed on. This is God's relational approach. He chooses a particular group in order to connect with other groups. When you focus on one demographic, therefore, you imitate God's preferred way of working.

This does not only mean selecting one group from the various segments of your life. Sometimes it may also mean selecting from *within* that group.

In the UK or Australian context, for instance, if you were thinking of starting a witnessing community in a school setting, you would need to ask whether you plan to serve the parents or the staff or the pupils, and, if the latter, which age group.

You can't serve everyone. Generally speaking, the more specific you are the better. You will be more able to respond to the distinctive needs of the people involved. Some Christians dream of a church for everyone – the wider the mix the better! But as soon as you fix a time, a venue, and the type of activity, you will include some people and exclude others. You will have a focus whether you like it or not. So you may as well do it intentionally.

Once you start, however, you may find that the group you gather is broader than you expected: you planned to serve the residents in a nursing home but some of the staff came too. In addition, once the group is confident in its identity, you will want to practise Christian hospitality to those who were not your original focus but want to come along.

Start with who you are

To help select your mission focus and imagine what you might do, start with who you are, what you know, and who you know. These are God's priceless gifts to you. How might you share them with others?

Who you are will include the passions of your life – what energizes you and gets you excited.

> In Poole, England, a common interest in felt-making brought together two people, who started to run felt-making workshops. These sessions developed into a monthly felt-making group, which seeks to draw people into the Reconnect Christian community.[2]

> When Methodist pioneer Lou Davis moved to Edinburgh, she sought to be open to the various ways she might serve people in Scotland's capital city. But she found that

> making things and being creative was so much a part of me that I couldn't let it go. Things have since moved on and I have got myself a studio at Portobello, the city's seaside! It is great for making friends and building community as a creative hub, a place where people are creating artwork in all sorts of different forms.[3]

Add in what you know and who you know

What you know may include something you are good at. If you are a soccer coach, for example, might you coach one of the local teams, pair up with a Christian friend to provide good food after training, and see what happens? Or what you know may include something ordinary that you are tempted to overlook.

> For eight years, a group of musicians used the St George the Martyr building in Toronto for public performances, but there was no living connection to the church.
>   Some church members asked how they might build

---

2 Michael Moynagh with Andy Freeman, *How Can We Be a Great Team?*, Fresh Expressions, 2011, p. 5.

3 www.freshexpressions.org.uk/stories/edinburghdreams

> bridges to these performances. What gifts could they share?
> (What did they know?) Their answer was that they could cook
> and organize meals. Who did they know? The musicians and
> members of the congregation who could help.
>
> So they laid on a free meal at 10 p.m. for those who
> had been to the performance. Fifty people came on the first
> evening. The Christians hope that community will form around
> the food, and that this will be the first of several communities
> originating from the church.[4]

In your neighbourhood, you may know another Christian and each of you may know a couple of other people. You could invite them for drinks and see whether they would be interested in meeting regularly – maybe once a month for a video and takeaway.

Stay focused

The best way to find a focus is to ask, "Who am I? What do I know? Who do I know? With these gifts, whom might I serve and how?" If you can begin to answer these questions, it could be a sign of the Spirit's call.

Assuming that proves to be the case, don't lose your focus! Be disciplined. Steve Jobs, the founder of Apple, said, "Deciding what not to do is as important as deciding what to do."

Find another Christian

Whether you are enthusiastic or anxious about starting a witnessing community ("It's not the sort of thing I've done before"), it may help to share your early thoughts with a trusted friend or colleague. Depending on how the conversation goes, you might ask whether you should do this together or with whom you might do it.

---

4 Diocese of Toronto, "A Missional Road Trip", YouTube.

Pooling resources with at least one other person is vital. In Genesis 2:18 God said, "It is not good for the man to be alone." Jesus shared his public ministry with his team of disciples. The Holy Spirit undertakes mission with the Father and the Son.

Indeed, the three persons of the Trinity always act together. This means that we best make God visible to other people when we act not as individuals but with fellow believers. If God is a divine communion-in-mission, we reveal something of his nature when we form communities-in-mission in faint imitation of him.

Finding a colleague is a key test of whether you are called to gather a witnessing community in the context you have in mind.

Size of team

When a new church or witnessing community is being intentionally planned, people sometimes ask about the best size for a team. The answer depends on the situation.

The bigger the team, the more contacts it will have with people outside the church. On the other hand, large teams can create a whirlpool effect, centred on a particular way of being church. Everything pulls towards this Christian culture. The team may develop a preferred style of worship that is out of sync with the culture of the people it plans to serve. Individuals with little Christian background avoid dipping their toes in the water, lest they get sucked in to a form of worship that fails to speak to them.

A smaller team may adapt more easily to the context. As individuals come to faith, the team can modify its worship to accommodate the new believers. Three Christians in a workplace may find that a fourth not-yet believer joins them. It will be almost impossible for them to plan, pray, and discuss Scripture without being sensitive to the new arrival.

Whatever its size, you will never belong to an ideal team. So be realistic, and pray for one or more colleagues who are:

- *Faithful* – they are passionate about their faith and inspired by the great commission (Matthew 28:19–20);

- *Available* – they can offer time and make the witnessing community a priority;

- *Conscientious* – they are reliable, work hard, and are often unsung heroes: "She always clears away after the shared meal";

- *Teachable* – they are willing to learn from Scripture, the people they serve, and their colleagues;

- *Servant-hearted*.[5]

"Who before what" is a good motto. Pray for a person with these "FACTS" rather than someone with a specific gift. A gifted person without these personal qualities could prove entirely unhelpful. Equally, the Holy Spirit may use someone with the right qualities but an unsought gift to take you in a surprising yet fruitful direction.

Beware!

Pitfalls to avoid include teaming up with individuals:

- who have pastoral problems, which become a distraction. These people certainly need caring for, but perhaps not in the community you feel called to start;

- who don't get on well with each other, have different spiritual bottom lines, or can't agree on the vision;

- who say they are available, but in practice are distracted by family, friendship or work commitments;

- who are unable to connect with the people you feel called to serve – they don't live in your neighbourhood (if that's

5 This list is adapted from Stuart P. Robinson, *Starting Mission-Shaped Churches*, Chatswood: St Paul, 2007, pp. 42, 46.

your focus), they are unable to identify with the particular demographic, or they fail to make time for the people involved;

- who are disgruntled Christians, more concerned with what is wrong inside the church than with mission opportunities outside it.

Once you have started, beware of well-meaning Christians.

> One person led a fruitful course introducing the Christian faith. At the end, the people attending said, "If only church was like this, we would come."
>
> She replied, "Church can be like this. Come next month on the same Thursday evening, we'll go on meeting every week, we'll eat together, discuss some input, and learn to worship, just as we have been doing. This can be your church."
>
> So they came, as did members of the church's worship group. The latter dominated the discussions, changed the tone of the evening, and made assumptions that the rest of the group were not ready to accept. Gradually the original members drifted away, till only the Christians remained.

Well-meaning churchgoers have been unhelpful on numerous occasions. So firmly discourage them from coming. You are not a zoo, where Christians can goggle at all the animals you've tamed!

Building community

As members of the team get to know each other, you should move from being a team to being a community. This is because the team is the embryonic heart of the larger community you are seeking to create. So drink together, eat together, go to the occasional film together, have fun, and share your lives in whatever way feels natural.

Don't be surprised by tensions and disagreements. They are part of life. Allow yourselves to have honest conversations drenched in prayer. If you find you cannot work together, do not despair. Paul and Barnabas disagreed and separated (Acts 15:36–40). It happens. Better to face your differences early rather than later, when the people you serve may be hurt. Separation has its advantages. It may enable the person who leaves the group to discover what God really wants them to do.

When the group meets, concentrate on your purpose and what you agree on. When you study the Bible, for example, if you disagree on an interpretation, listen respectfully to the other person, accept that other Christians may take that view, and suggest that you now search the passage for insights on which you do agree.

Community Bible Studies is a large North American network of local Bible-study groups, meeting weekly and drawing in people from every church background and sometimes none.[6] Think of all the potential for disagreement! Individuals make it work by concentrating on where they agree, listening respectfully to views they disagree with, and undertaking not to dwell on issues on which they have denominational or other differences. "Let's focus on our common ground" is the continual emphasis.

As we begin to develop witnessing communities, these steps of praying for a mission heart, finding a focus, and finding one or more Christians to travel with us will help to confirm us in our call and build the foundations we need.

Ask for help

Surrounding yourself with support is another way to reduce the hesitancy you may feel about forming a witnessing community, or to create checks on what might be your excessive enthusiasm.

---

6 www.communitybiblestudy.org

When Jesus left his disciples, he made sure they had continuing support through the Holy Spirit. Mountaineers also recognize the need for support. They set up a base camp with food supplies, first aid equipment, and other items they will require as they progress up the mountain.

So what base camp of support might you need? One person reckoned she needed the following support as a full-time pioneer:

- someone to cry and laugh with;

- a spiritual mentor;

- the prayers of other Christians;

- peer support from other pioneers who understood what she was doing (in contrast to many in the church who didn't);

- a mentor or coach who would listen, give her confidence, and provide wise advice;

- advice from others in a similar field – if you are starting a witnessing community in a café, for instance, might you talk to someone who has done something similar? www. freshexpressions.org.uk/stories could point you in the right direction;

- specialist expertise in finance, legal matters, child protection, and the like;

- real, supportive, and light-touch accountability.

Your needs may be different and the style of your support may be more informal. Rather than a coach whom you meet on a regular basis, for example, you could turn to different people at different times to seek mentoring-type advice, appropriate for the stage you've reached.

Whatever form it takes, do not short-change your support. Help from others will prevent mistakes, open doors, provide you with reassurance, sustain you through hard times, demonstrate your willingness to learn, and plug you in to the varied forms of guidance used by the Spirit.

As you consult others, you will have a growing sense of whether you are called to witness through a Christian community and how. The Spirit will build your emerging call into a reality.

What if my minister won't support me?

Here are some ideas to get your church leader on side and allay possible fears:

- Take accountability seriously – promise to keep your leader informed.

- Agree the parameters with your leader – e.g. whom you are seeking to reach and how accountability will work.

- Promise not to empty the church! Agree on the number of churchgoers who will be involved, and who they should be. Guarantee to discourage other church members who may want to join. Promise not to take members from ministries the leader values.

- Commit to staying focused on people outside the church. This will reinforce your promise not to sheep-steal from the existing congregation. Quote the statistics in Chapter 2: for every churchgoer in the fresh expressions surveyed, three non-churchgoers were involved.

With these understandings in place, what has the minister got to lose?

Keep listening

One person helping to lead a carers and children's group said, "Our leadership team sits around and discusses what holy goods we should offer the carers and mums who come. I've now realized that, instead of asking what we as Christians should do for the group, we should ask the adults, 'What can we do together?'"

Jesus spent thirty years in the society that would become the focus of his mission, but only three years on the mission itself. If his behaviour as a twelve-year-old is any guide, he spent those thirty years listening to, and learning about, the people he was going to serve. Aged twelve, Jesus listened carefully to the temple authorities and asked them questions (Luke 2:46). He wanted to understand the culture that would be part of his adult life.

Listening prayerfully to the people you feel called to serve should shape every aspect of your witnessing community's life. Usually this listening happens in a simple way – in informal settings as you chat with people and get to know them. Sometimes it can be more elaborate.

> Ryan Sim began by commissioning a study of Ajax, a growing suburb near Toronto. He collected age, education, income, and other data. He also learned about common values, buying habits, and responses to specific statements.
>
> I familiarized myself with the community by walking, driving, shopping, and enjoying community spaces, and reading about the history, official plans, and news of the community. I interviewed local civic and church leaders, as well as regular residents in more casual conversations.
>
> After observing and listening as much as possible, I began to interpret and look for common threads. It quickly became clear that Ajax has an extremely high percentage of young, multi-ethnic families whose adults commute long hours to work...
>
> In times of prayer, I would ask God to reveal needs that were not being served by existing churches in the area... Because of their limited free time at home, it became

apparent that any church events, no matter what the time or theme, were unlikely venues for such overcommitted people to learn about Jesus for the first time.

How could we reach commuters with the good news of Jesus Christ, even while on the move? An idea emerged in a moment of inspiration, so we conducted an online survey to test its potential, and decided to go ahead.[7]

Lou Davis did Twitter searches for Edinburgh and followed people online to see what they were doing.[8]

Heather Cracknell held regular curry nights in her house to get to know people in the neighbourhood. During the evenings, people suggested things they might do together, such as running sessions, picnics, quiz evenings, and "Stitch and Yarn", which "involves people coming together for crochet, knitting or some sort of stitch craft, a cup of tea, and a lot of chat".[9]

Look out for...

As you listen, ask yourself:

- How do people spend their time?

- Where do people meet?

- What are the joys and pleasures, hardships and difficulties in people's lives?

- What do people value and what do they put a low value on?

- What works and doesn't work round here?

---

7 www.freshexpressions.org.uk/stories/redeemerchurch

8 www.freshexpressions.org.uk/stories/edinburghdreams

9 www.freshexpressions.org.uk/stories/cringleford

- Who are the key networkers and opinion-shapers?

- What are the needs?

- Who – perhaps in a different part of the country – is meeting similar needs effectively, and what can we learn?

- What resources can we draw on?

- Who could give us advice?

Look out for gatekeepers – people who can open doors for you, give you permission, and put you in touch with others. These are sometimes known as "people of peace", a reference to Luke 10:6.

The proconsul of Cyprus, Sergius Paulus, seems to have been a door-opener for Paul and Barnabas after becoming a believer on Paul's first missionary journey. His family had large land holdings in the area of Pisidian Antioch. Was it a coincidence that Paul and Barnabas went to Pisidian Antioch after leaving Cyprus (Acts 13:14)? Or did Sergius Paulus gave them letters of introduction and pave the way?

Ask the people

Often people involved in witnessing communities ask, "What should we do?" The answer is to ask the people you serve. This is the golden rule. "One or two of us are thinking of starting so-and-so. Do you think it would work?"

If you don't feel able to ask, maybe you should get to know the people better. But if the answer is "Yes", that will be further confirmation of your call.

Seek help from those you serve

Perhaps you have had an idea: "Let's organize training courses for lawyers in the town, with free but optional spiritual advice at the end." Then you think, "There are only two of us!" The task seems beyond reach. Yet why shouldn't the two of you form the Christian core and invite other lawyers to help? Involving those you serve will lighten the load.

Loving and serving should not mean that you are doing something *for* other people. This can lead unconsciously to a condescending attitude at odds with the servant heart the Spirit wants to form.

Methodist theologian Martyn Atkins has warned against a "sloping" approach to mission. Mission slopes downward from the church to other people. The church starts from an elevated position. It assumes it has a gospel that everyone else needs. This then becomes a subtle superiority that puts others off. We need a more level attitude, serving people as friends and neighbours.[10]

This "level" approach will follow the example of Jesus. When he sent his followers out in pairs, he told them to take nothing with them. They were to depend on the villages they were going to serve (e.g. Luke 9:3–4). Mission was to be a partnership. So, in your context, why not invite the people you serve to help with the organization?

"We mustn't be too good!"

A professional couple has chosen to live in a neighbourhood with poor people. During their several years of building relationships, the wife gathered a small social-cum-Bible-study group of local women. Some have become Christians but others are still on a journey.

The women decided to start an occasional Saturday-afternoon event for families in the area. As people arrive there are games for the children, followed by a Bible story, prayer, and then a meal.

---

10 Martyn Atkins, *Resourcing Renewal: Shaping Churches for the Emerging Future,* Peterborough: Inspire, 2007, pp. 124–131.

Everyone is encouraged to bring food to share, even those on benefits. "We want them to realize that they, too, have something to contribute. If you are always being given things, you can feel inadequate."

Recognizing how middle-class they are, the couple made a rule for themselves. "Don't let's make it too good. Let's do it in such a way that the people who come think they can do it better. That way, they will be more likely to get involved and make it true to themselves."

It worked. After the first event, one or two people suggested improvements. "That's great!" came the reply. "Would you like to help?"

"Serve days"

One team planning to start a church organized "serve days" and a "serve week" in its neighbourhood. Individuals collected litter and performed other tasks that benefited the community.

The aim was not to mobilize fellow Christians to do this, but to involve the people who lived there (and had few church connections). Residents watched as team members, wearing special T-shirts, got the ball rolling. Quite a few joined in and became friends with the team in the process.

When some months later the team began worshipping in the local school, as a result of these relationships a number of the residents asked to come too – so much so that the gathering quickly grew to sixty.

The willingness of others to get involved is a sure sign that the (ad)venture you envisage will fly. So test out your ideas on people. If one or two volunteer to help, take this as a sign that the Holy Spirit is behind it. Define your mission as something that other people can help you with.

Find partners

Whatever its size, a witnessing community needs partners. Finding partners and befriending them should be a top priority. Partners will provide resources, put you in touch with people, supply information, give permission, and provide all kinds of other support. Partnerships are the soil in which fruitful initiatives grow.

Potential partners

The following list of potential partners may spark your thinking. You may not work with them all. Some you may not have considered to be partners. Are there any that you might neglect?

- *Prayer partners.* These could be friends, people in your local church, or other Christians you know. You might keep in touch with them through a regular email, and seek their advice or help from time to time – "Has anyone got a projector we can borrow?"

- *People of peace.* Individuals who are well connected or born gatherers of others, and who warm towards you and your aims.

- *Permission-givers.* These may range from the manager of a bar where you meet to your minister or representatives of the denomination whose support you need. Take time to discover their priorities and concerns. How might your initiative fit in with these priorities, and how might you answer their questions about your plans?

- *Holders of purse strings.* If you are going to raise money, ask how the income will be sustained. It may be better to start small and remain viable than to launch big and crash down when the funds run out.

- *Partnering organizations.* Sam Forster, who is working with a group of churches in Scarborough, England, has partnered organizations involved in debt advice, pregnancy counselling, and free food distribution to help initiatives become sustainable. Two of the agencies have contributed financially and trained volunteers.[11]

- *The public.* Enjoying "the favour of all the people" (Acts 2:47) witnesses to the kingdom, opens doors, and makes it easier to win backing for the initiative. To earn a good reputation, you need to be especially sensitive to legal requirements such as child protection, health and safety, employment law, and third-party insurance, and to ethical boundaries, which may apply especially to communities in the workplace.

- *The people you serve.* Rather than having a "sloping" relationship with them, you can invite individuals to share an interest, skill or possession as they become partners in the initiative.

Building a web of belief

In developing relationships with your partners, you will be creating a web of belief. Your partners will believe in you and your plans, just as you will believe in them.

This mutual belief will rest, first, on shared goals. Working with you will help the partners achieve their objectives. Second, it will have an emotional dimension. Partners will identify emotionally with what you are doing. They'll share your values and possibly admire the altruism involved. Your initiative may be the sort of thing *they* would like to have done.

Third, belief will be based on the credibility of you (if you are the leader) and the story you tell. Partners will want to know that your proposals are feasible, you have thought through the potential problems, and that you and your team have the

---

11 www.freshexpressions.org.uk/stories/scarboroughdeanery/feb13

capabilities and the resources to deliver. They will be reassured if you consider their advice.

Fourth, belief in you will be strengthened if you go the second mile for your partners – if you show that you are concerned for their interests. You can show concern by demonstrating that you have taken into account matters important to them. Or you can express it at a personal level, such as a card of appreciation if the manager of a community hall has faced a wall of criticism.

Or you can go the second mile through practical help. Penny Joyce won the confidence of the head teacher in her neighbourhood by volunteering to stuff envelopes. A café invited some Christians to run a weekly spirituality session because they had repeatedly helped to clean the place.

Webs of belief are built on a multitude of conversations and actions. So you need to make time for these conversations, and prayerfully express practical love towards your partners. Getting their support will further confirm that the Holy Spirit is behind what you have in mind.

Having prayed for a mission heart, found a focus, identified another Christian to work with, built a "base camp" of support, listened carefully to those you are serving, involved them in your planning, and forged good relationships with partners, you will be making real progress towards developing a witnessing community. There are, however, still a few more things to bear in mind.

Go step by step

Starting a witnessing community may feel like climbing Everest. You stare at the journey ahead and think, "I'll never make it." Or you may be so fixed on your ultimate goal – "It is my vision" – that you fail to adapt to changing circumstances or the comments of those you serve. It helps to focus on the next one or two steps instead.

Perhaps you have broached the idea of a witnessing community with a Christian you play sport with. You agree that the first step is to imagine various ways you could serve others in the club. The next step would be to try out these ideas on some of your friends. These two steps seem feasible. You decide not to think further ahead for the moment.

Following the Spirit is to be guided step by step, confident that when you have completed one stage of the journey you will be shown the next.

Beware of the blueprint

Some people start witnessing communities with a blueprint in mind – "It will become a church plant like the one we've heard about." Sometimes a model *is* replicable, as long as you adapt it to your situation. But though it is helpful to have hopes for the future, being too prescriptive is a mistake:

- It can make you anxious – "It's got to look like this, and I'll have failed if it doesn't."

- It leaves little room for the Spirit to work through unexpected events. One British couple thought they were called to start a youth gathering: they ended up with a community of people with disabilities. If God gives you an orange, don't make lemon juice!

- It ignores the obvious truth that you cannot predict the future.

> One foursome in Pittsburgh, Pennsylvania mobilized Christians to plant a church in an urban area. But the team became discouraged and gave up. The foursome then met some Christians who wanted to form a community in the basement of a tattoo parlour. From that "chance" encounter has grown a thriving church among people on the edge of

society. "You could never write this up as a plan," one of the leaders said. "It just happened."

7,000 on Twitter

One group of Christians used a pub as a base for an outreach activity during Holy Week. They gave out free coffee, hot cross buns, and leaflets about the Easter story to commuters walking to the station.

A member of the team tweeted about what they were doing using three keywords, Heaton Moor, Community, Caring. The tweets were picked up by people in the Heaton Moor area involved in community and caring, as well as by local radio. Before long the messages were retweeted to about 7,000 people.

Building on this, the pub agreed that a group – No Holds Barred – could meet monthly on its premises to discuss a variety of issues, with low-key Christian input.

Local minister Stuart Radcliffe comments:

I'm always reluctant to put labels on something like No Holds Barred because it's organic and I don't know where it's going to lead. If it leads us to a fresh expression of church meeting in a pub I'd be delighted, and I'd love that to be the direction it takes. What I'm starting to learn is that I get more out of it by letting it go where it wants to go…[12]

Others have had a similar experience – that it works best to have aspirations for the future, but not to be a slave to them. You may expect to travel on one of the journeys described in the last chapter, yet at the outset be vague about what the journey will look like.

Having some sense of direction will help you to be intentional

---

12 www.freshexpressions.org.uk/stories/noholdsbarred

about what you do – to put in signposts to Jesus, for example, as you listen, love and serve others, and build community. But being too rigid in your plans will prevent you from seeing the unexpected as an opportunity – a fresh idea from the Spirit.

God may be calling you, therefore, not to embrace the whole story of what you might do, but to take the first step and trust the Holy Spirit for what happens next.

Keep it simple

A meal-based church among students in Paris started with the hors d'oeuvre, during which people caught up with each other. A short talk on a Bible passage or a topic such as forgiveness followed, and was discussed over the main course. Matters for prayer were collected during the dessert, and after prayer people had coffee.

The convener's hope was that modelling something so easy would encourage students to start similar communities when they moved away.

This is a good example of keeping an initiative simple. Food-based church fits into what people already have to do, which is to eat. Getting the meal is straightforward – each person brings a dish. No one has to spend hours preparing a sermon: the talk can be simple and brief.

There is no need for a worship band, a special building, or a gifted preacher. Though these are valuable in other contexts, the more complicated you make your community, the more time and resources it will need. You will find it harder to start one in your everyday life.

Simple communities work with the grain of our busy culture. They fit easily into time-squeezed lives. They suit contexts where resources are scarce. They require less management time and skill than more complex initiatives (which is not the same as needing no skill). Failure is less likely because they are more doable. They feel less daunting, which encourages "ordinary" Christians to have a go. They put smaller demands on leadership, making it easier to multiply.

Keep it simple, therefore, is good advice. It puts your call to start a witnessing community within reach.

Connect up

But be aware of the limitations. Simple communities are simple only in part, as honest relationships within the group still have to be fostered. It will help to have someone who can facilitate the meetings.

The small size of the community may limit the range of spiritual input. You can use online and published resources, of course. But emerging Christians will be enriched if they can also meet with larger circles of believers, where they can receive more varied teaching, have a wider experience of worship, and learn more about God's extended family.

- Maybe two or three small groups can "cluster" together every few weeks to provide this wider experience. As groups multiply, additional clusters can be created within an expanding network. The network could pool resources and draw the clusters together for occasional celebrations.

- A small group might periodically worship with its parent church or another well-established congregation nearby.

- It could take part in town-wide Christian events or attend a Christian festival, conference or retreat. If one existed locally, it might join a coalition of new and established churches to share resources for mission and disciple-making.

- Christians in the group might invite emerging believers to their church on Sunday. Group members would belong to two worshipping communities. Both would be part of the one family of God. Supported by fellow believers, individuals would encounter Jesus in different compartments of their lives.

Might simple and connected be good words to keep together?

Make disciples from day one

Making disciples should not be an afterthought, popped in once people start coming to faith. Making disciples is the heart of the great commission (Matthew 28:19). It should be the core of your witnessing community, too.

Rather than making disciples being one aspect of the community's life, the community should form around the task of discipling others. Making disciples should be the thread that holds the community and its activities together.

At present, you may not be able to picture this in your situation. But perhaps you can envisage a process, such as *A serving-first journey*. Listening, a loving and serving activity, building community, exploring Jesus, having an experience of church, and doing it again is all about making disciples.

So include this process in your prayers. You do not have to see the whole journey in detail. It is enough for you to keep the outline in mind. Doing so will help you to move from one stage to the next. It will prompt you to ask, "Where have we got to on the journey? What would take us to the next stage? If we followed up this idea, would it be a helpful step along the path?"

Make disciples before you make Christians

The Bible does not say that you come to conversion first and you are made a disciple next. Coming closer and closer to Jesus is one process. There may be a point of conversion during the walk to Christlikeness, but the entire journey is about being made a disciple.

This means that you can begin to disciple people before they have explicitly entered the faith. You will need to do this sensitively, of course, without laying on them assumptions they are not ready to accept. Yet, with prayerful imagination, might you find a means of serving others that doubles up as discipleship? Like the Alcoholics Anonymous Twelve-Step programme, might your community support individuals in countering habits that limit their lives?

Scripture contains rich resources for addressing issues of everyday concern. The Sabbath theme, for example, can be applied to time pressures. A group of busy parents might support each other in practising "mini Sabbaths", short periods of rest, as well as more substantial Sabbath breaks during the week. "Mini-retreats" might work for some people, as one group found. A spirituality-at-work group might explore how the Sabbath concept applies to work–life balance: what would be practical in its context?

In exploring how to manage conflict, members of a group might be introduced to the Christian discipline of silence. How can the Spirit fill the silence, still your emotions, and give you a more detached view of the matter? Individuals might support each other as they learn, perhaps through role-plays, to practise short Spirit-led silences in the midst of conflict. Exploring longer periods of silence as part of a rhythm of life might be the next step.

Other themes also have potential, such as confession and forgiveness (in relation to office politics, for instance), spiritual resources for navigating life stages or changes in circumstances, and stewardship in relation to managing personal finances and ecological concerns.

Mindfulness

One opportunity may be the growing popularity of mindfulness training. Mindfulness has been described as:

"affectionate attention". It deepens our potential for kindness and understanding through developing our capacity to be present in each moment with an open-hearted attention to our experience. Mindfulness helps us to step back and see our situation more clearly. This allows us to make wiser choices and to take better care of ourselves... [13]

Individuals often seek mindfulness training to ease physical and psychological symptoms, cope better with stressful situations, and generate greater energy and enjoyment of life. Why should your community not respond to this demand by using resources from the Christian traditions of contemplation and meditation?

Employing Christian practices to serve people, introduce them to the kingdom, and form their characters before they fully own the faith must be done with care. You don't want to introduce people to a works-based faith. So combine Christian practices with continual pointers to Jesus. Teach them within a framework of grace, and respect people's right to disagree.

Tools for getting started

- Pray for a mission heart
- Find a focus
- Find another Christian
- Seek help
- Keep listening

---

13 www.mindfulnessforhealth.co.uk/mindfulness.html (accessed 17 October 2011).

- Involve those you serve

- Find partners

- Go step by step

- Keep it simple

- Make disciples

Conclusion

As you consider whether you are called to start a witnessing community in an area of your life, you may want to pray through the ten steps summarized above.

Can you imagine yourself beginning to take some of them, at least the early ones? If you can, that may be evidence of your call. As you meet with a Christian friend, pray together, and explore the options, other steps may come into focus. If they do, that will be further confirmation.

Don't forget the idea of making disciples from an early stage. It is a brilliant way to serve people – and it has one other advantage. Even if an individual never comes to explicit faith, he or she may have become more like Jesus.

This means that even if you never complete, for example, *A serving-first journey*, your efforts will still have been worthwhile. The kingdom will have become more present on earth.

So there is no need to stress and strain to reach the end point. If it feels as if the engine has stalled and you are only halfway along the route, relax! It is the Holy Spirit's work, not yours. Wherever you have got to, by serving the kingdom you will have brought joy to Jesus.

Chapter 6

MAKING DISCIPLES

"Write about new types of church that have lasted for more than five years," one of Britain's senior ministers urged me. "Sceptics claim that most of these churches are flaky and short-lived, and don't make disciples. How can I convince the critics?"

Maybe you have similar concerns. If you started a witnessing community, would it be too flimsy to draw people into mature faith? Would it have enough spiritual ballast to breed long-lasting followers of Christ?

Certainly there is anecdotal evidence that some witnessing communities live for only a short season. On the other hand, the Church Army Research Unit found that, of the new communities it had surveyed between 1992 and 2012, described as fresh expressions of church, only 10 per cent had died.

The great majority of the communities surveyed took discipleship seriously. Nearly four-fifths engaged in one-to-one mentoring, provided courses, ran groups or drew individuals into serving teams. Of the remaining fifth, many were too young to be forming new Christians.[1]

Discipleship – following Jesus faithfully – is a central call of the church. Christians are to "make disciples of all nations" (Matthew 28:19). Forming disciples was a priority for Jesus, so it should be a priority for you.

---

1 Church Growth Research Project, "Report on Strand 3b: An analysis of fresh expressions of Church and church plants begun in the period 1992–2012", October 2013, p. 49, 96, available from Church Army Research Unit.

Keeping discipleship at the front of your mind is vital if your witnessing community is to grow towards maturity. Healthy discipleship will encourage:

- new leaders to emerge, as gifts and ministries are nurtured within a supportive apprenticeship culture;

- new Christians to give generously to the community (as well as to other causes), as stewarding money and talents becomes second nature;

- the community to grow and reproduce itself, as Christians invite others to "come and see" (John 1:46).

To put discipleship at the heart of your witnessing community, what would you have to do? How would you work with the Spirit to help individuals to grow more like Christ?

The answer involves drawing new believers deeper into the Christian story through community, worship, instruction, shared leadership, and connections with the wider church.

Community

Nurturing believers' faith will start with helping new Christians to deal with the "rubbish" they are carrying from sin and negative experiences. As the Spirit frees them from their earlier lives, they will take hold of their new identity in Christ and move on to become genuinely fruitful.

But remember: many of these new believers may have little Christian experience. In the fresh expressions of church surveyed by the Church Army, leaders thought that people with no church background substantially outnumbered not-yet Christians with some background, who in turn outnumbered the Christians.[2]

---

2 George Lings, *Church Growth Research Programme,* London: Church Commissioners, 2014, p. 6.

Drawing people with little Christian background into the faith will be very different from discipling those who have been brought up in the church. You will have to assume much less Christian knowledge, and the journey may take a considerable time.

Shared lives

Community provides the womb in which the Holy Spirit can form individuals in the faith. To work with the Spirit, you need to be intentional in laying down pathways that will take people to Jesus.

If for example you come together once a month for all-age activities or in a weekly drink-and-discussion session, the first stone on the path will be to make the most of these times together.

Teachers talk about the "hidden curriculum". This is what pupils learn as a by-product of school life, such as the values and practices reflected in people's relationships. It is informal, very present but often scarcely noticed. Encouraging members of your witnessing community to eat together and share other forms of fellowship will enable them to learn through your community's "hidden curriculum".

A father whose dad never played with him might watch another father playing with his children and get some ideas. A person seeing someone apologize might learn an important Christian practice, even before this has been explicitly taught.

Paul Moore describes what happens at a Messy Church in his English church:

The meal that follows the celebration is an essential part of the programme where socialization is happening. Christian faith and values can be modelled, observed and discussed around the tables. It is also important community-building time, as we sing a special song for all those with a birthday during the month: "A happy birthday to you... Every day of the year may you feel Jesus near."

It has been suggested that more use could be made of the mealtime to explore discipleship, perhaps forming regular groups meeting around a table with a designated leader to facilitate discussion. To me this seems too formal and threatening for our context, as well as difficult to organize, but placing a card on each table with an optional question for discussion linked to the day's theme can easily be done.[3]

People can start to be disciples before they embrace Jesus. So develop your communal life. Put in extra social events, from fun days to film evenings, and create as many opportunities for informal Christian formation as you can.

Look at the "Twelve Gospel Values" in the box below. What practices might your community introduce to express some of these values appropriately?

Twelve Gospel Values

- Gospel of forgiveness: new beginnings.

- Gospel of welcome: belonging, adoption, new family.

- Gospel of calling and service: building, sowing, sewing, washing…

- Gospel of servant leadership: socially responsible, proactive, future-focused.

- Gospel of reconciliation: removing walls of prejudice, fear, and enmity.

- Gospel of solidarity in suffering.

- Gospel of healing: wholeness for body, soul, mind, community.

---

3 Paul Moore, *Making Disciples in Messy Church. Growing Faith in an All-age Community*, Abingdon: Bible Reading Fellowship, 2013, p.86.

- Gospel of courage: capacity to stand for justice, against injustice.

- Gospel of liberation: freedom and release.

- Gospel of transformation: change in priorities for people.

- Gospel of creation: God's pleasure in God's handiwork.

- Gospel of insight: knowledge, wisdom, truth that guides and opens.

Source: Paul Moore, *Making Disciples in Messy Church. Growing Faith in an All-age Community*, Abingdon: Bible Reading Fellowship, 2013, pp. 92–93.

Shared practices

When the community is ready, you can begin to make the "hidden curriculum" more explicit. You can encourage those who want to support each other in "disciplines" that will enrich their lives.

These disciplines could range from regular but short periods of meditation (perhaps using much-loved Scripture passages such as Psalm 23 or the hymn of love in 1 Corinthians 13), to reading and praying with children before they go to sleep, to the practice of forgiveness, to a disciplined approach to food.

For example, some individuals in the group might contract with each other to take regular exercise. Each person might say when they were going to exercise during the week, report back how they have got on, and maybe have fun rewards for those who achieve their goals.

Or the community might select a theme, such as generosity. Over a period, when the community gathers members might describe one act of generosity they have engaged in since the last meeting.[4]

"It's OK if you forget," the leader might reassure them. "For me as a Christian, one of the great things about following Jesus is that we don't get it 100 per cent right." Equally, there's nothing like having to report back to keep you on your toes!

These shared practices can become more permanent, perhaps, and more explicitly Christian as members of the group walk towards Jesus. Inspired by the monastic tradition, for instance, some communities have shared rhythms of life.

Again, this can be simple and members given the chance to opt out. Those opting in might agree to say the Lord's Prayer silently wherever they are at noon each day. Ian Adams used to send to his community a daily call to prayer by text.[5] The box below illustrates a more elaborate rhythm.

BELLS – Small Boat Big Sea's rhythm of life for individuals

B *Bless x three*   Three acts of blessing a week – to someone inside the community of faith, to someone outside, one spare to go either way.

E *Eat x three*   Table fellowship three times a week – with people inside the community of faith, with folks outside, one spare to go either way.

L *Listen one hour*   Spend at least one hour a week in contemplative prayer (knowing other forms of prayer will be practised along the way).

L *Learn*   Constantly
1) read and reread the Gospels,
2) read another book of the Bible,
3) read best books in any category,
Christian or not. Give up trashy magazines.

---

4 I am grateful to Brian McLaren for this suggestion.

5 Ian Adams, "Cave, Refectory, Road: The Monastic Life Shaping Community and Mission", in Graham Cray, Ian Mobsby & Aaron Kennedy (eds), *New Monasticism as Fresh Expression of Church*, Norwich: Canterbury Press, 2010, p. 46.

| **S** | *Sent* | See yourself as "sent" into every sphere of life. At the end of the day, answer in a journal reflection: 1) Where did I resist Jesus today? 2) Where did I work with Jesus today? |

Source: Alan Hirsch & Dave Ferguson, *On the Verge: A Journey into the Apostolic Future of the Church*, Grand Rapids: Zondervan, 2011, p. 182.

Christian character grows when the individual learns empowered habits. Your community can begin to form these habits, step by step, by offering a range of practices that individuals can opt in to and support each other in doing.

Small groups and one-to-ones

Having established your community, in time you may feel the need to add a second group for those who want to explore Jesus more intentionally. For example, a Messy Church might introduce "exploring spirituality" sessions between its monthly meetings.

> *Sorted, described in Chapter 3, began by making contact with young people through its schools work. Teenagers were then invited to Friday open evenings with activities, a testimony and a five-minute talk. Then it introduced small groups on Thursday evenings. Teenagers either study the Bible together or work on a fundraising project.*

In some cases, a group to explore Jesus might continue to meet for prayer and Bible study and become the spiritual heart of the community. If further small groups emerge – perhaps the first one becomes so large that it grows into two – the groups might meet together as a larger cluster once a month.

As these groups mature in the faith, they should be more

than cosy personal networks – otherwise they will be inward-looking. They should go beyond Bible study – otherwise they could be too theoretical. They will be countercultural when members hold each other to account for making Jesus public in their lives. Fellowship, study, and prayer should have this accountability in view.

Ideally, these groups should have a double focus. The first is a mission task, such as serving a specific area or a demographic group unreached by the church.

- This will stop the group turning in on itself.

- Mission, the priority for God, will stay at the forefront of members' minds.

- Members will be able to do mission activities they could never do on their own.

- The group will keep energized as members get to know new people, seek better ways of serving them, and welcome them into the kingdom.

The second focus should be on practical discipleship – helping members to live out the gospel concretely. Pastoral support should be framed by the challenge of leading a practical Christian life. Someone facing a personal crisis will receive emotional and practical support not only as ends in themselves, but as aids to living faithfully to Jesus and experiencing his grace within the crisis.

To keep this outward and practical focus, at each meeting the group could follow the sequence of

- purpose – planning its mission task;

- problems – supporting members in the challenges of discipleship;

- prayer and Bible study – undertaken in the light of the purpose and problems the group has just discussed.

Or else the group might reorder the four Ws of cell church into: welcome, witness, word (with attention given to practical application) and worship. Putting "witness" near the beginning will ensure that this is, literally, top of the agenda.

> As well as its main meeting, re:generation – a church among young people – has small discipleship groups, led by the young people themselves. Despite their natural ebbs and flows, the groups have promoted an honest sharing of personal concerns, mutual support and prayer.
>
> Alongside the groups, pairings between individuals of the same sex have encouraged further sharing and support. Some pairings have had a short life, but others have stood the test of time and become a valuable tool of discipleship.[6]

Like re:generation, many witnessing communities have found that alongside small groups, one-to-one mentoring is the bedrock of Christian formation. At the heart of Neil Cole's organic church movement, for example, are Life Transformation Groups. These groups contain two or three people who meet weekly to challenge one another to live an authentic Christian life.[7]

Worship

Individuals will be drawn into God's story as they journey into community and encounter him in worship. Many who are new to the Christian faith will have had little experience of worship and will need to be taught how to do it. This must be done patiently and sensitively.

6 Paper by Ruth Poch, 2011, available from the author, ruthpoch@ntlworld.com

7 Neil Cole, *Organic Church*, San Francisco: Jossey-Bass, 2005, pp. 27–28.

A path to worship

The journey starts with small tastes of worship, which can be described as "missional worship". This involves snippets of worship that connect with individuals who half believe, are confused, or have only a faint awareness of God. As we saw in Chapter 4, "missional worship" differs from "Christian worship" in having a mainly evangelistic intent.

Examples would be a sewing circle that added prayer to the end of its sessions and a group of teenagers, who were not-yet Christians but used contemporary dance to pray to God, as they understood him.

> In Mawsley village, Northamptonshire, England a monthly "café with a bit more", called SPACE, offers a quiet space to think, meditate or pray, a space for children with Bible-based activities, and a common space for everyone to enjoy a coffee, a bacon roll, and a chat.

> The Goth Church in Coventry, for groups of young people who listen to heavy metal music and wear dark clothing, offered the ancient Office of Compline on Wednesday evenings. The service included candles, prayer, silence, and the Peace, tailored to the missional context.

Fuller worship

Once people are ready, you can explore with them what a journey to fuller worship might involve. Worship draws people into the conversation between the Father, Son, and Holy Spirit. The Spirit prompts worshippers to sing and say words that resonate with the words exchanged within the Godhead.

As you ponder how the group can be drawn into this divine conversation, remember that the style of worship you are used to may not work for others in your community. The Christian songs you love may not connect with them.

It may even be that the traditional liturgy you thought you had left behind is the sort of thing that would engage your emerging Christians. One person working with an illiterate demographic found that people valued a set liturgy. They could learn the words and imbibe gospel truths as they repeated them – a reminder that this was one reason liturgies came to be written in the first place.

> By contrast, an Anglican church in Toronto had served meals to unemployed and other people on the edge of society. They decided to take a further step by inviting guests to a separate part of the church building for a simple act of worship.
>
> They initially used a lot of liturgy because, in the words of one team member, they wanted to be in control. But they have found it works best when they do not restrain the Spirit.
>
> The sessions have become more informal and fluid. The leaders don't teach in a didactic way, but rely on discussion lubricated by coffee. There is honesty, and sometimes a high level of discomfort in what is said, but also a growing sensitivity and willingness to minister to one another.[8]

Some principles to help you

If you have never done this before, introducing worship into your witnessing community may seem a bit daunting, but it need not be.

The starting point is to keep it simple and remember the golden rule: when in doubt, ask the people you serve. So share an idea for worship, ask people if they would like to try it, give it a go, ask for feedback, and then prayerfully decide whether you should continue with it, do it differently or try something else. "There is no such thing as failure, only feedback."

---

8 Diocese of Toronto, "A Missional Road Trip", YouTube

Whatever your situation, you may find it helpful to bear these five principles in mind.

Simple

Life may be too short to copy the complex worship of mainstream churches. The new monastic Gate Faith Community in Wales keeps it simple by "fitting in elements of worship, prayer, and reflection around our eating, laughing, and chatting together".[9]

If you meet over a bring-and-share meal, you could exchange your news, light a candle, welcome the Spirit, silently confess your sins, read from Scripture, and listen to a short talk about the passage. During the main course you could discuss the talk, over dessert you could share topics for prayer, and you could then pray together before having coffee and finishing up. No need to spend hours in preparation!

> The all-age worship of B1 in Birmingham, England often starts with a chant. This leads into silence, when not infrequently there is a tangible movement in the atmosphere.
>
> Confession then occurs in small groups, in which individuals look back over the last week, imagining it to be an Emmaus-like journey. For how much of the journey were they unaware of Jesus alongside them? When did they notice his presence? At what points did they recognize him? What do they want to say to Jesus about their failure to acknowledge him?
>
> This is followed by Bible-based discussion, often in age groups. Individuals are texted which passage to read in advance. They are encouraged to spend the week dwelling within the passage. When they meet together, they share their responses. Integrating private Bible study with public worship encourages personal devotions.

9 www.freshexpressions.org.uk/stories/thegatecardiff (accessed 4 June 2013).

The community then sings the Lord's Prayer and concludes
with a song or hymn. The whole event lasts for about an hour.

Holistic

This is a wholeness that comes from drawing on the riches of the whole Christian family. To keep your worship fresh and add depth, you could look at the ingredients of a conventional service.

Is there one you have not recently included – a confession or a creed, perhaps? Might you include it for a season? How would you make it work for your witnessing community? For instance, might you do some input about creeds, invite members to write their own, and suggest the group chooses one to use in its next few meetings?

A helpful resource may be www.freshexpressions.org.uk/guide/worship. It lists traditional elements of worship – from the welcome through to the blessing – and seven contexts in which worship may be held, such as children, café, and retired. It contains examples of each element in the different settings. The examples are intended less to be copied than to spark the imagination.

Authentic

To be a true offering, worship must come from the heart. So it must be real for the people concerned. Some people love singing Christian songs, for instance. But others feel awkward. If the group is not ready for sung worship, members might listen to Christian music instead.

> *One person started a monthly Christian apologetics meeting in a pub. After a couple of years, he invited some of the regulars to a Christian explorers group. After the initial six weeks, the members decided to keep meeting. They had been doing so for a year. "How do you worship?" I asked.*

> *"We've tried everything,"* he replied, *"and we still haven't cracked it."*

You may have to experiment for quite a while before you discover what is authentic in your context.

Relevant

If individuals are to be transformed, worship must connect with their lives. When you discuss a bible passage, for example, you might ask: What are the main themes in the passage? What can you learn to help you in the days ahead? When the group meets next, individuals might describe what they did with their takeaways from last time.

> *Where members have a social justice or ecological passion, why not do what Just Church did in Bradford, England? The church began with members writing letters on behalf of the charity Amnesty International, as part of their worship. Prayer became campaigning.*

Enabling

Worship should allow people to pool their gifts. Contributions may range from being responsible for reminder emails, to organizing the food (if you eat together), to finding online resources, to making prayer suggestions, to sharing spiritual gifts.

> *The Anglican Bishop of Buckingham, in England, described worship in a gathering of people with disabilities. Rainbow Worship "is rumbustious and celebratory some of the time, but hushed and awed at others. Comments are chipped in from all around as things happen, like an old- time revival meeting. Craft activities are built in, and the management has radically tried to break down the distinction between client and helper. On one occasion, as Noah's Ark was revealed*

> *in all its glory, a loud voice cried from the back, 'This is one*
> *I made earlier.'"*[10]

The acronym SHARE is a reminder that worship is shared with God (we are drawn into the eternal worship of the Trinity), shared with the world (not least through prayer), shared with the wider body (by including resources from the church at large), and shared by members of the gathering as they pool their gifts.

Markers on the journey

S might also stand for sacraments. Communities that seek explicitly to be church will want to celebrate the sacraments of baptism, where appropriate, and Holy Communion. These are increasingly common in fresh expressions of church, where even ordinations have sometimes taken place.

Though not everyone will find it helpful, some people may value opportunities to mark their arrival at a new stage of their spiritual journey, even if this stage is not baptism.

> *At one Church of England service, some candidates were baptized and then confirmed, others were confirmed, several renewed their baptism vows, and a few – in an unusual development – publicly committed themselves to a journey of exploring the Christian faith.*
>
> *All were given a narrative in which to interpret their varied experiences. They had an opportunity to mark publicly and symbolically the different milestones they had reached, and this helped them to take a step forward.*

Paul Moore suggests a more informal approach. In an all-age community:

---

10 www.freshexpressions.org.uk/stories/rainbowworship (accessed 4 June 2013).

Families could be invited to mark their first steps in following Jesus and discovering more about him by stepping with bare feet in a tray of paint and walking along a length of paper to leave their footprints, cheered on by everyone. A short prayer could be said for them, and a family would present them with a suitable book or Bible to read together at home. With permission, photos and videos could be taken and posted on YouTube and Facebook as a record of the event.[11]

Holy Communion

Though it will not always be appropriate, most witnessing communities will want to remember the Lord's Supper in some way. You may want to keep the SHARE principles in mind as you think how to do this.

If Christians in your community belong to a denomination that requires an ordained minister to preside at Holy Communion and you are not ordained, don't be dismayed. You have a number of options:

- Invite an "outside" minister to be a "chaplain" to the community and preside at Communion. The minister can symbolize connection to the wider church.

- Celebrate Communion jointly with your "parent" church from time to time.

- Use "Extended Communion", in which the bread and wine are consecrated at a main service in the parent church and distributed later to others.

- Introduce "Agape suppers", which remember Christ's death and resurrection during a meal but don't use consecrated bread and wine. You might want to make it clear that this is not a normal Holy Communion, as understood by some of the main denominations.

11 Paul Moore, *Making Disciples in Messy Church. Growing Faith in an All-age Community*, Abingdon: Bible Reading Fellowship, 2013, pp. 102–103.

- Britain's Methodist Church is prepared to authorize appropriate lay people to preside at Communion in mission situations.

- Be content that you are not celebrating Communion, because members of your community do so in their "home" churches.

Instruction

As members of your community begin to walk towards Jesus and start to experience worship, Christian instruction will become an important aid to discipleship.

To begin with, this can be one-to-one, and low-key. It may occur informally during conversations, or in discussion evenings about life or spiritual themes. If you belong to a group that watches and discusses films, for instance, from time to time you are likely to explain aspects of the gospel as you link your contributions to your faith.

Other forms of gentle evangelism may range from answering people's questions over a meal ("Why do you entertain so much?") to special events alongside the community's main meeting, such as debates involving Christians and not-yet Christians.

In time, these evangelistic events will be supplemented by more focused teaching on the Christian story and what it means to follow Jesus.

Following Jesus: shiploads of good practice (based on Acts 2:42–47)

- *Leadership* – both respecting Christian leaders and learning yourself how to lead (verse 42).

- *Apprenticeship* – continually learning how to follow Jesus by being a perpetual apprentice (verse 42).

- *Worship* – regular corporate and personal devotions, led

by the Spirit through the word and the sacraments (verses 42, 46–47).

- *Lordship* – allowing your prayers, gifts, and quality of life to be channels through which Jesus exercises his reign over creation (verses 42, 43).

- *Stewardship* – by using material possessions to benefit others (verses 44–45).

- *Fellowship* with other believers (verse 46).

- *Friendship* with the world, which includes serving others, resisting injustice, and working for the good of creation (verse 47).

- *Discipleship,* which encompasses all the above and anything else that enables others to follow Jesus (verse 47).

Remember the context!

Instruction will enable believers to grow to love this story. They will come to see themselves as a verse in one of its chapters. Equally important is that they acquire the skills to follow Jesus. Knowledge has a practical dimension. The big themes of discipleship, summarized above, must be turned into lived experience.

The great strength of witnessing communities is that they grow in the middle of life. So they are well placed to help new believers root their faith in the mud of everyday experience.

If discipleship is not contextual, applied to the actual circumstances of a place and its people, it is not likely to be discipleship at all because it does not touch real lives.[12]

---

12 Graham Cray, *Making Disciples in Fresh Expressions,* Fresh Expressions, 2013, p. 14, available from www.freshexpressions.org.uk

Christian instruction, therefore, must show new believers how to make connections between God's story and their specific circumstances. It must help them learn how to discern what general Christian principles look like in their situations.

Katie Miller, the lay leader of a fresh expression of church among adults and families in an area of social disadvantage in Norwich, UK, provides an example.

> Teaching is probably what is uniquely different in that we will break into small groups during the worship and do stuff; we may play games, we may paint something together, we may collect things, we may have a quiz.
>
> We quite often share in small groups, maybe about someone who was a good father to you and then whoever's leading will gather that back together and bring it into the lesson.
>
> It always starts with people, it always starts with people's experience, whether their experience of what we are doing on the day or their stories – their story of their life or of their faith – and we tie their story into the wider gospel story.
>
> So it's not someone from the front telling people what to think and believe; it's drawing out people's experiences and then relating those to the gospel.[13]

Preaching in different shapes and sizes

Clearly preaching and teaching will have a key role. The Gospels and Acts are shot through with references to preaching.

Jesus exemplified the creative teacher and preacher, using as he did a whole range of methods. His sermons sometimes have a conversational feel. Sometimes he adopts a more formal approach. He used actions as well as words to get his message across. His style matches the context he finds himself in.[14]

---

13 www.freshexpressions.org.uk/stories/marlpit (accessed 22 August 2013).

14 Norman Ivison, *How Should We Teach and Preach?* Fresh Expressions, 2012, p. 4.

Preaching and teaching will be shaped by circumstances. Though witnessing communities mostly have some combination of a talk and discussion, the balance between the two varies tremendously.

Sermons by discussion

The leaders of an all-age, café-style gathering in a poor community remarked, "You will rarely hear a sermon here, but we hope, pray, and trust that people will hear plenty of what God is saying."[15] The Spirit speaks through ordinary people as they discuss God's word.

The Reconnect Community of urban professionals in the heart of Toronto typically explores a topic through a Scripture reading, which individuals discuss at their tables. Teaching is then presented in a conversational style, followed by questions and answers.[16]

One witnessing community met around tables. The evening started with members exchanging news. There was sung worship, and then in their tables people discussed a Bible passage.

They were invited to answer one question: how will this passage make a difference to my life in the coming week? One table would share its answers with another. Prayer and food followed. "It is so easy to organize!" the leaders explained.

Some people wonder, "How can new believers do a properly informed Bible study when they know so little about the Bible?" Don't underestimate the Spirit!

You can ask a couple of people to read a Bible commentary. If a group gets stuck, they can invite one of the two to answer their

---

15 www.freshexpressions.org.uk/stories/e1cc (accessed 5 June 2013).

16 Diocese of Toronto, "A Missional Road Trip", YouTube.

questions about the text. Or one person in each group might read the commentary in advance.

Another possibility is to ask a group member to google information about the historical background to a Scripture passage. The group can discuss the passage's meaning and relevance in the light of what they have been told.

You can vary the input by using podcasts, YouTube clips, and other online resources. Might others in the group, suitably mentored, share in selecting the material? Leaders don't have to do it all!

If you don't have a gifted Bible teacher within the community, sermons by discussion may be your best option. But if substantial new knowledge has to be conveyed, such as an overview of Mark's Gospel, more extended teaching may be required. If the gifts for this do not exist within the group, why not invite an outside speaker from a nearby church? You might run a day-long course or a series of evenings.

Courses – but beware!

Used flexibly at the right time, published discipleship courses can be helpful. But you need the right course for your context. For instance, do the examples used in the course apply to the people in your setting?

If not, you may need to adapt the course – or even write your own, as witnessing communities are starting to do. For example Cook@Chapel, described in Chapter 3, is a community of teenagers who cook and eat together. The leaders are preparing their own taught course for developing and deepening the faith.

Beware of being too "programmic". A couple of agnostics in their mid-twenties attended a Christian apologetics course. They loved it and went to the follow-up.

After three sessions they stormed out, complaining: "Now we know the church is like every other organization. It wants people on its own terms. First we're told to come to church every Sunday. Now we're told to stop sleeping together. We've had enough!"

The teaching was not necessarily wrong, but it came at an unhelpful stage in their discipleship journey. They were not ready to take the steps being asked of them.

It's the Spirit's agenda

If you are part of a witnessing community and individuals are coming to faith, be sensitive to what the Holy Spirit is doing in their lives. Don't set the agenda for the Spirit.

You may think it is important that the new believer attends worship regularly. But the Spirit's priority may be that the person stops fiddling their expenses; regular worship may be something for later.

So when the group discusses an issue, remember that the Spirit never leaves identical fingerprints. If you sense that some people are struggling with the application, it may be a sign of God at work, but equally the Spirit may not be ready to deal with the matter.

You may want to remind the group that the issue could be top of the Spirit's agenda for some people but not others. This will place the responsibility where it belongs – with the Spirit and the individual. It will avoid new believers having to follow the Spirit at the same pace and through the same stages as everyone else.

In deciding what themes to study as a community and what matters to address, let the Spirit take the lead. Consult the group. Ask members what issues they face, give them options, and through their replies listen to the Spirit.

The day of unchallengeable experts has gone. Anyone with a smartphone can find an alternative view while you speak. Don't see this as a threat. It should be a spur for you to share your discernment with the community ("Let's seek God together"), which will help members to learn the practice of discernment themselves.

> Tubestation, among surfers, does not have a programme as such: the leaders may go through a Bible passage and explain it, but they're much more interested in where people are at and the questions they ask. So many things emerge as individuals look at Scripture together. [17]

Shared leadership

Your style of leadership will do much to shape new believers' faith. The Bible commends no one model of leadership. Different models seem to be appropriate in different circumstances. Yet it is striking that, in the Old Testament, the book of Deuteronomy offers a shared form of leadership as the ideal.

Extraordinarily for the time, responsibility is thrown back to the people. They are to take responsibility for administering and enforcing the law (16:18), identifying the Lord's choice of king (17:14–15) and discerning a prophet (18:21–23).

Likewise, within the early church, authority was quite heavily decentralized. Paul's churches had considerable autonomy. Within his communities, authority was distributed between apostles, prophets, evangelists, pastors, and teachers (Ephesians 4:11). Similarly, within the Corinthian church gifts were shared among the people (1 Corinthians 12:7–11).

> Peterson Feital has described how the people outside church he met in Nottingham were not attracted to worship services partly because there was nothing interactive or personal about their format.
>
> "Something else", which he started, was intended to have

---

17 Graham Cray, *Making Disciples in Fresh Expressions*, Fresh Expressions, 2013, p. 21, available from www.freshexpressions.org.uk

the character of a close-knit family. Participants described it as more like a party, "but we all had a feeling that, like any good party, it was up to us (the partygoers, not the event's organizers) to make it work."

To bring this participative community to birth, Feital drew together a committed team in which members had an equal voice, served each other, and modelled community.[18]

The serving team

According to the Church Army research, a third of witnessing communities draw emerging Christians into serving teams,[19] and these become settings in which individuals can learn how to follow Jesus.

Serving teams help lead the community, serve it, and become involved in the community's mission. Because the community is called to mission, these teams are likely to be outward-looking, which means that new Christians will be discipled in the context of mission. "If making disciples is at the heart of mission, then mission is the essential context for learning discipleship."[20]

Frances Shoesmith, a pioneer near London, introduced "Time Team" to encourage shared leadership. She developed the idea over several months in a series of open meetings. People were then invited to volunteer for the team, and were commissioned at a special event in the local community hall.

"The idea is that we will be mutually accountable for running our activities – both existing ones and some new

18 Peterson Feital, "Breaking free from individualism: Discipleship and community", in David Male (ed.), *Pioneers 4 Life: Explorations in Theology and Wisdom for Pioneering Leaders,* Abingdon: Bible Reading Fellowship, 2011, pp. 105–114.

19 Church Growth Research Project, "Report on Strand 3b: An analysis of fresh expressions of Church and church plants begun in the period 1992–2012", October 2013, p. 49, available from Church Army Research Unit.

20 Graham Cray, *Making Disciples in Fresh Expressions,* Fresh Expressions, 2013, p. 35, available from www.freshexpressions.org.uk

ones soon – and providing pastoral care.

"'Time' refers to people committing to one year, with the option to renew or leave after one year – or for new individuals to join. We didn't want people put off by being asked to sign their lives away.

"It's also the start of us doing some succession planning. I'm not intending to go anywhere anytime soon, but it's important that we work towards being sustainable."[21]

Sustainable leadership

Within the serving team, for example, or in a separate group for people exploring the Christian faith, encouraging sustainable leadership should begin from the earliest days. You don't want the community to depend too heavily on its original leader. If that person leaves, the community may flounder.

How you "midwife" individuals into the faith will create helpful or unhelpful patterns of dependence. If you are the leader, you will pray that new Christians will learn to depend on the Spirit, not you. You will want them to trust the word and value Christian gifts such as wisdom, discernment, and encouragement.

One person working with a group of less educated adults resolved, as far as she could, not to answer their questions.

"If someone asks, 'Who's John the Baptist?'" she said, "I'll ask them to google it. I want them to learn to trust their own resources and those of the group. In time, of course, they will discover that these resources are channels of the Spirit."

If you were convening a spirituality group, you might start by using a book of Christian meditations. After a few sessions, you might ask someone else to lead, using the next chapter, and

---

21 www.freshexpressions.org.uk/stories/stlukesinthehighstreet/aug13 (accessed 16 August 2013).

perhaps another person after that. You would have begun to share your leadership at a very early stage.

Connecting up

Individuals new to faith can feel isolated from the wider body. Often they are not plugged in to Christian networks. Sometimes they struggle to understand the behaviour and jargon of the well-established church. Feeling part of the whole Christian family may not come naturally.

Yet being actively involved in the wider church is vital.

- *It strengthens the believer's prime identity* – with Christ and his family – and allows that identity to be expressed.

- *Christian character can be formed by the entire church*, stretching round the world and back in time. God is too big to be revealed by a single community. It takes the whole church to reveal the whole Christ.

- *Specific needs can be met.* One gathering, however large, cannot meet everyone's discipleship needs. If a couple have a teenager with an eating disorder, they are unlikely to find another family in a similar position in their witnessing community. But if the parents connect with other Christians in the area, they could well find couples in the same boat and support each other.

- *Believers can contribute to the wider church* through their questions, insights, experiences, and, not least, their involvement in larger Christian initiatives. Scale is often required for Christians to help tackle major problems, such as the AIDS epidemic in Africa.

- *The public witness of the church is strengthened.* The New Testament Christians met in small communities, reflecting the social diversity of the city. They also met on a city-wide basis.[22] When the church adopts a similar pattern – of having culturally distinct communities on the one hand and joining up these communities on the other – it models a solution to one of today's biggest challenges: how to combine unity with social difference.

Connecting to the whole body is especially important, because not all witnessing communities will have a long life. A community in a workplace or among filmgoers may come to an end when a key member moves away. A gathering on a campus may dissolve when students graduate. A group with a mission may run out of energy. In areas of social disadvantage, membership and attendance may be so fluid that the initiative always feels fragile.

New believers, therefore, must be encouraged to have a wider church involvement. These relationships may help to sustain active church belonging if their witnessing community closes down.

Imagine that Jeremy and Anna meet on a prayer retreat organized by several churches in the area. Jeremy may discover that Anna worships on Sunday mornings at St Michael's. "Would you mind if I came with you one Sunday?" Jeremy asks. "I've been gathering with a small community on Thursday afternoons. But my shifts have changed and I can no longer go."

A cardinal part of making disciples should be attending carefully to the flow of new believers into the church at large. Finding a way for your community to serve the wider church would be a great place to start! Serving others creates connections.

---

22 This is discussed in Chapter 2 and more fully in Michael Moynagh with Philip Harrold, *Church for Every Context: An Introduction to Theology and Practice*, London: SCM, 2012, pp. 20–23.

Four ways of connecting up

One way for new believers to share in the life of the extended church is to have a blended church involvement. They can belong to more than one type of church. This is not pick and choose, but pick and mix. It is not about consumerism but about commitment – to more than one Christian community.

With one foot in a witnessing community and another in a conventional church, well-established Christians can invite emerging believers to their "weekend church" to give them a fuller experience of worship and teaching.

When she studied some of the Church of England's fresh expressions of church, Louise Nelstrop found that a significant proportion of the Christians involved had retained ties to their existing churches:

Some had intended to leave but the initial fragility of the "fresh expression" had meant that they had waited to see what would happen. Once they discovered that they could do both, much to their surprise, several actually felt more integrated into the parish system now that their sense of church wasn't limited to it.[23]

A second form of connection may be shared events between a witnessing community and its parent church. If a community has come out of a local congregation, its members will have a richer experience of church life by combining with the parent for social events, study groups, a short course, or outreach.

> *St Mary's in the east of England started a young adults group, with meal-based meetings. It drew in people from outside the church and numbers grew to about forty. The leaders did not develop a strategy for how the group would relate to the*

---

23 Louise Nelstrop, "Learning from Practitioners' Experiences of 'Fresh Expressions' : A Report on the Fresh Expressions Initiative", June 2008 (available from the author), p. 101.

Sunday-morning congregation. They simply raised the issue of identity: "What does it mean to belong to St Mary's?"

Links emerged organically. Some of the young adults contributed to the church's annual outreach event in the town. When the leader of the new group ran a "Kingdom Ministries" course for the young adults, several from the morning congregation came too.

Likewise, when members of the morning congregation started a Sunday-evening celebration, a number of the young adults got involved. These connections were not planned. They just happened by making sure that everyone knew what the others were doing.

Sometimes you may need to be more intentional. If so, look out for an opportunity to serve your parent church. Might your community offer to provide the refreshments for a church study day, for example? There is nothing like loving kindness to open people's hearts to you.

Thirdly, connection occurs when small Christian communities cluster together. St Thomas, Crookes in Sheffield, England is encouraging new missional cells, which meet together monthly as a cluster. The vision is for clusters to multiply, and then to gather for occasional celebrations and learning.

For a short period in one of Britain's police forces, Christian police officers – many of whom had fallen away from church – met for prayer and Bible study in a variety of small cells(!), roughly based on seniority. Once a month the cells met together in the canteen, with up to eighty people attending.

Rather different is the network of church plants based on Holy Trinity, Brompton in London. The network has an annual holiday week. Courses on work and family themes are open to people within the network and outside, and leaders share resources through learning communities.

Fourthly, believers can connect to the church at large through events run by local churches together – such as "street-pastor" schemes, which involve teams providing practical support to those "out on the town" late at night.

"Coalitions of the willing" – local churches that agree to work together – can enable a variety of outreach and discipleship initiatives. If there is a will, local cooperation is astonishingly easy to start. Churches can advertise among themselves events that individual churches already organize, such as a weekend prayer retreat or training for volunteer children's workers. As they get used to sharing activities, churches can become more ambitious. They can try initiatives that may be too specialized for one church, but become viable when open to several.

Conclusion

If you are starting a witnessing community, you can prayerfully draw new believers deeper into the Christian story through community, worship, instruction, shared leadership, and connections with the wider church.

These become means for the Holy Spirit to lead individuals towards Jesus. As believers become more like Christ, they will show him to the world.

Making disciples is a serious responsibility. If the leaders of a witnessing community are not being faithful disciples themselves, their efforts to make disciples will lack credibility. They will be a poor model for new Christians within the community.

Jesus set exacting standards. Lord Williams, former Archbishop of Canterbury, the most senior position in the Church of England, has given a flavour of what being a disciple would have meant in New Testament times:

The essence of being a student was to hang on your teacher's every word, to follow his or her steps, to sleep outside their door in case you missed any pearls of wisdom falling from their lips, to watch how they conducted themselves at the table, how they conducted themselves in the street. To be the student of a teacher was to commit yourself to living in the same atmosphere and breathing the same air; there was nothing intermittent about it.[24]

Jesus has set the bar high. He knows that most of us struggle to come anywhere near it. But in his gracious love he works with us, whatever our shortcomings. He is not the first to blame. Rather, he has sent the Holy Spirit, the encourager, to lead us the next step and to weave that step into his eternal plan.

24 Quoted by Graham Cray, *Making Disciples in Fresh Expressions*, Fresh Expressions, 2013, p. 6, available from www.freshexpressions.org.uk

Chapter 7

MULTIPLYING DISCIPLES

"You should meet Richard and Wendy," Ben urged me. "They started a fresh expression of church, but then realized that this was not enough. They had to do more."

Wendy had run a toddlers group, but found that the mothers and carers wouldn't come to church. So she invited women from toddlers and the school gate and others she knew to a Bible study in her home. Many came to faith, but they still wouldn't come to church.

So she and Richard gathered them into "breakfast church" on Sunday mornings. Numbers grew till up to sixty people were coming through their house at different times of the week. They had hit a ceiling.

She and Richard felt dissatisfied. Their vision was for a small expression of church in every street in their neighbourhood. They knew that this was the only way they could grow beyond their sixty ceiling. But they didn't know how to do it. So they took advice. Remember: when in doubt, always ask.

They found they had to unlearn much that they had taken for granted. A key moment was when Wendy met one of the mums in her toddlers group from several years back. The woman was interested in one of the Christian groups meeting in her home.

Wendy was on the verge of inviting her, when she remembered the new principles she had been learning. Instead, she asked if the woman had some friends who might be interested too. Might they meet in the woman's home?

When Wendy arrived, she found that the mum had invited three friends. After they had got to know each other, Wendy led them in a simple Bible study, which they enjoyed. They came back for more, and a simple church was started in the person's home. Wendy had helped to start one community, and now she had started another.

Multiplying Christian communities is a core ingredient of God's call to the church. It is the key to making disciples on a large scale, magnifying Christian witness, and transforming society. Why is it so important and how can you go about it?

Disciples make disciples

A vital part of being a disciple is to work with the Holy Spirit to make further disciples. Jesus was very explicit about this. When he bade his disciples follow him, Jesus promised that they would become fishers of women and men (Matthew 4:19). They would not just be his followers. They would enable other people to be his followers too.

Christians need to understand this. In their thinking, they must not stop at "I'm being discipled", nor at "I have become a disciple". They must embrace the notion, "I am making other disciples." Living out all three statements is crucial to the Christian life.

Jesus' last words to his followers were, "Therefore go and make disciples of all nations…" (Matthew 28:19). Jesus instructed the people round him not merely to *be* disciples, but to *make* disciples. They were to bring other people to Christ and encourage them to grow in the faith. Commentators stress that the dominant verb is "make disciples" rather than "go". This is the thrust of the instruction. Making disciples – being "fishers of men" – is the purpose of going.

You may be tempted to think that these words do not apply to ordinary Christians. They were spoken to the apostles, people who would go on to found the church. So they apply mainly to church leaders. But, unlike Luke's account in Acts 1:1–9, at the end of Matthew Jesus spoke to his followers as disciples rather than as apostles. Not every Christian is an apostle, but all *are* disciples – a term derived from the Greek word for learner or follower.

What was true for these immediate followers of Jesus applies to his disciples generally – to everyday Christians like you and me. Beckoning others sensitively towards Jesus is part of the Christian call.

New communities on the edge

Jesus summons disciples to make other disciples not only through their personal lives, but – very importantly – by multiplying witnessing communities. These Christian hubs are to attract non-believers by their acts of loving service, the quality of their community life, and their winsome descriptions of Jesus. As individuals come to faith, these hubs are to multiply once more. The church is constantly to move out.

Your witnessing community must not settle down and rely exclusively on drawing more and more people to itself. It must follow Jesus, who explicitly rejected a purely settled, attractional approach to mission. Though your community will want to be a magnet to others, it should also reach out by launching further communities.

Jesus on the edge

At the time of Jesus, the Jews saw their missional task as being to attract the nations to Israel. The Old Testament pictured God summoning the nations to himself in a great pilgrimage to Zion in the end times. Zechariah 8:20–23, for example, envisages people "from all languages" streaming to Jerusalem. It was a "come-to-us" approach.[1]

Alongside it are hints of a "we'll-go-to-you" approach as well. Jonah leaps to mind. But these hints are a sub-plot. From a New Testament perspective, they point to what would be fulfilled later through the church.[2]

During his public ministry, Jesus had begun to model an alternative approach to mission. He sent his disciples in pairs to the villages, a "we'll-go-to-you" strategy. But the disciples then returned to him. Jesus exercised a centripetal pull. While he remained on earth, people kept gravitating to him at the centre.

His ascension, however, changed everything. The centripetal pull was removed. There was no commanding figure physically present for the disciples to keep coming back to. The nature of mission had changed. The disciples were not to settle down in Jerusalem, but to go "to the ends of the earth" (Acts 1:8). They were to go out from Jerusalem to the edge. That is where they would find Jesus, because he was going to the edge too.

He was no longer to be tied physically to one place. Through the Spirit he would be present in all places. Jesus would be with them wherever they were (Matthew 28:20). Wherever two or

---

1 Christopher J. H. Wright, *The Mission of God: Unlocking the Bible's Grand Narrative*, Nottingham: InterVarsity Press, 2006, pp. 502–503.

2 Matthew 23:15's reference to scribes and Pharisees proselytizing, the only ancient source that explicitly ascribes a missionary policy to a Jewish group, does not necessarily refer to Jewish mission *to* the Gentiles. It may refer to the conversion of other Jews to Pharisaism, for example, or the attempt to turn God-fearing Gentiles in the synagogues into full Jews. See Michael F. Bird, *Crossing over Sea and Land: Jewish Mission Activity in the Second Temple Period*, Peabody: Hendrickson, 2010, pp. 66–70.

three gathered in his name, he would be there (Matthew 18:20).

Rather than going out and then regrouping at the centre, the centre – Jesus – was moving to the rim. He was turning his community of disciples inside out and transforming its entire way of being. Consolidating and remaining in one place became impossible as the community was stretched by its expanding edge.

Instead of being a single community travelling with Jesus, sometimes splitting off in pairs but always re-forming as a single unit, now there would be multiple communities, all travelling outward, across the world, with their Lord. The one group of disciples was to multiply into a plurality of communities that stayed connected.

This is how Jesus intends mission to be done. Remember Chapter 1: God himself does mission in community and wants Christians to do the same. He wants these communities to be located in everyday life. He wants them to be active as communities in witnessing to people nearby.

The first Christians did precisely that. Acts records how they followed Jesus to the edge of the church and beyond, forming new Christian communities as they did so. Churches sprang up on the frontiers of life, in people's homes. They were missionally active as communities, extending hospitality and meeting people's material needs.

Witnessing communities are to do likewise

Your witnessing community should multiply in the same way. It should avoid settling into a contented single community. It should follow Jesus to the edge. It should encourage new believers – and perhaps some members of its original Christian core – to go with Jesus and start new witnessing communities.

These communities will love and serve new groups of people and invite some of them into the faith. As individuals respond, the number of disciples will multiply, and some of them in turn will form further communities. As with the early church, there will be a constant multiplication of new Christian gatherings. Your witnessing community will contribute not just to an institution, but to a movement.

Already there are examples of this happening. One Family Fellowship in the city of Košice, Slovakia, quoted in the Introduction, has multiplied into scores of Fellowships across the nation. Stepping Stones, a witnessing community at St George's, Deal, England, has given birth to a further community, One Step Beyond.

> At St Thomas, Crookes in Sheffield, England one of their witnessing communities, called Emmaus, reached out to young adults and families. One of its members taught English to immigrants.
>
> An Iranian in her class asked how he could get conversation practice to improve his English. She suggested that he come to her community. He felt so welcomed that he invited other Iranians along.
>
> Soon they had Bible readings in English and Farsi, and alternated socials with European and Iranian cuisine! Several years later a separate Iranian, Afghan, and Kurdish community has branched off.
>
> Meanwhile, Emmaus spawned a second new community – white English and middle-class, like the original – on the other side of the city.

Withdrawal and engagement

Multiplying witnessing communities is not just imperative for mission, it is also vital for growing disciples. It allows "withdrawal" and "engagement" to be combined to bring new Christians to maturity.

New believers can withdraw into the witnessing community for worship and to learn about the faith. Then they can engage with the world. They can practise their faith – individually and *as a community* – where they lead their lives by forming witnessing communities themselves, introducing others to the gospel, and inviting those who respond into a similar withdrawal-and-engagement rhythm.

The withdrawal model

This withdrawal and engagement is far from the norm today. Believers tend to be formed in the faith mainly during times of withdrawal from the world. Christian character is shaped through worship, small groups, discipleship courses, and other aspects of church life. Christian practice – living out the faith on the frontiers of life – becomes the responsibility of believers mainly on their own. Christians withdraw into the church to be formed in the faith, but leave the congregation behind to engage with the world.

In itself, there is nothing wrong with withdrawing into the church to be shaped by Jesus. Through teaching and much else, the Spirit uses the gifts, example, and encouragement of other believers to form Christian character. Withdrawal is an important part of the discipleship process.

But withdrawal should not be the only arena in which the faith is passed on. As well as withdrawal, disciples should be formed while they engage with the world as Christian communities. This applies both to the Christian core of your witnessing community and to those who come to faith through the community.

Witnessing communities that do life are important for making disciples for three reasons.

The example of Jesus

First, Jesus did not rely on the withdrawal model alone to teach his disciples. Certainly there were times when he withdrew from the crowds to instruct his followers in private, as when he explained to them the meaning of the parable of the weeds (Matthew 13:36–43).

But Jesus also made a point of teaching them as a group in public, as they engaged with life. In Luke 6:20, he deliberately turns to his disciples to teach them, even though a large crowd is standing by (verse 17).

Luke 12:1 records that thousands of people were packed close to each other. Yet Jesus began not by speaking to the crowd, but by addressing his disciples. Subsequently in the chapter, Jesus goes back and forth between speaking to his followers and to the crowd.

In Luke 9:46–48, he draws out a child from ordinary life to settle his disciples' argument about status. In 18:18–29, a public exchange with the rich ruler immediately leads to an instructional conversation with Peter.

In Mark 12:41–44, Jesus observes people leaving their temple offerings and provides a commentary for his disciples. When a woman anoints him during a meal at the home of Simon the Leper, he publicly rebukes his disciples for their response (Matthew 26:6–13).

Jesus formed his disciples not only privately but publicly – on the front lines of life. By watching how Jesus attracted followers where life happened, his disciples could learn how to do the same.

Witnessing communities should perform a similar role today. They should form disciples in the public settings of life. Individuals who gravitate to the faith will do so within a community that is drawing people to Jesus while engaging with daily existence. By observation they can learn (even before they become Christians!) how to repeat the process – how to start witnessing communities themselves, attract people to Christ, and help these new Christians to grow in faith by witnessing alongside fellow believers in *their* everyday lives. Multiplication can be inserted naturally into their spiritual DNA.

Who's pulling your strings?

Second, relying on the withdrawal model alone ignores how relationships outside the church shape personal identities.

When individuals think about who they are, they understand themselves in relation to other people. Who am I? I might answer that I'm a male – I belong to the category of people who are men and not women. I'm British – I belong to the category who have British citizenship rather than those who don't. I am a Moynagh – I belong to a specific family.

During the week, we identify with the people we associate with – our families, networks, neighbours, workplaces, those with the same music preferences, and so on.

Christians get a strong reminder in church that their identity is supremely in Christ and they belong to his family. But, when they go into life on their own, their other identities come to the fore. They identify with their work peers ("I'm a security guard"), or their sporting friends ("I belong to the tennis club") or their neighbours ("I come from..."). At work or the club, for example, they are surrounded by signals that remind them they are a security guard, a tennis player, or whatever. Prompts that they are a Christian are almost non-existent.

Without fellow believers to reinforce their identities, it is difficult for individuals to let their Christian identities mould their secular ones. Individuals lack the everyday supports to behave in a distinctively Christian way – to show what a difference Jesus makes to their other identities. The believer behaves as a security person rather than a Christian security guard, as a tennis player rather than a Christian tennis player. One of our church members recently told the congregation, "I don't think of myself as a Christian professional at work, but as..." and she gave her name.

Yet does not being a disciple mean putting "Christian" in front of our other identities? Does not following Jesus involve subsuming our other identities under the identity he has given to us?

Being a Christian security officer or Christian tennis player will include going the extra mile in relation to virtues already recognized by the world, such as transparency, kindness, generosity, and being a team player. In their own behaviour, Christians at work or in the club will keep raising the moral bar.

However, as we have seen, it becomes difficult to do this on your own. It becomes all too easy for your Christian identity to be swamped by your other identities. In particular, when your distinctiveness as a Christian becomes blurred, it is much harder to make new disciples. Once you start to forget your identity, you become less inclined to invite others to embrace that identity.

On the other hand, if you meet with other believers where you are, you will have Christian support and drip-feed prompts about your identity in Christ. With mission as your witnessing community's raison d'être, you will be reminded that your Christian identity has a mission shape. It will be easier to remember that you are called to invite others to share that identity.

If you are a recent convert and your witnessing community seeks to multiply, you may start a community in another sphere of your life. As you meet up with one or two other believers, this new community will reinforce your Christian identity in that context.

Connecting faith to life

Third, the withdrawal model of forming disciples fails to address what is both a strength and a weakness of conventional church, exemplified in small groups.

In most Bible-study groups and the like, members face widely different situations during the week. This introduces welcome diversity into the group, but also means that discussion easily moves from the specific to the general.

Members do not fully understand each other's contexts, so they feel constrained in what support they can give. "It would be too difficult to describe my situation," someone thinks, "and I don't want to dominate the discussion, so I won't ask how this Bible passage might apply to my circumstances."

Another person concludes, "It would take too long to explain the problem I have with my boss and I'm not sure the others would understand. I'll just ask them to pray for my difficult work situation."

Finding it hard to engage with individuals' different settings, the group sticks to principles. Making disciples drifts into theory. Discipleship floats in the air rather than being earthed on the ground.

These general discussions are not to be sniffed at. Christians need to learn the principles of following Jesus, and a fair amount of sharing often occurs. But the group lacks the practical bite that can happen when believers get together with others in the same circumstances. Principles may fail to be rooted in the practicalities of making new disciples in a specific context.

Alongside the conventional church, however, witnessing communities provide a practical dimension to Christian formation. They focus not on the abstract but on the concrete: what does it mean to make further disciples in this particular situation? Individuals in the same setting can support each other in this task by their example, encouragement, and exhortation.

Being in the same context enables believers:

- to understand one another's circumstances and offer relevant advice;

- to notice how each other behave, making it easier to hold one another to account;

- to stand alongside one another in difficult circumstances – "Shall I come with you when you talk to your awkward neighbour?"

Paul Szkiler is a successful businessman in the City of London. He and his friends run A Call to Business, a growing community of people who believe that God has called them into this type of work.

He also knows his theology. "St Paul told us not to conform to the pattern of the world but to be countercultural. Most of us are subcultural rather than countercultural," he complains. "It is impossible to create disciples in the church structure, in pews, dipping into Scripture. Disciples can only be created in markets."

You can only change the markets, he argues, by being a Christian *in* the markets. And you can only discover what it means to be a Christian in the markets by learning alongside other Christians who are in the markets too.[3]

Encouraging others to become and be disciples must occur in the thrust of life, as well as during times of withdrawal from life.

A men's group, comprising Christians and not-yet believers, planned to improve their environment – to remove graffiti, clear litter, and enhance local amenities.

---

3 George Pitcher, "God is the new CEO", *New Statesman*, 31 May – 6 June 2013.

> *Members lived in the shadow of a Japanese car factory, where continuous improvement was the mantra. The convener had the idea that this should be the umbrella for the group's discussions over a drink after the men's hard work. "How can we improve not only what we do for the environment, but as husbands and fathers and in our work?"*
>
> *As they worked on the environment, individuals would get to know and trust each other. They would begin to talk about their lives. Opportunities would arise for Christians in the group to share their faith. Improving the environment and making and growing disciples would go hand in hand. Doing life and doing church would blend together.*

Withdrawal and engagement today

Witnessing communities allow the Christian core to be shaped by a rhythm of withdrawal into the church and engagement with the world.

This is not a one-is-better-than-the-other approach: witnessing communities are better than discipleship programmes in the conventional church, or vice versa. It is not either/or but both/and – formation both through Christian communities temporarily withdrawn from life and through communities actively engaged with life.

Your Christian core can practise this both/and through dual church involvement, for instance. They can serve and share the gospel with others in a branch of their daily life, while worshipping from time to time in their "weekend church". Or they can have a full-on commitment to a witnessing community for a period, before returning to a more intense involvement with a conventional local church. Later they might commit to a witnessing community again, return to a conventional church subsequently, and in time perhaps repeat the rhythm once more.

Keep reproducing!

The danger is that, as newcomers are drawn to Jesus, your witnessing community will lapse into being a conventional church for them. The community ceases to be a pole of the both/and rhythm. New believers treat it increasingly like a traditional local church.

A community formed in a café might witness effectively to the café's hinterland. A number of people come to faith. But the community is limited in how far it can serve others in that context. Gradually it evolves into an ordinary "church" that happens to meet in a café.

It retreats into a withdrawal model of Christian formation. Members turn to the community for teaching, worship, and other resources that will deepen their faith. They then go back to the rest of their life to witness as individuals. Because members come from different workplaces and neighbourhoods, discussions about applying the faith in those settings become rather general. Christian formation is stronger on principles than application. Café church becomes like regular church.

To avoid this, keep multiplying! As new Christians come to faith in the backwash of a community based on loving service and evangelism, encourage them to repeat the process – to start witnessing communities among *their* friends and contacts.

Be a good parent and launch your spiritual children into the world. Help them to form further communities either in the same context as the one in which they found Christ, or in another sphere of their life.

Let *making* disciples, not just *being* disciples, be the throb of their spiritual formation. Do this because multiplication is vital for mission – and mission is a first step for God. Do it also because withdrawal *and* engagement, both in Christian community, are the key to maturing in Christ.

There is nothing like mission to grow new disciples' faith! There is nothing like engaging with the world alongside other believers to echo Jesus' public model of Christian formation, to keep new believers' Christian identities at the front of their minds, and to help them apply their beliefs to the specifics of their situations, especially as they help other new Christians do the same.

So let new believers develop a similar rhythm of withdrawal and engagement to that of the original Christian core. Let them keep a foot in the witnessing community through which they came to faith while starting further communities. Or support them as they fully commit to a new community for a season, before returning perhaps to their original community.

Starting additional witnessing communities will stretch your new converts and make them more reliant on the Spirit. By following Jesus to the edge, they will retain an engaged model of Christian formation, bring the kingdom more fully into their ordinary lives, and introduce more people to Christ.

What story are you passing on?

If witnessing communities are called to multiply, for reasons of both mission and discipleship, how might you go about it?

The first thing is to be intentional – to have multiplication in your sites from the very beginning. If you start with the intention to multiply, you will be more likely to do it! You will be more likely to encourage others into the faith in ways that help them to start witnessing communities too. You will be more likely to give your community a reproducing DNA.

Second, you need to ponder carefully the story you tell about Jesus. When individuals choose to follow Christ, they are drawn into "his-story" through baptism and the Spirit's ongoing work in their lives. This presents a challenge: the story can be told in different ways.

The version new disciples receive will influence their expectations, often for years. It will shape their understanding of God, why they have decided to follow him, and what they understand discipleship to mean. Their understanding of the story will set their spiritual course, including whether they start further witnessing communities.

Becoming a gift

One version of the story says, "Come to Jesus and he will satisfy your needs." This is true in that, when the kingdom fully arrives, when we experience the glory of heaven, our needs will be completely met.

But clearly it is not an accurate description of being a Christian on this earth. Christians who do not enjoy good health, who struggle with addictions, whose poverty leaves them inadequately clothed and hungry, or who cannot get a job are not having their needs met, as we normally understand the phrase.

This version of the Jesus story sounds rather too much like a consumerist bargain: "Jesus died so that I can have all sorts of benefits. I must follow him in return." The emphasis is on what Jesus has done for me.

This version of the story can be told differently, however. Not only did Jesus die for me, but when I become a Christian I die in him (Romans 6:1–4). My ego dies in Christ so that I can bring a fuller life to others. I don't enter into a bargain ("You died for me so I will follow you in return"); I enter into a person.

Just as Jesus becomes a gift to the world through his death and resurrection, I become a gift to others by sharing in his crucified and resurrected life. Salvation is the joy of being made a more attractive gift. Following Jesus involves learning how to be this gift.

A gift to the kingdom

A second version of the Jesus story puts being this gift into the story of the kingdom. When Mark summarizes the message of Jesus, he reports Jesus proclaiming, "The kingdom of God is near. Repent and believe the good news!" (Mark 1:15).

The New Testament is clear that this realm is more than a restored personal relationship with Jesus. It is about restoring the entire creation. Jesus associates the kingdom with healing the blind, the lame, and the deaf, and raising the dead (Matthew 11:5, 12). When individuals are welcomed into this story, they are invited to join Jesus in creating a world where justice rules and love shapes everything. They are to be signs, foretastes, and instruments of his planet-transforming reign.

As the story has been told to me over the years (and I have told it like this myself), serving God's kingdom involves being salt and light in the world (Matthew 5:13–16). Supported by Sunday worship, Bible teaching, and the prayers of fellow Christians, we are to go into the week and witness to Jesus. The assumption is that we do this on our own.

Yet, as we have seen, this individualistic telling of the story says too much about me and not enough about "we". It plays down God's desire that mission be done in community, that witnessing communities be visible in everyday life, and that these communities be active in serving others and sharing the gospel.

A gift through kingdom communities

So a third version of the story might run like this: "Jesus longs to make you a gift to others. To be this gift, he wants you to join the Spirit in transforming the world so that it looks more like his dream society on earth.

"The first step is to repent of how you have often worked against this society rather than for it, accept Jesus as your personal saviour and Lord, and be baptized into his family.

"Then let the Spirit enable you to work for the kingdom in your daily life. You will do this in various ways, but one is vital. Find other Christians in a key part of your life. Join with them to serve other people and offer the gospel. Just as Jesus started his public ministry by gathering a community of disciples, you can start your public life with him by witnessing with fellow Christians.

"Don't be overambitious. One other person is enough. As a community of two, ask God to bring to mind one or two practical steps you can take to be a gift to others in your setting."

In our highly organized culture, micro communities, crawling through the undergrowth of life, are more likely to subvert the world for Christ than individuals standing alone.

Model and mentor

How else might you encourage your witnessing community to reproduce? As well as being intentional and including multiplication in the story you tell about Jesus, you should introduce people to the gospel in simple ways that they can imitate.

If you want a new Christian to share the gospel with their friends, you need to have shown them how to do it. The best way for them to learn is from how you did it with them!

If you rely solely on an Alpha course, for example, this will not be easy for most new Christians to replicate with their friends. Alpha may play a role in your community's evangelism, but you should supplement it with easy-to-use forms of discovery Bible study. Emerging Christians can then use (and adapt) these Bible studies with their friends. Having experienced the power of these studies themselves, they will have the confidence to use them with others.

You can start with stories about Jesus and build a simple approach, for example, around four questions. This is what Wendy did in the story at the beginning of the chapter. She introduced the women to the story of Zacchaeus, using this framework.

- *What is the story about?* After she had read the Bible passage (which she had photocopied for the others), Wendy invited members of the group to tell the story in their own words.

- *What does the story mean to you?* Wendy gave the women time to think about this before sharing their responses. She wrote down a one-sentence summary of each person's answer, and read the sentences back to the group as a preparation for the next question.

- *What will you dare to do now in the light of this story?* The women each took one meaning of the story and described how they would act on it. "I'm going to pray for sick people," one person said.

- *Who will you share this with?* Wendy encouraged the women to imagine simple things from the evening that they could share with a friend or family member – perhaps no more than "I met some new people the other evening, at the home of…" As individuals grow in confidence, they can be encouraged to share a bit more – a little of what they are learning and some of their experiences of Jesus.

The next time the women met, Wendy gave them time to catch up with each other. Then she asked them how they had got on with their "dares" and "shares". Each Bible study can start with this looking back, but within a supportive atmosphere. Challenge and encouragement should go hand in hand.

Mentoring

To insert the gene of multiplication into your witnessing community, the fourth thing you can do is to ensure that new believers are mentored as they seek to form witnessing communities themselves.

> Stephen (not his real name) was involved in a luncheon club for older people. The club had spawned two smaller groups, in which a mixture of churchgoers and people outside the church explored Scripture together.
>
> Stephen drew alongside one of the people coming into faith, Dorothy, who lived in an apartment. He suggested that she team up with one of the Christian helpers in the luncheon club, invite others in the block for pre-Christmas drinks, and see what opportunities emerged.
>
> After the party, in this elaboration of a true story, Dorothy asked some of those who came for their feedback. One person remarked, "I enjoyed having a good conversation." Dorothy asked, "Might we do this once a month? We could take it in turns to bring a bottle (or several!), choose a topic for discussion each month and see how we get on." People liked the idea.
>
> Stephen in his mentoring role described to Dorothy the process of listening, loving and serving, forming community, exploring Jesus, providing tastes of church, and doing it again. Over the months they brainstormed what signposts to Jesus Dorothy might include in the evenings, such as suggesting prayer as a discussion topic.
>
> In one of their conversations, Stephen asked, "Why don't you attend John's witnessing community for a while? Find ways to help out. Learn about its journey so far. Discover what has worked and hasn't. See if it gives you any ideas."
>
> This proved impractical, but Dorothy did visit one or two

communities elsewhere. She also read some of the stories on www.freshexpressions.org.uk/stories, connected with someone who had done something similar to what she was trying to do, and downloaded their wisdom.

As the temperature rose within Dorothy's little community, Stephen encouraged Dorothy to introduce some simple discovery Bible study, showed her how to lead it, and then taught her how to become a disciple-maker, echoing some of the ideas in the previous chapter.

In time, perhaps Dorothy would show some of her new Christians how to make further disciples. Multiplication would become a continuing process.

You may want to ask whether it is you or someone else who is called to this type of mentoring role. Making twenty-first-century disciples is more than bringing people to faith. It is more than teaching Christian truths. It is more even than teaching Christian behaviour. It includes helping new believers to repeat what you have done and start a witnessing community in a pocket of their life.

Multiplication rather than addition

The American Neil Cole, who heads up a network of "organic" churches, has described what happened after Sean became a believer through a Christian community meeting in Neil's home:

Sean came to church one night and announced that he had started a new church. It was meeting on Wednesday mornings at 3.00 a.m. in a supermarket parking lot in downtown Long Beach. Why would he start a church that meets at such a ridiculous hour and location? Sean was working as a security officer in the city of Long Beach. He found several people

> who [were] committed to Christ but who worked at night and
> sleep during the day, so now there was a church available
> for them.[4]
>
> *Cole encourages new believers to start small organic*
> *churches in the midst of their everyday lives. One even met in*
> *a strip club! By 2004, his movement had spawned close to*
> *800 churches in only six years.[5]*

Contrast this approach with the church worker who befriended residents in a low-income neighbourhood. After several years, she started a small gathering in her house on the edge of the apartment blocks. Numbers began to grow. The leaders decided to move the group to a school slightly further away.

They wanted the group to keep growing by adding new members. They hoped it would do this by also embracing people connected with the school. But the original members stopped coming. They were put off by the new setting and the group's larger size. Growth by adding people to the gathering proved less effective than Cole's strategy of multiplying gatherings.

As numbers in the church worker's house grew, might it have been wiser to start a second group in the home of one of the new members? The church worker might have led the group for a period while the other person hosted, sharing the leadership with others in the group from an early stage.

"Why don't you lead the prayers next week? Just do what I did today. Invite people to write down what they want to say to Jesus. Next give them a chance to read out what they have written. Then read out your own prayer as a way of bringing the session to a close." As individuals became confident in leading, the church worker could have reduced her involvement.

---

4 Neil Cole, *Organic Church*, San Francisco: Jossey-Bass, 2005, p. 14.

5 Neil Cole, *Organic Church*, San Francisco: Jossey-Bass, 2005, p. 26.

Reproduction is possible

A small number of witnessing communities are starting to reproduce. As described in Chapter 4, Sorted is a good example.

> *Sorted 1 emerged among young teenagers in an English school. After several years, the leader began Sorted 2 in an entirely different school. A year later members of Sorted 1, who were now young adults, began discussing how to start Sorted 3 among young teenagers in the school that they had attended.*

> *Thirst, described in Chapter 3, is a community of mothers and carers at St Philip's School, near Cambridge in England. As new members became bolder in sharing their often new-found faith, they began reaching out to others they knew in the local area. They wanted their families and friends to share their experience of relating to God and each other.*
>
> *The community meets every Friday at school, as well as on Tuesdays for prayer and Bible study, but many of those the women were trying to reach would not have been able to make it at those times.*
>
> *So the women decided to find a convenient time and setting for Thirst Too – a setting where these families and friends would feel comfortable. They approached Romsey Mill, a Christian charity with sufficient space.*
>
> *Thirst Too now meets there once a month on Saturdays from 5 p.m. to 7 p.m., and whole families are invited. These still tend to be drawn from St Philip's School, but they often bring friends with them as well. Within a year, attendance was averaging about fifty-five people.*

Making disciples involves teaching new Christians to make disciples. This includes helping them to start witnessing communities in their ordinary lives. They can do this as individuals. Or as a community you might start a second community or even a third. The communities can meet together from time to time so that members feel part of a larger whole.

Less theory, more action

A "disciple-shift" is under way. It involves making disciples not just within the conventional local church, but beyond it – within witnessing communities in everyday life. These communities should do more than help new believers to value and live out the Christian story. They should also encourage and enable them to "do it again" – to start Christ-bearing communities in *their* ordinary lives.

Encouraging the dynamic of multiplication is the key to producing, through the Holy Spirit, not an institution, but a movement – a movement with the potential to change lives and refashion society.

This picture of discipleship differs from the one I was brought up with. Influenced by a range of evangelical writers, I was encouraged to develop a Christian mind – to think biblically about issues in my work and in society at large.

Lesslie Newbigin, for instance, visualized "frontier groups", groups of Christians working in the same sectors of public life. They would meet to thrash out the controversial issues of their business or profession in the light of their faith.[6]

There is an important role for this. Yet imagine that a group of Christian accountants from different companies met together and discussed what a Christian tax system might look like. Unless they were incredibly influential, who would notice?

Say instead that they asked themselves, "How can we serve our fellow accountants in this town? What activities, such as

---

6 Lesslie Newbigin, *The Gospel in a Pluralist Society*, London: SPCK, 1989, pp. 230–231.

training events, would assist them in their work and improve their lives? How might we add a spiritual dimension to these events – a free session on spiritual resources to manage stress, for example?" *That* would make a difference. People *would* notice.

Witnessing communities do not ask mainly abstract questions. They ask one simple concrete question: "How can we serve the people around us and help to improve their lives?" This is the heart of practical discipleship. People are drawn to Jesus as a result, the number of disciples grows, new witnessing communities come to birth, and the process starts all over again.

Serving people in this way is not a romantic stroll. It entails overcoming lethargy, surmounting barriers, struggling against collective sin, and making sacrifices. As the American Jesuit writer Brennan Manning said, Jesus "knew that following him was as unsentimental as duty, as demanding as love".[7]

---

7 From the *The Ragamuffin Gospel: Good News for the Bedraggled, Beat-up, and Burnt Out*, Colorado Springs: WaterbrookMultnomah, 2005.

PART THREE

Tools for the wider church

Chapter 8

HOW CAN MY CHURCH GET INVOLVED?[1]

When Ben Edson arrived in his medium-sized church in Manchester, England, he was convinced that pioneering Christian communities should be fully integrated into the life of the existing church. There should be space for innovative communities to reach out to people beyond the church's influence.

Ben sensed an opportunity. One of the four congregations was struggling to find its identity. Yet members also desired authentic community and a deeper life of commitment to God and each other.

During his first few months, Ben worked with the congregation to listen to God and one another. He encouraged members to dream about what the congregation could become.

Members soon recognized that an attractional model of church would not effectively connect with the unreached. They asked how instead they could be a community in which individuals were committed to each other in mission, a common lifestyle, and prayer. They went away to explore what they could be.

Six months later, the community had begun to find its

1 I am especially grateful for the help of Vicky Cosstick, a business and church consultant who uses complexity theory, in preparing this chapter.

> *identity in three places – five rhythms of grace (in which individuals commit themselves to five practices, such as serving others and sharing their lives with others), two monthly gatherings (a shared meal and an evening of experimental worship), and mission and prayer.[2]*

As a leader, perhaps you think you could never bring about that level of change in your church. If this is the case, this chapter may come as something of a surprise!

It argues that pastoral, side-by-side leadership is exactly what conveners of witnessing communities need and that leaders of conventional church, paradoxically, do not have to be innovators themselves to encourage innovation.

You can fan the embers of the new through fruitful conversations, carefully tended experiments, inviting those involved to agree on a framework for these experiments, encouraging shared learning within which witnessing communities are held to account, drawing in others by fostering perplexity and hope, and helping to "nest" the new in the church's life.

"I'm called to a pastoral ministry"

Maybe you believe that you are called to a pastoral ministry, not to start innovative witnessing communities. You do not fully understand what these new communities involve. You think you lack the skills to bring them into existence or to encourage your church members to do so.

Yet you are uneasy about the status quo. Your church is not reaching many outside it. Maybe church decline in your area is chronic. You wonder if the church has much future.

Perhaps, too, you realize that the pastoral ministry has

---

2 www.freshexpressions.org.uk/stories/abide (accessed 10 June 2013).

changed. Thirty to fifty years ago your church would have been nearly full. Pastoral care would have meant supporting those you saw each Sunday.

Now, with numbers in church much smaller, those needing care are largely absent on Sundays. To offer them support, the church has to go out. A pastoral ministry will include being with individuals where they lead their lives, not waiting for them to come to church. Might witnessing communities scattered throughout life be a means of pastoring people outside the conventional church?

An expanded vision

The good news is that if you are gifted in pastoral care, your gift may be exactly what's needed. You are not the one to form communities in the daily lives of your church members because you are not with them through the week, but you can support your church members as they do so. You can be a sounding board, an encourager, a source of probing questions, a warning voice, and an advocate for what they are doing, especially to others in the church who do not understand.

Church innovators often feel fragile. By trying something new they risk failure, which can make them anxious. If they are "ahead of the curve", they may feel misunderstood or unappreciated. What they need are good pastors who understand them, sympathize with the ups and downs of the task, and provide a listening ear.

In other words, you do not have to be an innovator yourself. You can be a pastor to those who are. Your care can release those in your congregation who feel called to start witnessing communities.

Might you go further? Where it is practical, might you offer to be a pastor to these new communities? Might you offer to be a referral point for individuals with pastoral needs? Might you visit from time to time, and care for some of the community's members as you get to know them?

You don't need to be a gifted change agent. Nor do you have to be gifted in up-front leadership to encourage these communities. Many Christian books on leadership and descriptions of "successful" church leaders assume that the leader is a charismatic person, who casts a bold vision, persuades others to get on board, and fearlessly leads the church to renowned success. You may feel that you don't fit the bill.

The reality is that you do not have to. A growing stream of secular literature questions these top-down models of leadership and favours side-by-side approaches – leadership that draws alongside people. Using numerous case studies and going under the overall label of "complexity theory", these writers argue that in today's society change is not directed from the top.

> A good example is Coffee in the Living Room, a partnership between a church and a medical centre in England's West Midlands. On Thursday mornings about forty people – mainly elderly – meet in the church foyer, which is transformed into a café.
>
> They chat, drink cups of coffee, and play board games. They can use a prayer tree to request prayer by the leaders, while face-to-face prayer is offered for those who wish. The café is less than a year old, but some of those involved can already see the potential for more Christian input.
>
> The café is far from being the minister's brainwave. Three members of the congregation had been feeling that the church should do more to serve the neighbourhood. Unknown to them, doctors in a medical practice were discussing the success of an initiative in one of its branches.
>
> Patients had begun meeting for coffee-and-chat on the doctors' premises. Appointments with the doctors had

dropped markedly. It seemed that anxiety and loneliness were being dealt with through this social event. "Can't we host something similar here?" the doctors wondered.

A "chance" conversation between the associate minister and the medical practice's compassionate community coordinator enabled a member of the congregation to join up the dots. She spoke to the three who wanted the church to do more to serve the locality. Might partnering with the medical practice make sense? They hesitated.

Then one day, in a small-group discussion, someone totally unconnected with the other conversations exclaimed, "Shouldn't we have a café in church?" One of the group again joined up the dots. The original three could no longer hold back.

They held discussions with the practice and the café was born. It came into existence not because the minister had the idea or was directly involved, but because of scattered conversations, at first unconnected, inside and outside the congregation.

Church leaders do not have to crack it all. Change need not depend on command and control. All leaders have to do is to work with others and allow them to find the answers.

The leader as gardener

The leader is akin to someone who tends an organic garden. The gardener has an intention for the garden rather than a rigid plan. The ecological system is not forced in an unnatural direction by the gardener's constant interventions: the garden is shaped by natural processes. There is room for surprises. A bird drops a seed from two gardens away. Instead of ripping the flower up, the gardener welcomes it as an unexpected addition to what's already there.

In this approach, leaders:

- Have intentions, not plans. "I expect to start a community with twenty members in a year's time" would be a plan. An intention might be, "I would like to encourage witnessing communities, but I am not sure how and what they will look like."

- Look for where the energy is and flow with it.

- Seek to open up possibilities without controlling the outcomes.

- Are open to surprises, therefore. The outcome may be unexpected.

- Keep listening and asking questions. With any problem or opportunity, the leader's default response is to ask, "How do we understand the situation? What should we do?"

The approach is similar to Paul's model of shared leadership, reflected for example in his teaching about spiritual gifts in 1 Corinthians 12 – 14. It allows room for the Spirit to be active at all levels of the congregation.

Less pressure

Being diffident about your ability to bring change need not be a handicap. Swayed by top-down models of leadership, maybe you pull back from encouraging witnessing communities. You are unsure what to do, fear failure, and are afraid of conflict.

In the "side-by-side" model, however, you are not expected to know it all. Drawing on the wisdom of those who have trodden a similar path, and guided by the Holy Spirit, the group you work with finds the answers.

Learning becomes more important than getting it right. It enables you and your fellow leaders to adapt to changing circumstances. If getting it right matters too much, the group will never try something new in case it does not work. But, if learning is the priority, the group will adapt through trial and error. *Any* outcome becomes a chance to learn what the Spirit is doing.

Responsibility is not yours alone. It is shared by the group. If things do not turn out as hoped, you will not be to blame. The group made the decision. More to the point, blame is an inappropriate response. There is no such thing as failure, only feedback – "What is the Spirit saying to us through our disappointment?"

Conflict is not to be feared, but to be welcomed. It is a sign of the group's health rather than of failure: individuals feel safe enough to express their differences. Differences provide an opportunity for new solutions to emerge. Novelty is the unexpected combination of different elements, including opposing ideas. Kary Mullis, a Nobel Laureate in Chemistry, remarked:

In a sense, I put together elements that were already there, but that is what inventors always do. You can't make up new elements, usually. The new element, if any, was the combination, the way [existing elements] were used.[3]

Disagreement becomes an occasion not for one person to "win" and another "lose", but for new thinking as the group seeks to combine elements from both views.

Be aware of your influence

To approach change from this perspective, a first step is to become sensitive to how you use your influence. It is impossible for a leader *not* to have influence. Just being present in the group

---

3 Quoted by Jeffrey A. Goldstein, James K. Hazy & Joyce Silberstang, "A Complexity Science Model of Social Innovation in Social Enterprise", *Journal of Social Entrepreneurship*, 1 (1), 2010, p. 111.

will affect others. Far from being embarrassed by their influence, good leaders use it to release other people.

Perhaps the group waits for the leader to propose a solution. The leader might ask, "Where do we think the answer to this problem will come from?" By asking a question, the leader brings a hidden assumption to the surface – the leader will come up with the answers. Space is created for the group to rethink that assumption.

Becoming sensitive to your influence involves watching out for whether you try to empower others or take power away from them – for instance:

- In discussion, do you close down people whose views you disagree with?

- Do you set the meeting's agenda or do you invite others to contribute items?

- Do you keep a tight rein on your volunteers or encourage them to take initiatives?

- If your church members wanted to start witnessing communities, how much control would you want?

To become more self-aware, you might keep a journal or use prayerful meditation. Note "distractions" that cross your mind during prayer, and watch for patterns. A pattern may reflect an attitude to control. Being more aware of your attitudes and motivations can open you to the Spirit. You can hold less tightly to your personal agendas. "I think this is important, but let's see what the Spirit says through the group." You can become more receptive to the unexpected. You can start to behave in more empowering ways.

A pastoral approach to change

Your discomfort about leading change can become an asset as your uncertainties draw out other people. If you were to say to your fellow leaders, "I think we should explore encouraging the congregation to start witnessing communities," you might – in some situations – spark a defensive response. "Why? Aren't people busy enough already?"

A more invitational approach might get a warmer response. You might say, reflecting your own hesitancies, "I have been reading about some new forms of outreach. They sound interesting, but I don't know if they would work round here. Do you think we should explore them?"

At each stage, your diffidence about the next step will draw you closer to others who feel uncertain. It will become easier to stand alongside them in empathy. Knowing that you understand will help them feel safer, which will make them more receptive to change. As they open themselves to the new, you will become more confident. You will lead through a pastoral model of change, employing the pastoral skills God has given you.

Encourage fruitful conversations

Perhaps you suspect that God is calling your church to start witnessing communities in everyday life. Your *hope* is that these communities take off. Your *intention* is to explore the possibilities. Your *plan* is for the immediate next step – to have some fruitful conversations.

Your prayerful plan is not that these communities flourish. The moment you think like that you impose your agenda on the outcome. You shut down the possibility that the Spirit may lead in a different direction. You exclude others from the process of discerning God's path. You put yourself in an elevated position: "I know what God wants. My task is to persuade you that I know."

You eschew being alongside others, which is the proper place for a pastoral leader.

Instead, you plan to have some profitable conversations because, as we shall see, conversations are everything.

Making time

The starting point for these conversations may be to clear space in your diary. Some ministers are so swamped by their commitments that they cannot take anything else on board. One person overseeing a declining church asked, "How can I make space for midwifery while engaged in palliative care?"

Time may not loom as such a problem when you remember that change, if it is God's will, can well up from any corner of the church. You may not have to do much yourself beyond providing pastoral support.

Keep remembering the golden rule: when you don't know what to do, ask other people. If you do not know how to create room in your diary to get the ball rolling, ask your fellow leaders.

You might say, "I think God may be calling me to do more to help individuals become effective Christian witnesses in their daily lives. But I am struggling because my diary is so full. Have you suggestions about how I can clear some space?" During the discussion, you might conceivably throw in the thought, "If I were to leave tomorrow, who would pick up my responsibilities while you looked for a replacement? Might this suggest how I could free up some time?"

You make yourself vulnerable, of course, when you share your diary with colleagues. But side-by-side leadership requires vulnerability. Sharing control and empowering others feels uncomfortable at times.

So include this in your prayers. Ask for the Spirit's strength as you follow Jesus, who made himself vulnerable enough to go to the cross. Prayerfully share your vulnerabilities with a spiritual mentor or guide. Frailties become less threatening when you talk about them.

Sharing control twice over

Tim has discovered what it means to share control. When he arrived as the new minister, he knew he would have to work collaboratively. The church was tired of having things imposed. So he worked with the church council to produce an outline vision statement, which the whole church was invited to flesh out through small discussion groups. The council met to draw together the threads in an away-day.

In a significant sharing of authority, Tim allowed the day to be led by a lay member with the necessary gifts. The person summarized the church's input and, in the context of prayer and Bible study, facilitated group discussion. During the day, the church's disparate ideas became a coherent whole.

The lay person himself surrendered control. He refused to impose his own agenda on the material being discussed, which would have been easy to do.

This double dose of releasing control – by Tim and one of his lay leaders – resulted in a high measure of agreement and a sense of God's presence throughout the journey. The church engaged in conversations that were exceptionally fruitful.

Later, Tim commented that sharing his oversight had not been easy. He had been anxious about what would come out of the discussions. Not least, would he be able to own the results (which he was)? Sometimes he has been tempted to speed up the process (which always means collaborating less, he noted).

A retreat followed by a church holiday had proved especially helpful. He sensed God saying that he belonged to a community rather than a project. So church would always be messy and change lead to unexpected destinations.

That is what communities do, he had come to realize. They are not neat and tidy like projects. Commitment to community means living with uncertainty, loss of control and uniqueness: communities walk their own distinctive paths. He was called to lead a community, not projects.

Fruitful conversations

Change does not come through structures and plans. It comes through conversations because conversations are the lifeblood of organizations.

British theorist and practitioner Patricia Shaw, for example, says that organizations do not exist apart from their formal and informal conversations. Take the conversations away and you would be left with some buildings and legal documents, but no living entity. Values statements, vision documents, and strategic plans make no difference unless people talk about them, and unless they influence the outcomes of myriad conversations within the organization.[4]

Everything happens through conversations – whether face to face, online, by phone or inside your head. Ideas are hatched in one conversation, modified in subsequent conversations, and put into practice through further conversations.

"We've agreed I'll start a witnessing community. Let me ask so-and-so if they want to be involved," someone says to himself. "We've agreed" refers to previous conversations. Now there is a conversation in the person's mind as they consider what to do next. The outcome of this internal conversation is the decision to have a conversation with someone else.

The leader's task is to encourage fruitful conversations. These conversations will address challenges people face, use

---

4 Patricia Shaw, *Changing Conversations in Organizations: A Complexity Approach to Change*, London: Routledge, 2002.

metaphors and stories, engage individuals at a personal level, and bring invisible assumptions and feelings to the surface, such as perceptions of the church's identity and fears that this will change.

Rather than assume that one view is right and the other wrong, people involved in these conversations adopt a both/and approach. New ideas emerge in a discussion when different elements are brought together – café and church, for example.

Open-ended questions, which are not too intrusive, can encourage this type of conversation – for example:

- What was on your mind as you came to the meeting?

- What is energizing you and de-energizing you at the moment?

- What are the things and people you value most?

- What works well in your situation and what doesn't?

- What do we aspire to become?

- What makes you anxious about these proposals?

The outcome of fruitful conversations is often unexpected. Don't be afraid of these surprises. They may signal that the Spirit has worked through the whole group and not just through you.

If you remain uneasy about the outcome, why not say so when you next meet? It will be in keeping with your desire for honest conversations. Of course, if you can reopen a discussion others must be allowed to do the same, which could prolong the process. But better to take more time and get it right than reach an over-hasty conclusion.

With whom?

So, you intend to explore whether to encourage church members to start witnessing communities in their daily lives. You expect to do this through fruitful conversations. Who should you talk to?

In this complexity approach to leadership, a key principle is that you flow with the energy – push when it moves. Don't stoke up energy where it is lacking. To do so is exhausting, time-consuming and often unfruitful. Go to where energy already exists. Ask people with energy and who are open to change whether they would like to explore the idea of witnessing communities.

These people may be:

- *Your leadership team.* Perhaps they sense the church is struggling. Volunteers are few and far between. Existing leaders are overstretched. One more pressure, one more grain of sand, and the whole sand pile would collapse. Might they be ready to consider prayerfully a different way of being church?

- *Individuals who want to do something new.* One person described her lively church: "But all growth is just Christians moving in and … literally only three adult new converts in ten years – a shocking statistic. A group of us are keen to be more intentional in our missional living and have been hoping, praying, and asking for new ways of showing Jesus' love to our neighbours, friends, and work colleagues." One or two people like that are well worth a conversation!

- *Individuals who naturally welcome a challenge.* Think of people who might be able to include a witnessing community in what they already do. One hairdresser complained that she could never invite her friends to her cell church because they would feel uncomfortable. But she could imagine inviting some of her customers to pray with her about family and other issues, "especially if I promised to do the praying". Who in your congregation might rise to a challenge?

You do not need scores of people to get started. One or two is enough. If they are not in your leadership team, you would be wise to inform the latter. You might mention that you are talking with a few people about how they can be more effective Christian witnesses. This is part of your pastoral care.

As ideas emerge you might report that John, say, is planning to meet with Christians in his street to explore how they can serve their neighbours. Later you might casually describe what the group is doing and the results.

Keep it all low-key. There is no need to alarm the team by telling them the whole story in advance, especially as you don't know what the story will be. (You may want to admit that.) God has not revealed his whole story to us. So just recount each chapter as it happens. Your fellow leaders will be kept informed. Perhaps some seeds will be sown in their minds as the story unfolds.

Encourage experiments

All being well, these initial conversations will lead to one or two experiments. "Experiment" is a better word than "pilot" because it is more open-ended. "Pilot" implies that you expect to repeat it. "Experiment" denotes a certain detachment. You are not bound to do it again.

"Experiment" suggests that you will engage in reflective learning at the end: what worked and didn't? What have we learned? What should we do in the light of our experience? You cannot fail with an experiment because the aim is to learn something. Learning is more important than the outcome. This alleviates the anxiety people may feel. The experiment feels less risky.

Great advances have come from "failed" experiments. Penicillin, for instance, was discovered by means of a contaminated experiment. Even if it "doesn't work", who knows what will come from your experiment!

As you talk about the possibility of starting an experiment, listen hard to the others involved. Listening affirms the other person, encourages them to share their thoughts, and boosts their confidence. "Maybe my idea wasn't so stupid. She took it seriously."

Within this listening atmosphere, you will put in some of your own thoughts. Telling stories of witnessing communities will spark imaginations, give permission to experiment ("If they were allowed to do it, perhaps we can"), and inspire confidence ("If it was possible for them, why not for us?"). You could show a DVD, such as those available through www.freshexpressions. org.uk, or the Diocese of Toronto's "A Missional Road Trip" on YouTube. Or you might visit a witnessing community nearby.

You will also have to explain why witnessing communities are important.

- *God wants mission to be done in community* wherever possible. He is the divine communion-in-mission. Jesus did mission in community, and so did Paul.

- *He wants these communities to be visible* in daily life. Jesus took his community of disciples into ordinary life. The early home churches were at the nerve centre of life.

- *These communities are to be active* in serving others and sharing the gospel, as was the community of Jesus' disciples.

Keep emphasizing "the mixed economy" – the idea that existing and new expressions of church should live together in mutual support and respect. New communities with a fragrance of church are not better than the existing church. Nor need they be alternatives. New and well-established types of church have their own distinctive missions, and it is possible to be involved in both at the same time. Emphasizing the value of both will remove the fear that individuals are being asked to make a choice.

As conversations progress, you should be able to identify some people willing to trial a witnessing community. Initially, there may be just one or two experiments – perhaps a one-off event like the one outside an apartment block in Richmond, Virginia.

From ice lollies to church

Greg and the associate pastor at Graceland Baptist Church organized some games and handed out ice lollies to the children, while a team of visiting Spanish-speaking missionaries shared a brief message with the people living there.

The team encountered not only Spanish speakers but people of many different nationalities. Fifteen of the residents became Christians. As a result, this "one-off" has become a weekly gathering.

Every Friday afternoon a small group of people, some of whom first met at the original event, get together for church. They meet on Friday because (like 30 per cent of people in the US) they work on Sundays.

Through this gathering Graceland, a predominately Anglo congregation, has connected with Colonial Place Christian Church, a mainly international congregation in the neighbouring county.

Greg says, "You know it's a move of the Spirit when all of these informal partnerships start to spread. A few months ago, we did not know any internationals. Now, we're doing church together."[5]

If your initial conversations are with your church leaders and they catch the vision, you may decide to work not with a few individuals but with the whole congregation.

---

5 www.freshexpressions.org.uk/stories/upstart (accessed 11 June 2013).

Random Acts of Cake-ness

One church with several hundred members invited volunteers to form missional communities. These are church-based communities that seek to reach a specific group of people outside the church. The leaders were explicit that this should be for a trial period of three months.

The idea of a trial encouraged twelve communities to form. Each had a mission focus. Nine zoomed in on neighbourhoods to which the group had a connection, while three sought to serve a specific demographic – elderly people, children and families, and mothers and toddlers.

Most communities supported an existing involvement or interest of one or more of their members. In one group, a couple belonged to their school's Parent–Teacher Association. Others in the group became more active, too.

In another group, a couple loved making cupcakes. Under the banner of "Random Acts of Cake-ness", these became gifts to individuals nominated by others in the neighbourhood.

After three months, these experimental communities had proved their value. They were accepted as a permanent feature of the church's life. Inspired by their stories, other members of the church have formed further communities.

You do not need to be a large church to encourage missional communities. Two or three people in a congregation of a dozen could have a go. They could find a simple way to serve their apartment block or street, and watch the Spirit open doors for them to share the gospel.

Will my denomination back me?

If you are worried about this:

- Where possible, keep the experiment(s) under the radar and don't bring it to the surface till there is proven fruitfulness. Most denominational leaders are only too happy to bless success.

- In any report to your denomination, focus initially on the first stages of *A relationships-first journey* or *A serving-first journey*, described in Chapter 4. No one can complain about an initiative to serve people outside the church!

- As people come to faith and start experiencing church within the witnessing community, discuss the implications with the denomination, including the language you use to describe it. If leaders are squeamish about labelling it "church", call it a gathering.

Agree a framework

As a few individuals explore the possibility of trying an experiment, they will need to set boundaries without being overprescriptive.

Complexity writers stress the importance of keeping a balance between order and chaos. Too much order stifles innovation. Insufficient order leads to chaos. A balance between the two creates a safe space in which the Holy Spirit can bring something new. People will need boundaries that describe *what* the experiments are seeking to do and boundaries that explain *how* they will do it.

Remember: *you* do not have to come up with these boundaries. You are engaged in a process of conversation. The boundaries will be drawn as those involved talk with each other and share their experiences. Your contribution may be to get the discussion started.

Agree on the direction

Might the four characteristics of witnessing communities described in Chapter 1 capture the aims of your experiments? Leaders would seek to start communities that were:

- *missional*: they connect with people who do not attend church;

- *contextual*: they find culturally appropriate ways to reach people;

- *formational*: they intend to form disciples;

- *ecclesial*: they are not stepping stones to existing church, but provide flavours of church for those who attend.

Something akin to these objectives might become the core values of the experiments. They would create enough of a framework to provide a sense of direction without filling in so much detail that improvisation suffers.

Agree on the means

Leaders of experiments will also need help in understanding how to achieve these aims. So, as part of their conversations, the leaders may want to talk through, for example, *A serving-first journey*. Especially among people with little church experience, the *journey* suggests that witnessing communities emerge through:

- careful listening;

- loving and serving others;

- forming community with those being served;

- putting in signposts to Jesus and enabling individuals to explore following him;

- allowing an experience of church to emerge around those coming to faith, including connections to the wider church;

- encouraging new believers to start small Christian communities in their own lives.

Leaders will want to remember that these stages overlap and look different in different contexts. This is not a rigid model but an aid to thinking about what is involved.

This framework will help leaders to structure their imaginations – to glimpse steps through which the Spirit may bring a witnessing community to birth. Imagining these steps will release their creative juices. An element of "order" will spark novelty of thought.

At the right time, might the leaders also discuss some of the themes of Chapter 5? The more practical help they receive, the greater their confidence.

Throughout it will be a step-by-step process. But you never know where these steps will lead!

> Hot Chocolate, described in Chapter 1, started in 2001 with a small group of churchgoers taking hot chocolate to young people in the centre of Dundee. It now has six paid staff (two full-time) and around thirty-five youth-work volunteers annually and serves about 300 young people through the year.
>
> Charis Robertson has described how Hot Chocolate has developed:

Since the outset, it has been the young people who have made the decisions about how, when, and what happens... In a way, everything that has happened so far in the way of church community is completely accidental, and so tends to be quite different from intentional church planting models and approaches... It seems that every couple of months we stop and say, "What are you up to now God? It's changing again!" ... Hot Chocolate experiments: not recklessly, but without anxiety of failure. There is a strong culture of reflection, vulnerability, and learning together, even when we have made mistakes.[6]

Learn together

You would be wise to gather the leaders of the experiments into a simple "learning community". Even if there is only one experiment, the minister or a lay leader can form a learning community with the leaders involved.

The community would have two purposes. The first would be to learn from each other's experiences. Your meetings might look back and look forward in the context of Bible study and prayer.

Looking back could be framed around the pastoral cycle (or spiral):

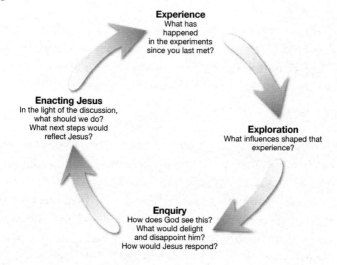

Experience
What has happened in the experiments since you last met?

Exploration
What influences shaped that experience?

Enquiry
How does God see this? What would delight and disappoint him? How would Jesus respond?

Enacting Jesus
In the light of the discussion, what should we do? What next steps would reflect Jesus?

6 www.freshexpressions.org.uk/stories/hotchocolate (accessed 14 June 2013).

Looking forward could include questions about strategic direction, using perhaps *A serving-first journey* – for example (at the appropriate time):

- Who else should the Christians involved listen to?

- How might the initiative love and serve people in the context?

- How might these people experience community?

- How can the team help individuals explore Jesus?

- What type of worship will be appropriate for new believers?

- Are new Christians being helped to make disciples?

- How can sustainability be built in – for example, by sharing leadership?

Ideally, two members of each experiment would attend the learning community. During the meetings, the pairs would set goals for the period ahead and report at the next meeting on how they got on.

Having two people from each experiment will make it harder for one person to exaggerate its achievements – the other person can inject a note of realism! The two can also support each other when they feed back to their community what they have learned.

Accountability

The learning community's second purpose would be to ensure accountability. Accountability in the context of learning feels more like "We're in it together" than reporting to a severe boss.

You will be rightly concerned that these experiments remain faithful to the gospel and do not bring the church into disrepute. Indeed, these concerns may be holding you back. "What happens if things go wrong? Dare we take the risk?" The best response is proper accountability.

Accountability should be mutual. If you are the minister, not only should leaders of the experiments be accountable to the church through you, but you should also be accountable to them for providing appropriate support – such as:

- championing the experiments;

- reporting on them to your fellow church leaders;

- negotiating with the denomination, where appropriate (see box below);

- helping the experiments to find expertise – from the wisdom of others who have trodden a similar path to financial and legal advice, such as child protection.

> ### Questions a denomination or network might ask about larger initiatives
>
> - How will the initiative be governed?
>
> - How will leaders be appointed and for how long?
>
> - What are the financial expectations and requirements (e.g. insurance)?
>
> - How will appropriate safeguarding policies be implemented?
>
> - How will progress be reviewed?
>
> - How will the initiative be "protected" if leaders of the parent church change (often a problem)?
>
> - How will the sacraments be celebrated (in denominations where only an ordained minister can preside)?

Accountability should be light-touch. You and others in the learning community should not second-guess the leaders of each initiative, but use wise questioning such as, "Do you have a biblical basis for your proposed approach?" "How would you explain your decision to others in the church if asked?" "What are the potential pitfalls?"

You might start with just one rule – leaders come to every meeting of the learning community. Over time and in the light of experience, the community might develop a code of good practice – "What seems to work well for us."

VentureFX

VentureFX is the UK Methodist Church's pioneering ministries scheme to encourage fresh expressions of church. By 2012 fourteen pioneer ministers were involved. They are networked together in a learning and support peer group.

As well as the group meeting monthly Ian Bell, who coordinates VentureFX, meets regularly with each pioneer. The oversight session is nearly always over a meal, where discussion ranges from what has happened since they last met to reflecting on the good and bad along the way.

It is not about telling pioneers what they should or should not have done. It is more like a mentoring relationship, talking about the challenges ahead, and "joining the dots".

Ian and the pioneer will explore opportunities that may have arisen, tease out possible implications, and see how the opportunities might fit the bigger picture. Ian aims for supportive supervision rather than "over-control".

In a local church, "supervision meetings" can be subsumed within a learning community, with occasional one-to-ones as necessary.

Be realistic

Accountability will help the experiments to stay on track. But there is no foolproof way to avoid accidents and mistakes. Look at Paul's difficulties with the church at Corinth!

When you try out something new you *are* taking a risk – hence the value of working collaboratively. The learning community can be a place where problems are shared and solutions prayerfully sought together. The risk need not fall on the minister alone.

Encourage wider support

Alongside fruitful conversations, experiments, boundaries, and shared learning, you will want to encourage the congregation to welcome this approach to mission. You will pray that others will catch the vision – that your initial experiment(s) will open the door to further initiatives.

Tilling the soil

To create a readiness for the new, as you begin to experiment you should encourage perplexity within the congregation. All change is rooted in perplexity. When individuals are puzzled and want to find answers, they become open to novelty. Jesus' parables work like this. They create bewilderment ("What's this about?"), which paves the way to see things differently.

The best way to encourage perplexity is to ask questions. If you feel that members of your church are complacent, you might ask, "Most of us are getting older. Who will be left in this church after we've died?" Or "We are a growing and apparently successful church, but who haven't we reached? Are we a bit smug?"

You might count the numbers who have joined and left your church in recent years. If there is a pattern of decline, you could show the figures to your leadership group and ask for reactions.

If you are a growing church, you might list those who have joined over the past year. How many came from other churches nearby? How many had moved into the area but belonged to a church before moving? How many were lapsed churchgoers? How many had virtually no church background? Again, you might show your fellow leaders the figures and ask if they are content.

If your growth is from people in the first three categories and church attendance in the area is declining, you might ask what will happen if this lopsided pattern continues? For how long can your church expand if it fails to reach people with little Christian experience? Would Jesus be content to attract so few of the never-churched?

You might invite one or two people from outside the church to describe to your fellow leaders their honest perceptions of the church.

As you bring these missional realities to the fore, an open-ended question such as, "How do you feel about this?" may allow feelings of disquiet and bafflement to be expressed. If people say that they feel uneasy about the situation but are at sea about how to respond, that is your opportunity to ask if they would like to explore possible ways forward.

Balance perplexity with hope

A Methodist chapel in Norfolk, England was on the edge of extinction. The new minister gathered the dozen or so elderly members and invited them to read the description of the early church in Acts 2:42–47. Members discussed how far their own experiences of church matched the one portrayed in the passage.

Feeling safe because of the way the minister had introduced the discussion and knowing each other quite well, individuals began to express their disappointments with church – the boring sermons, for example.

The minister encouraged them to imagine how church might be different. Some of them had heard stories about

> *café church. They decided to worship on Sundays in café*
> *style – sitting round tables and including more discussion.*
> *Over the next months numbers roughly doubled.*

Members of the chapel felt perplexed – they knew church was not working for them or their friends. The minister encouraged them to express these feelings. But that was not the end of the story. Individuals were not left in despair. Instead, they were shown a possible solution and they gave it a try.

So, while encouraging perplexity, you should point to possible solutions. Tell stories about what others have done. Show them some of the DVDs I've referred to. Talk about the experiments you are nurturing. Bring the challenge and the hope into your conversations, your committees, your Sunday notices, and your email updates. As the experiments start to bear fruit, invite some of those involved to provide descriptions.

Don't overhype what is happening. One minister fell into that trap. His exaggeration undermined the credibility of his stories of fruitfulness, allowing his successor to reduce support for the witnessing communities he had encouraged. So be honest about disappointments and mistakes. Remind people that experiments don't always "work". Learning happens through trial and *error*. It is what you learn that counts. The congregation will respect your honesty and have more confidence in you.

Repetition, repetition, repetition

Don't underestimate the importance of repetition. For you as leader, the church will be constantly in your mind. But others will have plenty of other things to think about.

So keep talking about the challenges your church faces – the threat of decline or the reality behind apparent growth. If you mention this once, they will forget it. You have to keep it on the agenda – and the possible solutions.

Find every opportunity to raise the questions. Constantly explain why the church cannot go on as it is. Keep describing the alternatives. Keep doing this as you start some experiments and await their results.

One minister resolved every couple of months to invite someone with experience of witnessing communities to come and preach. The congregation would be constantly challenged, but not always by him! (And there would be one less sermon for him to prepare – another way to clear his diary.)

Embedding the new

When I had finished speaking about the witnessing communities emerging today, a woman in the front row commented, "My church started one of these a couple of years back. It has had a big impact on us as a church."

If your initial experiments bear fruit, your church as a whole will feel the effects. The impact may be small-scale – such as the minister who invited recent converts to be among those having their feet washed during the parent church's Maundy Thursday service.

Or it may completely transform the church, as with St George's Church in Deal, England. To engage with people who would not cross the church threshold, in 2002 St George's launched what have become "missional communities" of anything from fifteen to sixty people.

Each community serves a specific group of people and has its own worshipping life. To allow time for both mission and worship, members do not meet with the rest of the church every Sunday, but from time to time. Forty new missional leaders have been released to run these communities.

People who previously were sitting in the pews – along the

lines of a "provider client" type of model – are now doing all kinds of things that they never dreamed they would be doing. As they've gone out and taken on these new roles with new responsibilities, they've discovered the need to depend upon God. As a result they've grown spiritually and in their discipleship as well.[7]

Selecting leaders

To nest your experiments in the church's life and to encourage other church members to follow suit, you will have to address a number of questions. One will be selecting appropriate leaders. Initially you may have done this "on a wing and a prayer", but the church will rightly expect criteria to guide future appointments.

In discussing potential criteria, you may find it helpful to consider the following. Leaders should be:

- *Grounded spiritually.* They should have a faithful walk with Jesus, and be committed to their local church if acting in its name.

- *Gatherers of people.* They should be able to gather a (small) team and help to attract around it the people the team serves.

- *Gifted in drawing out others.* They should be aware of their limitations, able to involve others with complementary gifts, and be willing to release people to use their gifts.

- *A good fit for the culture.* They should be at home in the context because they are already in it, are familiar with a similar culture, or gifted in cross-cultural mission. Pay special attention to someone who has sensed God's call to a specific demographic for some time.

---

7 www.freshexpressions.org.uk/stories/stgeorges (accessed 14 June 2013).

Creating space

You may well hear the cry, "How can we start something new when it is hard enough to find volunteers for what we are already doing?"

Jesus spoke about the need for pruning to allow spiritual growth (John 15:2). In a similar vein, as support for witnessing communities grows, some things may have to be cut back.

You might encourage the church to develop a releasing mindset: if a person doing a task feels called to a witnessing community, they should be released from that task whether or not someone can step into their shoes.

This could be a big ask! So might you invite the congregation to do a thought experiment: what would happen if the person had to move away for family or work reasons? The church's life would have to carry on. Might members see helping a witnessing community as equivalent to moving away? Of course, the person would not be leaving completely – and you never know how their community might enrich the church in future.

> One post-Alpha gathering seemed to drift out of the orbit of its parent church. The congregation felt rather sad. Then out of the blue the gathering offered to contribute to the church's budget – music to a church treasurer's ears!

So each time someone with a responsibility feels called to a witnessing community, why not treat them as if they were leaving the area? It could be an investment in the church's future.

Naturally, the parent church will have to sustain its life, which may require some creative thought.

- A Methodist Church, for example, might ask whether certain ministries could be left in the hands of another church in the circuit. "We can't find someone to run the Thursday young teenagers group. Should we join forces with so-and-so nearby?"

- The principle could be extended to a "like-minded" church in a different denomination.

- Might the task be undertaken by someone who has been drawn into a witnessing community?

- If the church loses a particular ministry, might it rejoice in its other ministries, especially its new witnessing communities?

Remaining faithful

Another concern may be that the new communities will slide away from your church's spiritual priorities. There would be a loss if these priorities were diluted.

The best ways to safeguard your values are the careful selection of leaders, building accountability into the leaders' meetings, and Spirit-filled teaching and worship when the whole church gathers.

Some churches have relaxed the expectation that believing members of "missional communities" will worship with the whole church each Sunday. To allow these communities time to develop their own worship and mission, members are asked to worship with the rest of the church just once or twice a month.

This concerns some leaders, who fear that church members will be under the word less often and that it will be harder to pass on the church's spiritual DNA. Yet meeting on Sunday less often may not be a big step in practice. Church members are often available for witnessing communities during the week but are tied up at weekends. It may be easier to prioritize one or two Sundays a month than to be present every week.

In addition, if they feel common teaching is important, ministers can video Sunday sermons for witnessing communities to discuss when they meet. This will strengthen communities' links with the centre. Social and other events involving the whole church will reinforce these ties. The church's spiritual values will be passed on informally through deepening relationships between long-standing members and new believers.

Transitioning leaders

Transitioning from first- to second-generation leaders is often a critical phase in a new community's life. It should be managed with special care.

Surveying fifty-seven stories of new Christian communities in the UK since 1999, the Church Army Sheffield Centre found that fourteen had ceased to exist. In about three-quarters of these, the founder was not replaced, a poor appointment was made, or the community was too dependent on the founder to survive that person's departure.[8]

> *An example of good practice was a pioneer who had helped start a Christian community in an area of social deprivation. She was aware that the sudden departure of a new community's "midwife" can be profoundly painful.*
>
> *So when it came for her to leave, she withdrew gradually. She shared more and more tasks with others in the team. After she had left, she continued to be available to her successor. She refused to follow the example of her co-leader who had left the year before and avoided further contact. Instead, she stayed in touch with members of the community. They felt less abandoned.*

The departure of the parent church's minister can be a particular problem. On a number of occasions a new minister has arrived with a different vision, has withdrawn support, and new communities have died.

If you are the minister, before you plan to leave you may want to discuss this danger with your fellow leaders and perhaps

8 *TSC Research Bulletin*, Winter 2011/12, p. 2.

with the denomination. What might be done to lessen the risk? Might the job specification for your successor include continuing to support witnessing communities?

From gathered to scattered church

Local churches need pastors who will love them into change. In a local church, witnessing communities can emerge through:

- fruitful conversations;

- carefully tended experiments;

- an agreed framework for these experiments;

- shared learning within which leaders are held to account;

- a combination of perplexity and hope that encourages others to get involved;

- nesting the new in the church's life.

The secret is for church leaders to keep asking the people involved. This is good news for leaders who are diffident about managing change. They do not have to shoulder all the responsibility themselves. They can share it with others, and in doing so feel more integrated into the church community.

Tim, mentioned earlier, has found that sharing his leadership has paid off. When he arrived, the church employed a children's minister, who started a thriving Messy Church on Wednesday afternoons. Around 100 children, mothers, and carers attend. Several dads arrive for the meal at the end. Two baptism services have involved several families who had been prepared in advance.

Hard on the heels of Messy Church has been Tiddliwinks, a mini Messy Church on Friday mornings for the under-fives and their carers. When the children start school, a significant number find their way to Messy Church.

A new lay pioneer minister has developed Zone, with around sixty young people from outside church on a Friday evening. She has taken some of them to Soul Survivor, a large Christian conference in England, and is asking what church might look like in this group.

As well as Coffee in the Living Room, described earlier, a couple who love walking have just started Stepping Out, a "missional community" centred on walking. They have gathered a Christian core who invite others to join them on walks once a month. These are opportunities for conversations that scratch below the surface. In time, might they lead to a fuller experience of church based on these monthly walks?

A senior citizens' lunch is followed by a few hymns, prayers, and a short talk. A monthly "Outlook" for the over-fifty-fives, most from outside church, aims "for a new perspective on life". Visiting speakers usually introduce a spiritual dimension.

This is an ordinary local church gearing up for mission. From being in touch regularly with 200–250 people, after just three years the church is now regularly in touch with over 500. This growth is due to the bubbling up of new initiatives. At the heart of these initiatives are small groups of Christians who are taking Jesus from Sunday morning into the community. Normal church is becoming church in normal life.

Chapter 9

WHAT SHOULD MY DENOMINATION OR NETWORK DO?

Decline casts a shadow over much of today's church. In Australia, Britain, Canada, parts of the United States, and elsewhere, the denominations are waking up to the reality of an ageing membership. The twenty- and thirty-somethings are scarcely represented.

Unless trends are reversed, in much of Europe the bottom will drop out of church attendance between 2015 and 2030. When the baby boomers have passed away, the pews will be almost empty. In some areas, the bottom has nearly disappeared already. Other parts of the global North are just one or two generations behind. To many, the future looks bleak.

Yet the mushrooming of new witnessing communities is starting to tell a different story. Continued decline may not be inevitable. Might we be entering a spring of fresh hope?

If you are involved in the leadership of a denomination or network of churches, perhaps as a lay person, how might you and your fellow leaders contribute to this story and fan the flames of hope? How might you prayerfully help to create a welcoming climate for witnessing communities and provide them with support?

A new missional imagination

You might start by asking what narrative has the upper hand in your denomination or network – a narrative of decline or a narrative of hope.

Trapped in decline (in attendance, clergy numbers, and finance), morale in denominations and networks is often low and many clergy seem passively resigned to the ebbing away of church.

Coping with the effects of decline is often higher on denominations' agendas than reversing decline. Shrinking financial and management resources are spread ever more thinly around existing congregations. The escalating demands of a complex world – from safeguarding to human resources – make "keeping the show on the road" hugely time-consuming. Little energy is left to pull the denomination around.

Shifting resources from ageing churches to initiatives for growth is seen as a risk. "What will happen if the new is unfruitful?" sceptics ask. "Will the church as a whole be weakened?" Institutions have an instinct for self-preservation. Spending on a new venture means putting resources into something that does not yet exist. No one misses the money if it is not spent. But withdrawing money from an existing activity produces squeals of anguish.

So, despite lip service to growth, the real action is in managing dwindling numbers – closing churches, merging them, and making do with fewer clergy. A narrative of decline has become deeply entrenched.

A missional imagination

Yet challenging this narrative are the stirrings of a new missional imagination.[1] Churchgoers are starting to envisage new types of

---

1 In articulating this, I have been especially helped by John Paul Lederach, *The Moral*

Christian community rooted in everyday life. In neighbourhoods and networks where the church is a fading presence, they are beginning to imagine initiatives that work for individuals nearby, create lively communities, draw people to Christ, and provide transformative experiences of church.

This new imagination is a willingness to bring to life something that in its very birth changes the world and how people see it. It conjures up an alternative future to emptying churches and withering Christian influence. It journeys to a horizon of active Christian presence in every fragment of society. It champions communal Christian witness alongside individual testimonies-in-life.

It is an imagination that is starting to reshape some of the mainstream churches.

The sound of change

Around 1990, Britain's Salvation Army took a hard look at itself. Its research showed that membership was plummeting so deeply that, on current trends, by 2020 it would no longer be viable. Senior staff revisited this around 2005–06 and saw that the trend was continuing.

Over the previous half decade, the organization had begun to restart work in places it had abandoned. Instead of sending one officer or a married couple to these areas, it had sent teams of four to six. Some twenty plants and outreach units had been born.

Though encouraging, the process was too resource-heavy and slow to reverse the decline. So in 2010 the Salvation Army decided to encourage non-officers, as well as officers, to explore new mission opportunities and innovative ways of being a Christian community.

Imagination: The Art and Soul of Building Peace, Oxford: OUP, 2005, esp. Chapters 3 & 4.

> The leaders launched a series of strategic conferences to explain their thinking and galvanize support. In 2012 they backed the initiative with £2 million a year, an astonishingly large sum by British standards and for such a small denomination. They made arrangements to identify, train, and fund leaders to undertake new ventures.
>
> Influenced by this decision and the discussions that led up to it, some eighty new initiatives were under way by 2013. They included leaders of a church beginning to be Salvation Army in a new area, a church starting a ministry among adults with disabilities, and the launch of a Salvation Army café in an inter-generational centre.
>
> Many could be described as witnessing communities – working with people outside the church, in a way that fits the context, seeking to make disciples, and allowing people to have an experience of church where they are.
>
> It is too early for non-teetotallers to pop the champagne, but there is new mission energy around. The Salvation Army is beginning to serve areas it had left. New expressions of Christian care and witness are replacing the threat of extinction.

The role of denominational leaders

What can other denominations and networks do to encourage this new missional imagination?

In parts of the UK, North America, Australia, and elsewhere, this fresh picture of mission is starting to emerge through a combination of local vision and an environment of permission and encouragement. Alongside this experience are insights from the increasingly influential complexity school of organizational change. Put the two together and what can we learn?

First, it seems that denominational leaders need not *direct* change – for example by casting a vision and inspiring others to get behind it. This "transformational" approach to leadership is popular in some Christian circles. But at a denominational level it appears not to have been crucial – so far – in the development of witnessing communities. These communities had begun to emerge in the late 1990s and early 2000s before most denominational leaders had even heard of them!

Their emergence has accelerated since the mid-2000s not because denominational leaders have beaten an inspirational drum for them. Relatively few have done so. What seems to have been more important – at least in the UK – has been the culture of permission that has been created in a growing number of denominations.

This has led some to suppose that giving permission is enough. But, again in the UK (and in some other countries), the quickening spread of new types of Christian community has been associated with more than top-down permission. Some denominational leaders have actively encouraged innovative forms of church by highlighting stories of good examples to encourage others, appointing staff to catalyse change, and helping the church to make sense of what is happening.

It seems that a combination of local initiative and a supportive culture can be prayerfully encouraged in a fourfold way: socialize the new missional imagination, try it, amplify it, and resource it.

Socialize it

Sculpting change is not a matter of writing a vision document, a statement of values or a strategic plan. These have their place, but are nothing if they are not talked about. Statements and plans come alive only if they enter into conversations.

This is because conversations – face to face, online, and inside people's heads – are the lifeblood of any organization, as we saw in the last chapter. Without its conversations, an organization would be a shell. New ideas emerge through conversation and their implementation is surrounded by conversations.

The trouble is that committee and other official meetings are frequently routine and stagnant. The most interesting conversations occur by the coffee machine during breaks in the formal business. Yet often the thoughts expressed in these informal conversations are not brought into the official meeting. So energy is dissipated rather than harnessed for change.

The challenge for denominational leaders, therefore, lies not in writing a strategic plan, valuable though this can be. It is to encourage imaginative conversations about witnessing communities, in which honest exchanges can breed new ideas and generate energy to carry these ideas forward.

If this is to happen in the myriad conversations of a denomination, leaders must use their agenda-setting influence to excite individuals and get them talking. How might they do this?

Getting people involved

As we all know, people are more likely to be engaged if they have an opportunity to contribute. If leaders come up with a plan and paint much of the detail themselves, individuals may feel they have little to offer. Having failed to add their own brushstrokes, they will be less inclined to own the final picture. On the other hand, if they are given insufficient direction, individuals will be unsure what the picture is about and will not know where and how to add their mark.

So leaders need to provide a framework within which, through conversations, individuals can improvise. At the core of this framework will be clarity about what people are being asked to imagine.

Some of us involved in Britain's Fresh Expressions team, which has been tasked with encouraging new and different forms of church, would say that one of our early mistakes was not to provide that clarity in relation to "fresh expressions of church". As the term spread, it was used so loosely that almost anything was covered by it. One church even redesigned its noticeboard and hailed it as a fresh expression! The phrase became flabby and lost credibility in some quarters. People were unsure what it meant.

If people are to have intelligent conversations, they must be clear what they are talking about. Whatever language the denomination uses to describe witnessing communities – whether "fresh expressions of church", "missional communities", "planting church", or "new contextual churches" – the definition must be both transparent and open enough for conversations to flesh it out.

Might the UK team's definition of "fresh expressions of church", referred to in Chapter 1, be a help? A denomination or network might encourage its members to imagine communities that are:

- *missional* – they work mainly with people who do not belong to church;

- *contextual* – they are appropriate to the culture of the people they serve;

- *formational* – they aim to form disciples;

- *ecclesial* – they aim to give the people they serve a taste of church where they are.

Perplexity and hope

In addition, people begin to get excited when they talk about something that brings hope to their underlying concerns – when they engage in conversations that address their perplexity.

Many church members have a sense of "lostness" – a feeling that the church is at sea amid the baffling changes that have flooded society. The church seems estranged from the world, often unable to reach out to it or to speak its language.

Church leaders will want to articulate this perplexity. They will point to signs of the church being lost – to the decline in overall attendance and the failure to engage with younger age groups in particular. They will keep reminding people of the gloomy picture ahead if current trends continue.

Encouraging church members to discuss their perplexity will challenge complacency. Awareness will spread that things are not fine as they are and must change. Those who know that change is needed will be given confidence to explore what change might look like. There will be a sense of urgency.

Complacency never leads to action, but perplexity can. Perplexity involves unease with the status quo. It is only when people feel this unease that they look for an alternative. Many of today's new Christian communities originate in dissatisfaction with the existing church.

> *Messy Church, attached to Christ Church, Oshawa in Toronto, is just one example. Some members of Christ Church recognized that the church was failing to serve many parents. So they started Messy Church, a monthly gathering with craft activities for all ages, simple Christian worship, and a shared meal. Numbers have grown from twenty to sixty.*
>
> *If you poke your head round the door, you will see churchgoing members with their grandchildren who never go to church, and parents who have stopped going to church accompanying their children.*
>
> *The community works by being a very different type of church. It was born because some Christians recognized that existing church could not cater for everyone on its doorstep. Dissatisfaction was a spur to action.[2]*

---

2 Diocese of Toronto, "A Missional Road Trip", YouTube.

So, where decline has set in, leaders will be wise to shout the church equivalent of "Fire! Fire!" – "If we go on as we are, a growing number of our local churches will not have a future." They will encourage the question: "We're in trouble, so what can we do?"

However, many leaders are rightly aware that, when you shout "Fire!", some people freeze in panic. If there are no exit signs, others rush around confused. Merely sounding the alarm can be counterproductive.

So alongside perplexity must be a story of hope. As well as shouting "Fire!", leaders must point to the exits – to the examples of how Christians are starting communities that combine loving service with evangelism, how they are meeting the challenge of "lostness" by finding a new way. These stories of hope will become more persuasive when they are embedded in a theological rationale – such as:

- Mission is an eternal first step for God, and should be a first step for the church.

- Just as God does mission in community, individuals should do mission in community wherever possible.

- These communities should follow the example of Jesus and his disciples and be visible in ordinary life.

- This visibility should come through corporate acts of loving kindness and sharing the gospel, again like Jesus and his disciples.

When leaders articulate perplexity, they describe the reality others in the church also see. When they tell stories of hope, they prevent perplexity from turning into despair.

Perplexity and hope can be springboards for a new missional imagination. They can bring excitement because conversations become relevant and positive. People can start to address problems creatively.

Different agenda

The excitement will be greater if these conversations connect with church members' varied priorities. Competing agendas may paralyse leaders who seek to affirm them all. Drawing a strategic focus from agendas that are moving in different directions is far from easy. But an imagination that embraces these agendas can affirm them and offer them a fresh framework.

For example, the idea of witnessing communities can speak to people with a passion for social justice or the environment. Witnessing communities can be campaigning vehicles. When individuals come together for a cause, such as combating developing-world debt, their concern can be enriched by the resources of the Christian faith. Writing campaign letters can become a form of prayer, for instance, as we saw in Chapter 6.

Christians who are cheerleaders for specific groups of people, such as those who are deaf, can be invited to see witnessing communities as an additional means of serving these constituencies. Denominational members who wave the flag for diversity can be encouraged to see witnessing communities as an opportunity to welcome minorities into a more heterogeneous church.

Believers who cherish traditional forms of church can be reassured by the concept of the mixed-economy church. There is room in the kingdom for both the new and the current. One is not better than the other: each has its distinctive ministry and mission. They complement one another, and should value and support each other.

Leaders will be wise to encourage a new missional imagination to be couched in terms of the mixed economy. The imagination should not all be about new forms of Christian community. It should also affirm what already exists. The Church of England's Liverpool Diocese uses the language of rivers and lakes. Rivers of fresh expressions flow in and out of the lake of existing church, renewing the waters in the process.

Embodying the tradition

There will be excitement about a new missional imagination if it resonates with the denomination's identity – if "it's part of us". The imagination must be owned as an authentic expression of the denomination.

Britain's Methodist Church, for example, sees fresh ways of being a Christian community as a reworking of key themes in the Methodist tradition. They include the conviction that the Church should be structured for mission, and be able to respond pragmatically when new needs or opportunities arise. Their original "method" was the development of new discipling communities:

Not without self-criticism, therefore, the Methodist Church, pointing to its own origins and to Scripture, holds to the conviction that the Holy Spirit leads the Church to adapt its structures as it faces new situations and challenges. This flexibility is itself an important principle, rooted in Scripture, theology and experience.[3]

The Anglican Church connects fresh expressions of church to the historic role of the parish, which was intended to ensure that the church was available to every section of the population. Prison, school, industrial, and other forms of chaplaincy emerged to fill gaps in the parish system as society changed. Fresh expressions take the logic of chaplaincy a step further.

When I described how new Christian communities were

---

3 Faith and Order, *The Missional Nature of the Circuit*, London: Methodist Church, 2008, para. 2.1.

emerging in every part of life, including the workplace, an Oxford academic looked distinctly alarmed. "How subversive!" he exclaimed. "They're infiltrating our lives without us realizing." Then he paused. "I suppose it's no different to the chaplains we've had in Oxford colleges for centuries..."

A clear but open definition, articulating perplexity with hope, tying the new missional imagination in to existing agendas, and framing it with the denomination's or network's identity will encourage conversations about where the church is now and how it can grow into God's future.

Leaders should keep injecting into people's conversations the question of how to imagine local mission. They should raise it in their one-to-one exchanges, encourage churches to discuss it, put it on committees' agendas, and include it in their public addresses and presentations. Getting everyone to talk about this new imagination will socialize it.

Try it

At the same time, experiments should be cultivated to inspire, test, and refine this new way of thinking about mission. Stories from even young experiments can feed into conversations about what it means to be a missional denomination or network. They can provide clues to what works and why. They can be sources of hope and words of warning.

When it experiments, a denomination takes a leaf out of God's book. God has chosen experiments to propel human history. Civilization is the product of successful experiments – houses that stay up, cars that work, and systems of government that are less disappointing than the alternative.

Experimentation is part of being human. So it should be second nature for denominations and networks to "try and try again" to express Christian community in the textures of life.

Giving permission

A growing number of church leaders are giving permission to lay people and clergy to experiment with new forms of community. As the Anglican Bishop of Toronto said, "I am giving you the keys of the car. Now drive it!"

This is a hugely important start. Most Christians see the current shape of church as a given. They need permission to imagine something new. Without permission, they lack the confidence to try a different approach.

But, as many church leaders have to come realize, permission is not enough. How many head teachers, for example, have turned a school around merely by "blessing" good practice in the classroom? Effective heads take the lead in introducing best practice, mentoring teachers, and articulating a vision. Their leadership is proactive as well as permission-giving. The same is true of other organizations. "You don't get to be a leader by being a tracker."

A trial-and-error culture

Proactive leadership will include prayerfully encouraging experiments. Their aim will be:

- to provide proof of concept – witnessing communities bear fruit;

- to discover what works and what doesn't;

- to give confidence to others – "I know someone who started a café church"; "Why don't we try something new?"

Creating a trial-and-error culture requires several elements. First, "experiment" is a better word to use than "pilot". As we saw in the last chapter, "pilot" implies that you intend to do it again. "Experiment" does not have that implication, so it is a more gradual approach.

It puts the accent on learning. The point of an experiment is that you learn something. Experiments can be a way of learning how to be a better church – how to serve God and the world more effectively.

Second, to encourage experimentation, leaders must keep repeating that individuals have permission to fail. They should constantly explain the paradox that a failed experiment need not be a failure. If an experiment teaches you something, it will have been a success.

In her research into successful entrepreneurs, the American academic Saras Sarasvathy found that failing is an integral part of venturing well. Entrepreneurs are willing to fail. They outlive failures "by keeping them small and killing them young… the success/failure of the entrepreneur does not equal the success/failure of the firm".[4]

Successful entrepreneurs are more important than successful enterprises. Effective entrepreneurs learn from their mistakes. Indeed, often it is only because they have made mistakes that they have successes. Failure helps them to flourish.

Henry Ford's first venture, the Detroit Automobile Company, collapsed. So did his second, the Henry Ford Company. But these failures taught him valuable lessons about the importance of pricing and high-quality products. The Ford Motor Company, his third venture, changed the world.

Though pioneering in church is not the same as in business, there are lessons here for denominations and networks. Attention should focus less on the initiative and more on the individual. Is the person learning from their mistakes? Are they becoming a better pioneer?

Experiments should primarily be a way of breeding successful practitioners, with fruitful initiatives as the by-product. If you

4 Saras D. Sarasvathy, *Effectuation. Elements of Entrepreneurial Expertise,* Cheltenham: Edward Elgar, 2008, p. 17.

reverse the order and aim always for successful initiatives, like happiness, your goal may become harder to achieve. Practitioners who might in time have been successful may get discouraged, give up, never put into practice the lessons learned from their mistakes, and so fail to plant the fruitful communities you prayed for. Individuals should be invited to try and try again. Leaderships must be patient while mistakes are made.

One Anglican diocese has laid down timed milestones for the pioneers it supports, with questions to evaluate whether the milestone has been reached. Broadly, the pioneer of a new church is expected to spend:

- the first six months mapping the context and the network possibilities;

- the next eighteen months engaging with some of these networks and forming a core team;

- the next twelve months forming a Christian community;

- the next two years laying the foundations for sustainability.

It is understandable that a denomination should want to see spiritual fruit from their financial investments. But a focus on outputs and timescales leaves little room for pioneers to learn from their mistakes. It puts pressure on pioneers to avoid mistakes lest they fail to reach the next milestone.

The denomination risks losing pioneers who have become discouraged. It may end up investing more heavily in a project than in a person. Rather than achieving the goal of encouraging mission initiatives, the denomination may fail to grow the pioneers on whom these initiatives depend.

Might it be wiser to develop evaluation questions in relation not to project milestones, but to pioneers' learning?

Leaders should keep explaining the value of failure to give

people confidence to have a go. Individuals need not hold back through fear the experiment won't work. The whole point of experimenting is for individuals to learn and to share their learning with others. It may be only a slight exaggeration to say that when a denomination or network focuses on learning rather than on outcomes, the outcomes will largely take care of themselves.

Network the experiments

A third key element will be capturing the learning from fruitful and less fruitful initiatives. This can be done by networking the leaders of experiments into learning communities so that they can support and learn from each other. Each member becomes both learner and teacher.

One model is for two or three leaders from an initiative to meet with teams from other initiatives several times a year. More than one person is important. Team members can support each other when they report back on their learning, hold each other to account for describing their initiative accurately, and ensure continuity. If one person is ill, the other(s) can still attend.

The aim is to have honest conversations in an atmosphere of discovery. Each session is supported in prayer by friends and colleagues of team members. The process takes the team on a journey, structured around three questions:

- *What is?* This includes asking, "What have we done since the learning community last met? What barriers did we encounter? What have we achieved? What have we learned?"

- *What could be?* This is about looking to the future imaginatively. What are the possibilities? Who do we know who has tackled this problem and could advise us? If we were to achieve the objectives we have set ourselves, what would we have created and what would we have stopped?

- *What will be?* This involves concrete planning for the coming months.

For each question, teams initially work alone. They feed back to the wider group. Then they send scouts to one or two other teams whose feedback sparked their imagination. Being aware of one another's experiences and plans encourages teams to explore crossovers between meetings.

Teams are invited to keep pressing towards the principles behind their answers to the three questions. Outside input during the sessions can help with this.

Drawing leaders of experiments into learning communities will enable:

- the experiments to learn from each other;

- the denomination to capture and disseminate the learning;

- the denomination to gain experience of learning communities, so that the next wave of practitioners can be networked into effective learning communities too.

Put it in your job description!

Fourth, to promote a culture of experimentation, denominational staff must be catalysts. They must encourage experiments, for example through:

- storytelling, both to broaden the imagination and create confidence - "We could do that";

- vision days to excite people and let them know they have permission;

- weekend or evening courses to introduce the principles involved;

- bringing opportunities and individuals together;

- using one-to-one conversations to give practitioners confidence;

- being advocates for pioneers of witnessing communities, speaking up on their behalf, and explaining to others in the church what they are doing and why.

As support for experimentation grows, the denomination should put this catalytic role into staff job descriptions. Say a youth-officer post becomes vacant. Why not write into the new person's job description, "Promote experiments in forming Christian community among teenagers with no church background"?

If "Encourage witnessing communities" was added to the job description every time a staff vacancy arose, the denomination or network would be transformed! Staff could be held to account for identifying potential practitioners, looking for volunteer churches, and providing mentoring, training, advocacy, and other support.

When a church leader says that fresh expressions of church, or church planting or whatever term they use, is one of their priorities, I ask myself, "Is it in anyone's job description?" If it is not, I wonder how seriously to take the claim. Job descriptions are a means by which priorities burst into action.

Understand the pioneering mindset

Finally, and perhaps most importantly, church leaders need to remember that one of the secrets of pioneering success is that pioneers of witnessing communities think differently.

They do not have an organizational mindset. This way of thinking starts with a well-defined goal, and works back to the steps and milestones needed to achieve it. It is appropriate once an organization has been established.

By contrast, research suggests that pioneers do not start

with clear goals because they do not know enough to define their goals.[5] The outcomes of their decisions are unpredictable, a change in the environment can blow them off course ("The manager said we could use the café but now she has left"), and they do not know which aspects of the environment to pay attention to and which to ignore.

Instead, pioneers are very pragmatic. They start with what they have got – who they are, what they know, and who they know. They proceed on a trial-and-error basis. They have some idea of what they want to achieve, but usually it is vague and only becomes more definite as they work with other people, try different possibilities, and change course.

If they are inspired by a model (such as a café church they have heard of), they will adapt the model as they collaborate with others and listen to the context. The final result may be very different from what they imagined at the outset.

The next chapter discusses this more fully, but the implication for church leaders is clear: they need to understand this pioneering mindset. They will find it difficult to encourage experiments if they don't.

Amplify it

Complexity theorists describe how stable organizations damp innovation. Various strategies and arguments are used to resist novelty – "Let's appoint a committee", "We mustn't risk our reputation", or "We can't spare the resources." Significant change becomes possible only when the organization is less stable. Instability is a sign of openness to the new. Instead of rigidity, flexibility creates space for novelty.

For an organization to become receptive to change, small

---

5 Saras Sarasvathy, *Effectuation: Elements of Entrepreneurial Expertise*, Cheltenham: Edward Elgar, 2008. As discussed in the next chapter, the research is based on business pioneers but many of us would recognize a similar mindset among church pioneers.

innovations must be amplified. The stronger the amplification, the greater the momentum, and the more likely it is that resistance will be overcome.

Amplification occurs through feedback. The effects of small changes feed back through the organization and influence future actions. Positive feedback creates a cycle of self-reinforcement. One change increases the likelihood of further similar changes.

Spread the news

Leaders encouraging witnessing communities are likely to see small changes coming from two directions – from conversations about a missional imagination and from experiments in these new types of Christian community.

The fruits of these conversations and experiments can be amplified by means of stories about them. Insights from a gathering to imagine new forms of mission, for example, can be relayed through conversations, blogs, tweets, YouTube clips, and much else. Likewise, social and other media can be used to report on experiments.

Leaders have a key role because others pay attention to what they say. So when they use sermons and talks, councils and committees, media, and personal exchanges to broadcast the outcomes of conversations and experiments, they ramp up amplification. Change may well up from below, but the advocacy of leaders feeds it and helps it flourish.

So does good research. It can enable a denomination to track experiments, evaluate their fruitfulness, pinpoint factors behind "success" and "failure", and become aware of initiatives under the radar.

A good example is the role played by the Church Army's Sheffield Centre in Britain. Between 1999 and 2012, its quarterly publication series, *Encounters on the Edge*, disseminated stories about new types of church. These stories became the evidence base for *Mission-shaped Church,* the 2004 Church of England report that kick-started denominational support for fresh expressions of church around the world. One reason the report was so influential is that it described what was actually happening on the ground.

More recently Church Army research, partly funded by the Church of England's Church Commissioners, has demonstrated the very significant contribution of these fresh expressions to British church life. The research has been credited for encouraging the Church of England in 2013 to substantially increase the sum it was willing to invest centrally in promoting these new types of church.

Spreading the results of research – through how-to-do-it resources, for example – can also help those starting from scratch. It can enhance the process of change by making it easier for others to get on board.

As news about witnessing communities spreads, support will grow. In 2012 Britain's Methodist Conference held some crucial votes on funding fresh expressions of church. The laity proved the main advocates for fresh expressions because they had seen and heard about fruitful examples. A substantial sum was voted through.

Strategic appointments

Key appointments are also crucial in escalating change. An excellent example is the appointment of Revd Dr Martyn Atkins as General Secretary of the British Methodist Church in September 2008. A keen supporter of fresh expressions, Dr Atkins has played a vital role in pushing this agenda forward within the Methodist Church.

The appointment of Dr Rowan Williams as Archbishop of Canterbury was similarly crucial within the Church of England. As Bishop of Monmouth, Williams had been vexed by the disconnection between the church and the bulk of the population, and had direct experience of some imaginative church plants in the diocese.

This set him on a path of reflection that prepared him to make *Mission-shaped Church* a priority when the report was published soon after his move to Canterbury. His time at Canterbury saw the appointment of a significant number of bishops who also played key roles in supporting the fresh expressions agenda.

These national appointments have begun to be reflected in strategic appointments on the ground, such as enablers of pioneer ministry who have clout within the denomination.

The Church of England Diocese of Liverpool is beginning, in addition, to identify "hub" churches. These are churches with a specific calling to multiply communities in the microcosms of life and to encourage other congregations to do the same. It plans to appoint ministers with suitable gifts and experience to lead such churches. Or it will send a pioneer with expertise in witnessing communities to a well-run church that wants to move in this direction but lacks the know-how. Once the pioneer has passed on their expertise, they will move on.

More generally, as vacancies occur a denomination might start to appoint "mixed-economy" ministers to local churches. These would be clergy who were committed to new, as well as more traditional, expressions of Christian community. Those initially appointed might join two or three ministers already in post with a similar vision. As they work together, they would share their experiences of encouraging witnessing communities in their churches and receive input on good practice.

They would seek out and support lay people who wanted to form one of these communities. These lay people in turn might form a separate learning community, again sharing insights and receiving input. In time, members of the two groups might facilitate the same process with other ministers and lay people.

Where full-time pioneers are appointed – for example, to start a church in an area of new housing – their job specs should include doing something for the existing church. A pioneer might be the secretary of the meeting of a local clergy group, for instance. This will have a big impact relationally, and magnify the pioneer's influence within the wider church.

Champions

Champions for witnessing communities are another means of amplifying change. The Church of England's London Diocese, for instance, has committed itself to starting 100 new worshipping communities in seven years by 2020.

These communities will include a variety of models – from taking over a church building about to close, to church in schools (among parents, pupils or staff), to church among specific demographics (such as French- or Spanish-speaking congregations), to church in unreached neighbourhoods, to "missional communities" serving a specific demographic or area.

Key to the initiative are champions. Each deanery – groupings of churches in the diocese – will have a champion, as will each model of worshipping community. These champions will be advocates for growing new communities in their deanery or for their model. By raising awareness, giving advice, assisting with training, helping to mobilize support for specific initiatives, and trouble-shooting, champions have the potential to become megaphones for new witnessing communities.

Young adults

One other way to spread change, for example, might be to bring together every so often promising young adults from across a region, especially where few young Christian adults exist and they feel isolated.

The aim would be to help individuals grow in their faith, and to develop the skills and knowledge to form Christian communities in never-churched territory. They would continue to meet as their initiatives flew or floundered, supporting and learning from one another.

In 2013 a report into fresh expressions of church among young adults in the Church of England grabbed attention. It suggested that posts be created to help young adults form experimental communities. It also recommended that more should be done to encourage open and supportive links between the wider church and fledgling communities started by this generation.[6] Gathering young adults together would be one way of providing this support and connection.

Resource it

As experiments bear fruit and snowball, the growing number of initiatives will need support. This will raise questions to do with finance, the type of support required, selecting leaders, and training.

Releasing resources

If a denomination or network is cutting its budget, which is often the case today, finding the money for something new is bound to be difficult.

In some cases, funds can be made available by selling property. If a minister's house or a church is sold because the congregation has come to the end of its natural life, some of the proceeds can be put into a mission fund. Church decline can finance church growth.

Britain's Salvation Army, for example, has an explicit closure

---

6 Beth Keith, "Authentic faith: Fresh expressions of church among young adults", www.freshexpressions.org.uk/resources/authenticfaith

policy. When a centre is shut (because it no longer meets a need), the money is put into a mission pot. Initiatives that have been funded for an initial three years can apply to this fund for up to seven years of further support.

The Anglican Diocese of Toronto has taken this in a radical direction. Between 1961 and 2001 its membership more than halved, with the decline accelerating. Facing a stark choice of grow or die, the diocese adopted a policy of pruning in order to grow.

Beginning in 2009, it classified churches into:

• Sustainable. These have the leadership, resources, and energy to meet the challenges of the communities they serve, and are financially self-sustaining.

• Strategic. These are strategic for the diocese. They are strategically located, make a significant contribution to the wider society, are mission-minded, and are in line with the diocese's priorities. Some will not be financially sustainable – because they serve an area of social disadvantage, for instance. But their strategic importance entitles them to call on the wider church for support.

• Static. These are inward-looking and have no clear mission focus. But they are able to sustain themselves financially. The few that have the potential to become sustainable or risk becoming unsustainable receive support. The rest are left to their own devices. They are not a financial drain on the diocese. Neither do they currently have much potential for growth.

• Unsustainable. These churches are not mission-focused and are not financially sustainable. They are depleting their capital reserves or rely unduly on outside funding. Informally, they are referred to – rather cruelly – as "vampire parishes": by being a financial drain, they suck the life out of other churches. Their futures are reviewed, and between 2009 and 2011 ten were closed or amalgamated.[7]

Human and financial resources have been tilted away from unsustainable parishes to strategic and sustainable ones. Bishops, for example, are giving the latter more of their time and they are sent more able clergy.

This has been generally welcomed in the diocese. It is widely recognized that growth requires pruning, and that unsustainable congregations cannot keep draining resources from the rest.

The lesson, perhaps, is that it is better to prune earlier than later. The longer you wait, the more savage the cuts may eventually prove to be. As decline sets in and possibly accelerates, more churches will become financially unviable. Larger numbers will have to be closed. The risk is that if you leave it too late, widespread closures become inevitable, yet the pain is too great to allow additional pruning to free resources for growth. You end up balancing the budget but failing to invest in the future.

What type of support?

Once some money has been put aside for growth, how should it be spent? Some denominations have invested in flagship projects. They have poured money and support into a handful of new Christian communities, led by someone employed full-time.

But experience suggests that this may not be the wisest course.

---

7 "The Anglican Diocese of Toronto: Diocesan Council's Report to Synod on the Priorities and Plans 2009-2011", 2011, pp. 3–4, www.toronto.anglican.ca

- It is expensive when budgets are tight.

- Relatively few projects can be supported.

- Once the money has been spent, what happens next?

- Little is learned about seeding these new approaches among "ordinary" clergy and lay people, which is the main challenge.

What is proving more valuable is to prayerfully appoint a dedicated staff member. The appointment will show that the denomination is serious about encouraging this type of mission. Ideally, the person will be an advocate, a catalyst, an aide, a fixer, and an enabler of others. If these gifts are not all present in one individual, it may be sensible to appoint two part-timers.

The Anglican Diocese of Toronto, for instance, has created two part-time posts. The Bishop's Officer for Mission encourages initiatives to help every parish become "mission-shaped", while the Missional Coach works with two outside consultants to help ministers and congregations relearn the skills and behaviours needed to be missional in the twenty-first century.

The person (or two part-timers) will explain and help shape the emerging missional imagination. They will come alongside people with little or no understanding, spend time listening, patiently answer their questions, and gently stir their imaginations.

They will look for opportunities to bring in the new. They will link people together, and show denominational leaders how witnessing communities can help to solve some of the problems they face: "You're wondering what to do with this near-empty church? I know someone suitable who is looking for a job. Might they use the building to start a new Christian community?"

They will be midwives to individuals giving birth to these communities. Perhaps supported by a special group, they will seek pathways through the quagmire of unhelpful rules and processes. Britain's Methodists appointed a Fresh Ways Working Group, whose remit included addressing institutional roadblocks to fresh expressions of church.

Experience has shown that such a person will need a strong steering group, which has clout in the denomination. Ideally, the person will be a member of the denomination's senior staff. If not, the steering group should include members with influence at the highest levels. Novelty needs support at the top if it is to crash through resistance and inertia below.

Selecting pioneers

As support is made available, denominations will want to appoint staff with gifts of innovation to pioneer witnessing communities within an existing church or to spearhead a new initiative. In making these appointments, they may be tempted to look for candidates who have pioneering traits.

Yet researchers into entrepreneurship have found it extraordinarily difficult to identify agreed personal characteristics that are peculiar to entrepreneurs. Efficacy – the ability to make things happen – seems to be the one that stands out. However, even this should be treated with caution:

- *Entrepreneurship is a team process.* Efficacy may be held within the team rather than by the leader.

- *Entrepreneurship is highly contextual.* Making things happen may require different skills and qualities in different contexts. A Puerto Rican woman may not be much of an innovator on Wall Street, but be highly effective among her fellow ethnic women in East Harlem.

- *Entrepreneurial ability may be widespread* in the population, but remain hidden because circumstances have not drawn it out.[8]

---

8 Some of this research is summarized in Michael Moynagh with Phil Harrold, *Church for Every Context: An Introduction to Theology and Practice*, London: SCM, 2012, pp. 230–231.

So, rather than looking for pioneering characteristics, it may be better to look for a record of innovation. If they are real pioneers, even twenty-one-year-olds will have innovated in some way at school or college. For example, the twenty-three-year-old person responsible for Youth and Young Adults in one Church of England diocese started a Christian Union at her school as a young teenager.

In its criteria for the selection of ordained pioneer ministers (who have a special calling to start fresh expressions of church), the Church of England now looks for "a <u>demonstrable</u> track record of innovation and initiative" in the candidate's past.[9]

Might a denomination extend this principle? Lay people might be encouraged to pioneer witnessing communities in their daily lives. If a person has demonstrated fruitfulness doing this in their spare time, the denomination might offer to employ them for one or two days a week so that they could expand their ministry. If the Spirit continued to bless the initiative, the person might be employed full-time to develop it further. They might connect with other Christians, for example, to energize further communities in similar contexts. Funding would follow blessing.

Training and support

Individuals who start witnessing communities step out with the Spirit. Even so, they can feel uncertain about what they are doing, anxious about some of the difficulties they face, and isolated from the church at large.

Lay and ordained pioneers of new communities will benefit from four types of support. The first is an introductory course in the theology and practice of witnessing communities. The second is being networked into learning communities, where they can receive input and the support of their peers. The third is

---

9 "Criteria for Pioneer Ministry", www.churchofengland.org/

some form of coaching or mentoring, especially at critical times in their community's life.

Neil Cole's astonishing multiplication of churches is based on mentoring.[10] *He advocates a just-in-time approach:*

- Never teach a skill till there is a need for it.

- Never teach a second skill till the first one is learned.

- Never assume a skill is learned till it is taught to another.

Cole uses the MAWL method (see box), and within that framework adopts the following principles:

- First things first – he addresses glaring areas of weakness first.

- One thing at a time – individuals learn at a different pace.

- Always one more thing – he keeps asking God what is next for the person.

The MAWL method of mentoring

- **M**odel: I do, you watch, we discuss.

- **A**ssist: We do, we discuss.

- **W**atch: You do, I watch, we discuss.

- **L**eave: You do, someone else watches… (The process begins again.)

Source: adapted from Neil Cole, *Organic Leadership: Leading Naturally Right Where You Are*, Grand Rapids: Baker, 2009, p. 248.

---

10 Neil Cole, *Organic Leadership: Leading Naturally Right Where You Are*, Grand Rapids: Baker, 2009, ch. 17.

The fourth form of support is connection to the wider church, especially where individuals are leading witnessing communities beyond the reach of a local congregation. As well as through learning communities, this connection can be achieved by the formation of longer-term networks linking the initiatives together, and by drawing individuals into the life of the denomination.

As witnessing communities proliferate, denominations may need to appoint a growing number of "connectors" to join people up. Spare-time lay leaders of witnessing communities will have few hours left to network into the denomination, so supervising ministers or denominational staff may have to make connections on their behalf.

What lies ahead?

To counter the narrative of decline, in many denominations and networks the Spirit is bringing to birth a new missional imagination centred on witnessing communities. It may sound trite, but one way to prayerfully work with the Spirit in creating this imagination is to follow the STAR:

- *socialize the imagination* by encouraging members to talk about what the denomination could become;

- *try it* by promoting experiments;

- *amplify it* by feeding the results of these experiments into the denomination's conversations;

- *resource it* by providing lay and ordained pioneers with support.

These are not sequential steps, but will be taken alongside each other and will reinforce one another.

Tasks for leaders

Three things stand out from this approach, which is rooted in complexity theory and in the emerging experience of fresh expressions of church.

Firstly, *leaderships must destabilize rather than stabilize the denomination or network.* They must eschew the temptation to be content with keeping the peace, minimizing conflict, and discouraging disruption. Change – to a greater or lesser extent – *is* disruptive. Often it provokes conflict. Sometimes the last thing you want is peace, if peace means nothing alters.

Rather, leaderships must encourage the denomination to sit at the "edge of chaos" – not to be so orderly and rule-driven that the new cannot emerge, nor to be so full of change that denominational life feels out of control. Leaders must shake things up enough to encourage innovation but without bringing the house down.

Secondly, *leaderships will encourage others to innovate rather than being the innovators themselves.* Leaders will not assume the responsibility for new ideas. They will not say, for example, that such-and-such is the best model to follow. They will encourage others to come up with ideas and try them. They will allow others to discover which models work best. Leaderships will then describe what is happening, make sense of it in relation to the denomination's history, and enable lessons to be learned.

It follows, thirdly, that *leaderships will interpret change rather than create change.* They will propose theological frameworks for understanding the new witnessing communities that emerge. They will explain how these communities are consistent with the denomination's DNA. And they will create language that helps the denomination's identity to evolve as it embraces the new.

Looking ahead

As witnessing communities move towards centre stage, what might a network or denomination expect to see? First, networks will proliferate, as is happening now – in particular:

- *"Conversations"* will be groups of people who are exploring the idea of witnessing communities and wondering whether to dip their toes in the water.

- *"Committed"* networks will comprise leaders of witnessing communities. They will include specialist hubs of leaders focused on particular demographics or types of area – such as inner city, suburban, workplaces, and schools. Some may produce their own resource material.

- *"Covenant"* networks will consist of leaders and members of witnessing communities who have a deeper commitment to each other. They will reflect different spiritual traditions – catholic, Celtic, charismatic, and so on. Influenced by the "new monastic" movement, some will share a simple rhythm of life. Like the other networks, they will have their own conferences and events. Some will produce resources, for example on discipleship.[11]

Second, a "single-economy" church in the future is improbable. Some people hope that novel forms of Christian community will evolve into traditional versions of church, which will revive and remain dominant. Others believe that the latter will eventually wither, leaving the field open to the new.

Neither seems likely. The mosaic nature of people's lives means that many new and existing believers will not choose between the old and the new, but welcome both – such as the "heavy metal" congregation that worships monthly with its

---

11 I am grateful to Canon Phil Potter for encouraging me to think on these lines.

Anglo-Catholic neighbour.

The old and the new will bless each other not by becoming more alike but by remaining different. Enriched by their varied experiences of church, a growing number of Christians are likely to worship in two "local" churches – one at weekends and the other "in life" during the week. Blended church will thrive within the "mixed economy".

Third, as Christian communities multiply in the hubbub of life, the church will connect more closely with believers' everyday experiences, its service to the world will be tailored more precisely to the needs of different settings, and its presence will become more visible to people outside.

Instead of trying to bring about change by seizing the commanding heights of power and influence, as it often has in the past, the church will follow Jesus into the fissures of society. It will become a subversive influence from within.

Chapter 10

THE KEYS TO SUCCESS

Lack of confidence can be the biggest barrier to starting a witnessing community. You fear you will get it wrong and be judged: "You should have gone about it differently." "You are not being faithful to Scripture." "How many have come to faith?" In the background is the killer: "Have you succeeded?" "Have you been stupid?"

If you harbour these fears, perhaps you will make excuses and, like Jonah, turn away from God's call. You may be too anxious to follow the Holy Spirit's promptings. That would be a shame. It is possible you are being ambushed by a mistaken notion of success. You may be sinking into the quagmire of viewing success as setting a target and hitting it. Failure becomes the lack of attainment.

When it comes to starting a witnessing community, this idea of success does not make sense. To understand why, we shall start with some secular research and then see how to follow the Spirit when developing a witnessing community. The keys to success are a try-and-see mindset, seeking the Spirit, and finding the Spirit through relationships.

The try-and-see mindset

Saras Sarasvathy is an academic who has written a ground-breaking book with the somewhat formidable title *Effectuation: Elements of Entrepreneurial Expertise* (Cheltenham: Edward Elgar, 2008). She took thirty highly successful entrepreneurs and looked closely at how they made decisions. A clear pattern emerged.

Entrepreneurs act in situations of great uncertainty. The outcomes of their decisions are unpredictable, their goals are at best vague, and they don't know which aspects of the environment to pay attention to and which to ignore.

So they do not launch out with clear objectives and plans to achieve them. They begin with the here-and-now, with what they have got. They start with who they are, what they know, and who they know. On the basis of their identity, their knowledge, and their networks, they have a go. They get together with one or two others and see what works. They will have some idea of what they want to achieve, but their goal becomes clear only as they work with other people, try out some ideas, and build on what seems to be effective.

A medical entrepreneur

A surgeon – for instance – may sense that a different type of surgical instrument could perform his favourite operation better. He talks to some of his colleagues, and their conversations begin to crystallize his thinking.

Two or three of them agree to work with him on a prototype. The first prototype does not work very well, but they learn from it. They try two or three more (the goal changes a bit), and eventually develop an instrument they are pleased with.

They believe there could be a market for it – think of the number of surgeons around the world who perform this particular operation! But they don't do any market research. That would take up too much time and they would not trust the results. People might *say* they would buy the instrument, but would they actually do so when the crunch came?

Instead, they show the instrument to some of their colleagues, who express an interest. So they seek out an engineer.

(There are agencies that help with this.) The engineer, with his contacts, works out how to manufacture the instrument.

Again, using an agency, the engineer makes enquiries about which company would be prepared to do this. The company suggests some modifications to the instrument – the goal has been changed again. It calculates the cost of producing the instrument. Conversations with distributors indicate what the instrument would sell for after distribution costs and the like.

The surgeons go back to their colleagues and ask if they would buy the instrument at that price. If their colleagues look cautious, they ask a few others and then perhaps call it a day. It is not going to work. But if there is enthusiasm, they test the idea further and take the plunge.

The process is very pragmatic. The surgeon starts with who he is, what he knows, and who he knows. The idea of the new instrument emerges through conversations and through trial and error. The decision whether to take it to market is likewise based on a process of testing. The entire approach is experimental – "Let's try it and see if it works."

Two mindsets

On the basis of Sarasvathy's research, there seem to be two distinct mindsets. There is what I would call the pioneering mindset, which is based on what you've got. It is experimental, step by step, and pragmatic.

By contrast, the organizational mindset is driven by goals, it seeks plans to achieve those goals, it is systematic (it will do market research, for example), and it is less experimental. It knows where it is going and has a strategy for getting there.

One mindset is not better than another. They come into play in different contexts. If you are starting something new, you will probably find that a pioneering mindset is helpful. But if you are consolidating what you have established – the doctor is now running a surgical instrument company – the organizational mindset will be more appropriate. The surgeon will set production and financial targets, and check regularly that these targets are being met.

Observation suggests that both mindsets can be found within the church. Individuals who found something new tend to adopt a pioneering approach, whereas denominational leaders and administrators frequently have a more organizational mindset.

Hot Chocolate, described in Chapter 1, is a good example of the pioneering mindset. The leaders had no initial plan. They simply took hot chocolate to young people in the centre of Dundee. The community has grown from there, step by step, in response to suggestions by and comments from the young people involved.

> *St Luke's in the High Street, Walthamstow, near London provides hot and cold drinks, homemade cakes, and somewhere for customers of the Farmers' Market in the high street to sit, chat, have lunch, and watch the world go by.*
>
> *Offering free drinks was an unexpected breakthrough. The drinks draw in men and women who hang around the town square and are dealing with loneliness, mental health problems, addictions, family breakdown, long-term unemployment, and other challenges. There was no big plan to reach this group. It just happened.*
>
> *On Sunday mornings Breakfast, Bible and Chat takes place in a local café. One Sunday the group offered to buy breakfast for one of the guys from the town square. From there it snowballed. Instead of attracting ten people, numbers shot up to twenty-five. Some pay; the others get paid for. Again, this was not planned. It happened unexpectedly.*
>
> *The wallet containing donations has never emptied,*

> *and the group takes this as a sign to keep going with this*
> *Sunday ministry. It is a step-by-step approach. "Something*
> *unexpected has developed. We've got the money. So let's*
> *keep going and see what happens."*[1]

Beware of distinguishing too sharply between the two mindsets. When the initiative is up and running, a pioneer may become more organizational in her approach, while a denominational leader may be thoroughly pioneering at times. The distinction is between mindsets, not people, though some people may be more at home with one approach than the other.

The nature of success

So what does this mean for success? On the one hand, it blows apart conventional notions of success. When you are starting something new, such as a witnessing community, typically you won't have a clear goal. The best you may have is a sense of direction, and this may well change as you go along. So you cannot say whether you have achieved your objective. Success or failure in relation to a goal does not make sense when the goal is unclear.

More important is that central to the pioneering mindset is trial and error. It is not trial and success. It is trial and *error.* Failure, if you want to use the word, is built into the very process. Successful entrepreneurs expect "failures". As Amazon boss Jeff Bezos said, "Willingness to invest requires a willingness to fail and to be misunderstood for long periods of time."[2]

If going through the process "successfully" requires "failure", if "success" involves "failing", is the language of success and failure very helpful? When a scientific experiment does not work, do you blame the scientist for being a failure? Likewise, if you dipped

---

1 www.freshexpressions.org.uk/stories/stlukesinthehighstreet/aug13 (accessed 16 August 2013).

2 *The Sunday Times,* 11 August 2011.

your toe in the water, joined another Christian to explore starting a witnessing community, and found that it was not going to work, would it make sense to say that you had failed?

Why not call it success?! You would have had a look and drawn a sensible conclusion – given what you have got and the circumstances, a community does not look possible. Even if you were to take several steps down the track and decide to go no further, this would still not be failure. You would have drawn sensible conclusions at each stage.

In the process, of course, you would have talked to people, listened to them, got to know them better, and perhaps blessed them through your conversations. You would have no idea what the Spirit had done, unseen, in those conversations.

"But," you may ask, "what if we start something, and it ends up being chaotic and people are hurt?" The answer is that you would be in great company! It is exactly what happened to Paul. Look at the church in Corinth! The best way to avoid being like Corinth is to stay humble and seek advice along the way.

When you adopt a pioneering mindset, "success" and "failure" are not the most important considerations. What *does* matter is learning, because experimentation is all about discovery. For disciples of Jesus, for whom learning is the essence of discipleship, the heart of this learning is discovering what God is up to. Christians have called this type of learning "discernment".

Seeking the Spirit

The key to success is not a magic formula to achieve a predetermined goal. It is discovering what the Spirit wants you to learn from your experiences and what you are being called to in the future. Success is about being in tune with the Holy Spirit. It is about being filled with the Spirit in every part of your life, especially in your decision-making.

This means that discernment should be central to your planning. Your inability to see more than one or two steps ahead does not mean that you will avoid planning. Dwight Eisenhower, the World War Two general and later US president, said, "In preparing for battle I have always found that plans are useless, but planning is indispensable."

Planning as discernment

This is especially true if you are starting a witnessing community. Discernment, as a central part of your planning, is crucial because it involves a path of discovery, of learning how the Spirit is leading you. In particular, planning as discernment is:

- *A spiritual means of learning from experience.* Through prayer and reflection in the light of Scripture, you can take stock. "What has happened since we last met? What has surprised us? What have been the difficulties? What can we celebrate? What is the Spirit saying to us in all this?" "What should we do in the light of our learning?"

- *A spiritual tool to chart your course.* Again in the context of prayer and Scripture, learning from experience can help you to discern what the Spirit is calling you to next. "This seems to be working well. It's not what we expected. But maybe the Spirit wants us to focus on it."

- *A spiritual aid to using resources well.* In the rush of life, you and others in your community will not have time and energy to waste. As the leaders of St Laurence, Reading found, it can be easy to take lots of initiatives but see little fruit. Chapter 4 described how it was only when they evaluated what they were doing, with the help of a senior church leader, that they found a way to plan activities that did prove fruitful.

Planning is not an optional extra, therefore. With discernment at its heart, it can be a vital spiritual discipline for navigating the journey – for spotting what the Spirit is up to.

As part of this discernment, you might ask, "What would fruitfulness look like? Not after two or three years – we can't yet imagine that, but after two or three months. If we looked back over three months, what would it mean to say that it has been a fruitful period? How would we recognize this fruitfulness?" Recognition – identifying traces of the Holy Spirit – is at the heart of planned discernment.

Imagine, for example, that two or three of you feel called to work with a community of migrants. You imagine together how you might listen to the migrants you know, how you could talk to one or two of the secular agencies familiar with this community, and how you could contact other Christian groups who have worked in similar contexts.

As you discuss this, you ask what fruitfulness would look like after three months. Perhaps it would comprise the results of conversations with three migrants about their longings for and frustrations with life, the outcomes of talking to one agency about the opportunities and pitfalls of working with this community, and identifying one Christian group you might speak to.

Having agreed that these outcomes would be fruitful, you make them your aims. You do not start with more distant goals and ask how you would achieve them – an organizational mindset. You start with the here-and-now, ask what you can do next, and turn the outcomes of these next steps into your goals. It is through these outcomes that you pray the Spirit will speak.

Milestone reviews

You can make planning a process of discernment by having regular milestone reviews. In the context of prayer and Bible study, reviews are times when you look back, look forward, and decide on the next steps. They are the Spirit's engine for driving the initiative forward.

So whether you are talking informally in a café or are in a more structured meeting, why don't you base your review on these three questions (which we also came across in the last chapter)?

- *What has happened?* When we last met, what did we imagine that fruitfulness would be like in the coming months? What have we done since then? What else has happened? Have things turned out the way we prayerfully hoped? So what is the Spirit teaching us?

- *What could happen?* As we look forward, what are the possibilities? What are we anxious and hopeful about? Where might the Spirit be leading us? What would fruitfulness look like?

- *What will happen?* In the light of our discussion and prayer, what steps shall we take?

From time to time, you may want to stand back and take a longer view. You could look back over the year and forward to the next one (perhaps longer), asking the same three questions. Subsequent planning meetings should keep this more distant horizon in mind. "We thought fruitfulness in a year's time would look like so-and-so. Three months into the year, is that what we are starting to see? Is the Spirit calling us to change our expectations?"

Your experience will not be driven by a distant, well-defined goal: as you adjust your expectations, your goal will be clarified by your experience.

Finding the Spirit through relationships

In these milestone reviews, how might you recognize the Spirit? The answer is that no neat formula exists! The more closely you walk with Jesus, the more likely you are to get a second sense of where and how he is at work. But, even then, God can be like a creature in the undergrowth – present but hard to spot.

Drawing on Scripture, Christians have been much clearer about the relationships involved in discernment. There may be no simple formula, but there are relationships. These are the interlocking relationships at the heart of the church – with God, with the world, with the wider body, and within the fellowship, all focused on Jesus. We discussed these in Chapter 2.

Your milestone reviews should be the hub of these four sets of relationships:

- *with God* directly through prayer and Bible study. Many Christians who start witnessing communities make these a regular part of their planning;

- *with the world* by continually listening to those you serve and others in the context. For example, you might plan over the next few weeks to test your ideas on some of the people you are seeking to serve;

- *with the wider church,* such as your prayer partners, others who have started an initiative like yours, Christians whose wisdom you respect, and, if appropriate, the leaders of your parent church;

- *within the fellowship.* As planning is shared within the Christian core, it will be enriched by members' gifts.

Discernment happens as God speaks through these sets of relationships. The central task of your planning process is to listen to what is being said, draw together the different threads, and prayerfully sift through all that you hear. What patterns seem to emerge? Do they have a Jesus shape to them? What warms your heart and gives you energy? If Jesus was visibly with you, how might he respond to all that you are hearing?

There is no formula to discernment because discernment happens through relationships. Relationships can never be boxed in. They always take you by surprise.

The secret of success

So, in starting and growing witnessing communities, what are the keys to success? First, adopt a pioneering mindset. Go step by step. Learn to be comfortable with trial and *error*. Experimentation will be the crux of all you do. Allow it to be God's voice to you, and learn from each step you take.

Second, turn this mindset into a process of discernment. Have regular milestone reviews, whether formal or informal. Put prayer at their heart as you look back and forward. Keep asking, "What is the Holy Spirit saying to us?"

Third, root this discernment in your relationships with God through prayer and Bible study, with the people you serve, with those in the wider church who have wisdom to share and are praying for you, and within the Christian core of your initiative. Turn your milestone reviews into a voyage of discovery, steered by the Spirit through these relationships.

You will find that witnessing communities are glorious opportunities to make Jesus public in every aspect of life. More and more Christians are getting involved. In ten Church of England dioceses, these communities comprise 15 per cent of all the churches. The majority are led by lay people, often in their spare time, usually in small teams, which can be as tiny as two or three.[3] Most have been started in the last ten years.

---

3 "Church Growth Research Project, "Report on Strand 3b: An analysis of fresh expressions of Church and church plants begun in the period 1992–2012", October 2013, p. 26, available from Church Army Research Unit.

The Spirit is doing a new thing, and ordinary Christians are leading the way. So why sit on the sidelines and miss out? God's church works, not in a theoretical, disembodied way, but through relationships in the messiness of life.

So, as you listen, assess, change course, and trust God to bring your work to completion, remember that the church is God's gift to the world – a gift to encourage, to heal, to provide foretastes of heaven, and to signpost the time, the promise ahead, when Jesus will complete all things and God will be all in all.

APPENDIX: HOW TO EVALUATE PROGRESS

Evaluation has had a bad press in the secular world. Frequently targets are imposed from outside, are not owned by those involved, and privilege some stakeholders (such as funders) over others (often those served by the initiative). Surely we do not want the same culture creeping into the church?

However, if rooted in healthy theology, evaluation in the church can feel very different.

- It will be welcomed by the witnessing community as a tool for discerning the Spirit's guidance.

- It will not be done *to* the community, but will be a shared process, owned by all the parties involved.

- It will be an instrument of the Spirit, not of a particular stakeholder.

Why evaluate?

For evaluation to be a positive experience, the first step is to move beyond the standard pragmatic rationales. These often rest on the requirements of those who have an outside stake in the initiative.

A local church, denomination, or network, for example, will understandably want to know that the community is remaining faithful to the gospel, that it is progressing towards agreed objectives, and that it is proving fruitful. Especially if funding is involved, decisions can then be made about whether the community warrants continued support.

On this model, evaluation becomes a tool for judging whether to keep backing the initiative. Assessments are made about whether the community deserves support. No wonder it can feel threatening to those being scrutinized!

A different starting point is to see evaluation as a contribution to the process of spiritual discernment. The purpose is not to assess whether support is justified, but to discover where and how the Spirit has been at work. Evaluation becomes a means of learning from experience, a tool to chart your course, and an aid to using your resources well.

On this view, evaluation is a process of recognizing fruitfulness. These fruits do not appear once a witnessing community is serving the people it is called to. Fruitfulness can be present at every stage of the journey beforehand.

Fruitfulness can be understood as the results of your decisions and actions. A conversation can be fruitful if you learn something or get to know the other person better. An experimental barbecue can be fruitful even though hardly anyone showed up: a throwaway remark during the evening gives you another idea to try.

Fruitfulness, therefore, is much more than the outcomes of your initiative – the number of people your community reaches, how well they are being served, the numbers coming to faith, and so on. Fruitfulness certainly includes these, but it goes beyond them. It includes signs of the Spirit at work during the journey.

"Results" get redefined. They are not something you see only at the end. They are something you can look for all the way through. A "result" is when you say or do something and the outcome has a flavour of the Spirit. Discernment is the process, week in and week out, of identifying these flavours to help you recognize what the Spirit wants you to do next.

Evaluation contributes to discernment by looking at the recent past. It is a stocktaking exercise: "Let's stand back and see where the Holy Spirit has been at work." It can be both low-key as part of milestone reviews, and something more periodic and substantial.

Who decides?

Witnessing communities do not grow on their own. They may be part of a local church or under the wing of a denomination.

Even if they are independent, they should still have links to the wider church. They should be backed by a group of Christians praying for them, their leaders should have made themselves accountable to a mature Christian outside the context, and they should be in fellowship with other Christian groupings.

This involvement of the wider church can raise difficult questions about evaluation. Where does final authority lie? How far can evaluation be left to each witnessing community? How much attention should be paid to the larger church, whether the parent denomination or the leader's mentor?

Two blind alleys

One extreme is to think that your witnessing community somehow floats free of the universal church. Some Christians behave as if the Spirit came at Pentecost, went to sleep for the next 2,000 years, and has now woken up to guide them uniquely in their gathering.

This is patently absurd. The Spirit has been active in the church for two millennia. Witnessing communities belong to a rich spiritual history. You cannot airbrush out the wisdom accrued over that time. Nor, unless you are independent, can you ignore the DNA of your local church or denomination. You may be able to stretch the expectations of your parent church (and that may prove a blessing to it), but you cannot presume that the latter will have no boundaries at all.

The other extreme is to believe that the existing church should call the shots. Having listened to the emerging community, it should draw on its repository of wisdom to have the final say. But why should the existing church be immune to human frailty? Its views and approaches have their share of fallibility. Indeed, God often calls the new to challenge the old – think of the long history of revivals.

The existing church should remember that it brings to the world a gift from God – the gift of life with Jesus inside the kingdom. It is in the nature of giving that you cannot dictate the terms on which the gift is received.

If I give my four-year-old grandson a toy plane, then spend the afternoon holding his hand and showing him exactly how to play with it, it ceases to be a gift to him. It becomes in effect a gift to me, a chance for me to relive my childhood.

In the same way, once believers have passed on the gospel, how the gospel is received, understood, and lived out in Christian community must be left ultimately to the recipients, as they listen to the Spirit through Scripture, prayer, and careful deliberation.

In the global South, new believers have often ended up using Scripture to criticize those who brought them the gospel. Zulu Christians, for example, used Genesis 3:21 to justify their habit of dressing in skins. They criticized the missionaries for not being properly dressed! Elsewhere, African Christians complained that missionary churches were unfaithful to the Bible, which allows dancing in worship.[1]

At the risk of overstatement, when new believers use the Bible to correct those who introduced them to Jesus, there is a sense in which the bearers of the gospel have finished their job.

---

1 Lamin Sanneh, *Translating the Message: The Missionary Impact on Culture*, Maryknoll: Orbis, 1989, p. 176.

"Success" is not Christian communities that conform to existing expressions of church, but communities that have the capacity, through the Spirit, to criticize existing church.

It is only through mutual correction – the old challenging the new and the new challenging the old – that the whole church can grow into a fuller understanding of Christ.

Discerning together

Evaluation, therefore, should be a shared journey – shared by the witnessing community coming to birth and the existing church from which it is being born. Inevitably this will be a messy process, sometimes with tensions and differences of view. No satnav exists to provide step-by-step guidance, but there is wisdom gleaned from how the first believers faced a similar situation.

The early church was at first almost entirely Jewish. Believers understood their faith in Jewish terms. They continued to worship in the temple, for example (Acts 2:46). But when a growing number of Gentiles started to find Jesus, the leaders faced the challenge of welcoming believers from very different backgrounds, with different understandings of what it meant to follow Christ. Not least, these Gentile Christians did not expect to be circumcised, whereas circumcision was central to Jewish identity.

The situation was not dissimilar to today. Through new Christian communities, people with little or no church background are streaming into the faith. In the Church Army Research Unit's survey, two-fifths of those attending fresh expressions of church had no significant church experience.[2]

Many who are new to church, and some who have been instrumental in bringing them to faith, have an understanding of

---

2 Church Growth Research Project, "Report on Strand 3b: An analysis of fresh expressions of Church and church plants begun in the period 1992–2012", October 2013, p. 6, available from Church Army Research Unit.

what it means to be a Christian community that is very different from that of people in more traditional church. They put a greater emphasis on eating together, for instance. Preaching and other aspects of worship can take new forms. Community may be more about keeping in touch between meetings than about gathering every week.

How did the early church rise to the challenge of welcoming new believers who saw the faith through different spectacles? Acts 15 describes the Council of Jerusalem, where some of the issues were thrashed out.

- There was "much discussion", which gave time to air different views.

- Both sides spoke openly and directly.

- People listened.

- Stories were told and interpreted in the light of Scripture.

- The Holy Spirit was seen to have been involved.

- A solution was reached that gave something to both parties – Gentiles did not have to be circumcised but were to observe certain Jewish food laws. Honest conversation led to give and take on both sides.

Paul did not go off and lead a breakaway Gentile church. Instead, time and again he made strenuous efforts to remain in fellowship with the more "traditional" Jewish believers. In Acts 21 he returned at great risk to Jerusalem and took part in the Jewish purification ritual.

Equally, the Jewish leaders in Jerusalem did not impose circumcision on Gentile converts. They did not seek to turn the new Christians into Jews. They respected the Gentiles' cultural distinctiveness. They recognized that church would look different among them.

Nor did they prescribe lots of detail. They laid down a few requirements in Acts 15:29, but explicitly avoided "burdening" the new Christians with anything more (verse 28). They adopted a low-control, high-trust approach. Paul's new churches were free to develop their own ways of following Jesus, guided by the Spirit and the Scriptures of the day (our Old Testament), and under the supervision of Paul and his team.

Shared evaluation

How these lessons are applied today will depend on circumstances. Where witnessing communities are largely independent, the existing church may have little direct involvement. Involvement, such as it is, may come through the community's prayer partners, the leader's accountability to a mature Christian, and believing members' involvement in the life of the wider church. Values and expectations of the larger family will filter into the community.

For communities linked explicitly to a local church, denomination, or network, the involvement may be more direct, not least through some form of accountability.

However the wider church and witnessing communities relate to one another, they should learn from the first Christians. They must talk honestly with each other, listen carefully, tell stories, interpret these under Scripture, involve the Spirit, where there is disagreement look for give-and-take solutions, remain committed to one another, and adopt a light-touch approach to accountability.

Some in witnessing communities may be tempted to feel that this is rather constraining. But their relationship to the wider Christian family will also be a huge source of strength, especially as they draw on the church's store of spiritual and practical wisdom. Witnessing communities should celebrate the gifts of the whole family.

They should welcome, too, opportunities to share their own experiences of walking with the Spirit. These can be a blessing to the wider church. So much of what we treasure today was given to the wider body by new expressions of church. Remember the Reformation! Sharing evaluation can be a journey of giving and receiving on both sides.

What should be evaluated – and how?

Some people, often church authorities, emphasize numbers – how many people are served by the community, have come to faith, attend the main meeting, and so on.

Numbers can certainly play a part. When Jesus sent out the seventy-two disciples, he encouraged them to go to where people responded. If they were welcomed by the town they were to stay there. If not, they were to move on (Luke 10:8–12). Response mattered. Counting heads can be a means of evaluating whether there is a positive response.

The danger is that concentrating on numbers leaves out too much else that is important. What is counted becomes all that counts. The kingdom is too multifaceted to be reduced to figures.

Others emphasize quality, such as Christian maturity. Ephesians 4:12–13 envisages that the church will be built up till its members become "mature, attaining to the whole measure of the fullness of Christ". If that is a mission statement for the church, they say, we should evaluate whether we have achieved it.

The trouble is that Christian maturity is an elusive term. Put ten churchgoers together and you will get ten descriptions of maturity! The concept is too slippery to measure easily.

Behind both approaches lies a bigger problem. Too much stress is placed on outcomes – numbers or maturity – and not enough on the process. The emphasis is on results instead of helping you to learn. Evaluation becomes more like marking the paper than preparing you for the exam. It gets close to "pass or fail". It feels like judgement rather than support.

Formative or summative?

Educationalists talk about formative and summative assessments.

Formative assessments help to form students. They aid them in their learning. Feedback on a test or essay enables the student to identify weaknesses and work on them.

Summative assessments summarize what the student has learned. They measure student learning against a benchmark or standard. They have a "pass-or-fail" element.

Evaluation should mainly have a formative purpose. It should help you learn what the Spirit is doing. As you reflect on your community's journey, evaluation should help you to recognize where the Spirit has been active (and where not), so that you can discern the direction in which the Spirit is leading you next.

A theory of change

For evaluation to do this, you need an understanding of the journey – an outline map. You must be able to recognize when you have reached a milestone and have some idea of where the next one lies.

In the voluntary sector, this map is sometimes described as a theory of change. To evaluate effectively, organizations need to understand what change they are seeking to accomplish and how. If a project is working with drug addicts, for example, its leaders should have a "theory" about how it will promote change.

The theory might be that a drop-in centre will be available to addicts, who will build relationships with the case workers and other addicts. Through these relationships addicts will be invited to a support group. Once they attend regularly, they will meet with a case worker who will help them to access other forms of support. By means of this support, they will address what lies behind their addiction and eventually become less dependent on drugs.

Evaluation will then centre on the journey addicts are expected to make:

- Is the first step working? Are addicts coming to the drop-in centre? If not, why not and what should be done?

- Is the next step working? Are addicts being invited to a support group? If not, again why not and what should be done?

- Is the third step working? Are addicts attending the support group regularly? Again if not, what could be done to increase their commitment?

- Further steps on the journey will be addressed in a similar way.

Evaluation becomes a "formative" process. It becomes a means of assessing whether each stage of the journey is achieving its aims and how the stage can be improved.

There is likely to be a "summative" element as well, and funders will almost certainly require it. This will consist of measuring how many addicts break free of their dependence and for how long.

Yet the summative assessment will not stand alone. It will be part of formative evaluation and contribute to it. Leaders and funders will use the results to check whether the journey as a whole is effective. Are addicts coming off drugs?

If the summative evaluation suggests that few are doing so, the leaders might question their theory of change. Is there something wrong with it? Does the theory ignore other factors that help to free addicts from drugs? How might the journey be adapted to take account of these factors?

Used like this, summative – and formative – evaluation can aid learning. If the results were disappointing, a funder might say, "This is not a reason to withdraw funding. We have confidence in the leaders of this project. We know the project is experimental. So let's discover what the leaders are learning about their theory of change and how they are developing it."

A serving-first journey

In Chapter 4 we thought about several theories of change in relation to witnessing communities. For example, communities serving people who have never been to church are likely to travel on *A serving-first journey*, as in the diagram below.

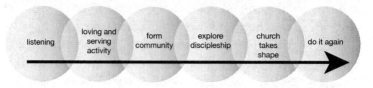

This is very much an outline. Each community will fill in the details differently. Some of the stages may overlap to a considerable extent or be taken in a different order.

Often you will not know what each stage looks like till you get to it. Even so, having this map may help you to see the direction of travel and provide a framework for your evaluation process. "The Spirit has led us to this point in the journey. Where might we be heading next?"

Discernment becomes a matter of imagining concretely what the next stage will look like. Evaluation will help you to assess whether your expectations have been met.

A medical café

Suppose two or three of you are talking to your local medical centre. As with "Coffee in the Living Room" described in Chapter 7, you are thinking of starting a weekly café for patients of the medical practice, especially those who feel lonely.

At the outset, you might imagine that "listening" will include requesting the minister for use of the church, asking the patients if they would be interested, and approaching some potential volunteers. Evaluation becomes very simple: did these things happen and what were the results? What might you learn from your findings?

As you head towards "loving and serving", perhaps you start to plan the café. At the end of each meeting you visualize what would be a fruitful few weeks before you next meet – what conversations you need to have, what outcomes you hope for, and so on. You turn these into concrete steps. At the next meeting, evaluation involves each person describing what happened as a result of the steps they took.

So you go on till the café opens. Then you evaluate whether the café is achieving your hopes for it at this stage. As you approached the opening date, you will have described what fruitfulness would look like for the café in its opening weeks – how people would hear about the café, the numbers you hoped to attend, how guests would be welcomed, the seating arrangements, the refreshments, and so on.

After the café has opened, you evaluate whether your prayerful hopes have been realized. Where things have not worked as you expected, you discuss how to put them right. Perhaps the numbers coming are not as large as you thought. Were you over-optimistic? Has there been a hiccup in the publicity? Are health-centre staff doing enough to invite their patients?

As you take the next steps – to "form community" – you continue to approach evaluation in the same way.

Annual reviews

Gradually, the *serving-first journey* takes shape. As it does so, maybe you imagine what fruitfulness in the café would look like in a year's time. You keep this in mind as you plan your next steps during the year. After taking each step, you evaluate what happened and periodically ask whether you are on track to see what you expected at the year end.

After twelve months, you see where you have got to. How close is the café to what you expected fruitfulness to look like? If there is a divergence (which could well be the case), why has that happened? What can you learn from the journey you have been on?

Used in this way, evaluation is common sense. It is what anyone does if they are planning well. You look forward to the next step, prayerfully imagine what that step will comprise to be fruitful, and then – through evaluation – see if what you hoped for has occurred. At the end of the year, you supplement this formative evaluation with an evaluation that has a stronger summative feel.

From time to time, summative evaluations may involve a more substantial review, centred on "How can we do things better?" You might ask an outsider with suitable experience to cast some fresh eyes over what you are doing. Or two of you might visit a comparable initiative to garner some ideas.

Some questions to ask

To help you imagine this evaluation process, below are some questions you might ask, using *A serving-first journey* as the template. The questions mainly have a formative purpose, but some summative ones have been included as well.

I have separated out "Qualitative" and "Quantitative" questions, though some overlap. This is because most people leading witnessing communities prefer a qualitative approach.

However, a denomination (or network of churches) or a funder may require some figures. Numbers are concrete and appear objective. You may of course dispute their value, but equally you may not have a choice. So I have also included some "Quantitative" questions.

Both sets of questions are no more than thought-starters. Some may not apply to your situation, and no doubt you will think of others that do.

Denominations, networks or funders may require you to relate your measurements to your objectives – what you hoped to achieve during the period being reviewed. And you may want this, too. So under each heading you may wish to list some simple objectives.

Under "Listening", for example, you might say, "We aim to speak to fifty people in the coming year (one a week), have three conversations with at least twenty of them, and one in-depth conversation with seven of them." If you set such precise goals, remember that the Spirit will often blow you off course. So, in your review, don't be worried about this but be willing to explain why things turned out differently.

Some good examples of objectives and further questions you might ask, using a slightly different formative journey, can be found in the Toronto Diocese's "Missional Waymarks", www.toronto.anglican.ca/uploads.php?id=4f32e4c3209ba

Listening

Qualitative

- What themes stand out?

- What are people's hopes and longings?

- What opportunities to serve them can you envisage?

- How have they reacted to your specific proposals or what you have tried?

- Where are they on "A post-modern path to faith", described on p. 144?

Quantitative

- How many people have you spoken to?

- How many were men and women, in specified age bands, and in other demographic categories?

- What is the average number of conversations you have had with each? For how long?

- Where were these conversations held (number in each category)?

- How many were churchgoers and how many were not? Of the latter, how many have had significant church experience and how many not?

- In some of your qualitative findings, how many people said what? (E.g. among the reactions to your proposals, can you categorize the responses and state how many respondents were in each category?)

Loving and serving

Qualitative

- In what ways have you been loving and serving people?

- What stories reflect well and less well on what you have been doing?

- For the team, what have been the high and the low points of the past year?

- What were your hopes at the start of the year and how far have they been achieved?

- What has surprised you and what have you learned?

- What ideas for improvement have people suggested?

Quantitative

- How many people in your network or neighbourhood do team members meet regularly?

- What are the average numbers at your main event – at the start of the year? At the end?

- What is the overall number of people you are in touch with (e.g. you see them at least once or twice a year)?

- What are the results (in relation to your service) of your satisfaction survey, if you have done one?

Community

Qualitative

- What form(s) does your community life take?

- What do you do to encourage community?

- What comments have people made that reflect well or less well on your community life?

- What stories illustrate the strengths and weaknesses of your community?

- What criteria would you use to assess the health of your community (e.g. a warm welcome, plenty of chance to chat, no pressure, opportunities to do things together), and how well do you think you are doing in each case?

- What suggestions have individuals made that would improve your community life?

Quantitative

- How many attend regularly? Occasionally?

- How many of those you serve have regular responsibilities in the community?

- How many help occasionally?

- In evaluating the health of your community against your criteria, how would the team rate each of the criteria on a scale of 1–5 (5 is outstanding)? E.g. welcome is 4.

- What are the results (in relation to community) from your satisfaction survey, if you have done one?

Explore discipleship

Qualitative

- What signposts to Jesus have you put in place, such as those discussed in Chapter 4 (acts of kingdom kindness, stories about Jesus, prayer and healing, and missional worship)?

- What feedback have you had from these activities?

- Who are these signposts engaging and who are they not?

- What stories/comments have you found encouraging and less encouraging?

Quantitative

- Can you put figures to the number of people involved in any of the signposts you have described above?

- Looking at "A post-modern path to faith" on page 144, can you roughly estimate how many are at each stage?

- Can you estimate how many have moved from one stage to the next?

Church takes shape

Qualitative

- What experiences of church are the people you serve beginning to have in your community?

- What intentional steps are you taking to make disciples (e.g. one-to-one mentoring, small groups, courses, drawing people into the worshipping life of the core team, shared spiritual rhythms)?

- What is worship beginning to look like?

- What are the signs that the four interlocking relationships of church (described in Chapter 2) are emerging – with God directly, within the fellowship, with the world, and with the wider church?

- What spiritual practices are you focusing on?

- In what ways are new believers being involved in some form of leadership?

- What feedback have you had? What stories/comments have been encouraging and less encouraging?

- What were you hoping to see by this stage? How much of this has happened? What has surprised you?

Quantitative

- How many people are involved in each of your intentional steps to make disciples? At the start of the year? At the end?

- How many on average attend your act of worship? At the start of the year? At the end?

- How many do you estimate occasionally attend your worship?

- Can you put figures to any other items in the "Qualitative" list – e.g. numbers involved in some form of leadership, numbers giving positive and negative feedback, numbers who in some way are connecting with the wider church?

- Of those involved, for what proportion is it their only expression of church? How many are also involved in another church?

Do it again

Qualitative

- What are you doing to encourage people to start another witnessing community?

- What stories/comments indicate positive and negative responses?

- What opportunities do you see to "do it again"?

- What are the obstacles?

- What witnessing communities can you envisage being born in the next year or two?

Quantitative

- How many witnessing communities has your community given birth to over the past year?

- How many are currently being considered? Are in the process of being formed?

- How many communities can you envisage being formed in the next year or two?

Ways of capturing this information include:

- Discussion by the core team.

- Discussion during the community's main meeting.

- A focus group drawn from the people the community serves.

- A simple questionnaire for those involved in the community.

- A "mystery visitor" to the community. This could entail the person talking to members of the community about an agreed list of topics.

- A focus group of people from completely outside the community – how do they view what you are doing?

How to keep evaluating

As your initiative develops, you will pray that it will serve others effectively, that community will form and grow and some people will come to faith, that as they do they will have a taste of church where they are, and that some of the new believers will start witnessing communities in another slice of their lives.

When this all happens, your community will have come to the end of *A serving-first journey*. To be sure, *individuals* will still be travelling through the circles – new people will be loved and served, drawn into the community, and find Jesus. But the community as a whole will have reached the final circle. What happens to evaluation then?

Four sets of relationships

You may want to adopt a different framework. Though you may not think of your community as a church or congregation, you may want to base your evaluation on the four sets of relationships at the heart of church and which are centred on Jesus:

- UP: relationships with the Father, Son and Holy Spirit.

- OUT: relationships with the world.

- IN: relationships within the fellowship.

- OF: relationships with the wider Christian family. You are part *of* the body of Christ.

If individuals are finding faith and your community is becoming church for them, you will want them to experience these four sets of relationships, and you will want other Christians in the community to be growing in these relationships too. The more your witnessing community is maturing in these sets of relationships, the better it will represent the body of Christ.

Be specific

Using this as your framework, evaluation will be similar to the approach you used during *A serving-first journey*. But it will be less pragmatic and more structured around goals. In terms of the two mindsets discussed in Chapter 10, it will have a stronger organizational flavour.

Perhaps at the start of the year, you and others in the community will prayerfully imagine what growth might look like in each of these four sets of relationships.

You will want to keep it simple – and concrete: every time you come up with a suggestion, ask yourselves, "How would we recognize this?" So instead of saying, "We would like to see people growing in their discipleship", ask, "In what two or three ways would we like to see growth in discipleship?"

Being specific will help you to picture the steps you might take to encourage these forms of growth. It will enable you at the end of the year to recognize – and thank God for – the growth that has taken place.

Evaluation will be the process of looking back, recognizing the fruit you have prayed for, recognizing also the absence of certain fruit, and perhaps identifying fruit that you did not expect. "We prayed that our new Christians would come once or twice to 'weekend church', perhaps as a step towards dual church involvement. Instead, they warmed to our Saturday prayer retreat."

Some possibilities

Imagine your "medical café" has travelled on *A serving-first journey*. The Christian core has begun to have lunch after the café closes at the end of each Thursday morning. Several people are coming to faith and have joined the core for lunch, where there is prayer, Bible study, and other flavours of church.

One early January, you suggest that the core group spend lunch prayerfully dreaming about how the group could grow in its spiritual life during the coming year. You invite members to think about the four sets of relationships at the core of church. For each set of relationships, what one or two steps might be a sign that the Spirit had been at work in their lives?

Perhaps the group comes up with something like this:

- *The UP relationship:* deepen our worship by including Holy Communion occasionally and running a short course (in the evening?) to introduce the gospels. The latter would help our Bible study, which could be based on the gospels.

- *The OUT relationships:* survey café guests on the themes, "How could we serve you better? How else could we serve you?" Use the results to inform our prayers during lunch, and see where the Spirit leads us.

- *The IN relationships:* introduce a couple of social events for café guests, one in the spring and the other in the autumn, and prayerfully reflect on the response. Does there seem to be an appetite for this sort of thing? What else might we do?

- *The OF relationships:* invite the minister to lead Holy Communion to strengthen the link with our parent church; try listening to three podcast talks as another way of connecting with the wider Christian family.

Towards the end of the year, the group might evaluate these suggestions. Did they all happen? What were the results? Were there other signs of growth? What gaps remain in the community's life? What is the Holy Spirit saying through all this? In the light of this prayerful discussion, what might growth in these sets of relationships look like over the next twelve months? For example:

- Should we be paying more attention to the spiritual gifts?

- Should we encourage the community to support a project in the global South?

- Should we be more proactive in inviting café guests to initiate or help with social events?

- Should we as the core group attend a particular conference that our denomination or network is organizing?

Putting some numbers to it

The above approach is largely formative. You may feel that there should be a stronger summative element, with numbers where possible. Your denomination/network or funder may also require this.

If that is the case, you may be able to develop some proxy measurements of your community's health and progress. These proxies would certainly not tell the whole story, but would be an improvement on many existing numerical measurements – for example:

The UP relationship with the Father, Son and Holy Spirit:

- What is the average attendance at the community's main worship event?

- How many people are involved in Christian discovery groups, and in Christian formation or accountability groups?

- How many people are giving financially to the community on a regular basis? On average how much? How have these figures changed over the last two or three years?

- How many are involved in the community's mission activities? (If mission is a priority for God, it will be a priority for those who are nurturing their relationship with him.)

The OUT relationship with the world:

- How many people are being served by the community in an average week?

- What feedback are they giving through your satisfaction survey, if you do one?

- How many people left the community last year (and why)?

- How many new people have started coming regularly to the community's main event – from another church? Once-churched? Never-churched?

The OF relationship with the wider church:

- How many of the community's leaders and members attended events in the wider church last year?

- How many of these events did they attend?

- What proportion of the community's budget is spent on supporting Christians in the wider church?

The IN relationships within the community:

- How many people attend the community regularly and identify with it? (This might be the basis of an "affiliation list", whose total would be used in denominational returns.)

- What proportion of the list usually attends – for example – weekly, monthly, three-monthly?

- What proportion of the list keep in touch with each other between meetings, face to face or online?

- What proportion of the list volunteer within the community?

NB: Especially in larger witnessing communities, you may need a survey to capture some of this information.

Seven reasons to do it

This overall approach to evaluation has a number of advantages:

- *It is straightforward.* It is the sort of thing that you would be doing anyway if you were planning prayerfully and carefully.

- *It is not an extra burden,* therefore. Evaluation can be easily incorporated into your community's life.

- *It introduces some discipline and rigour* into your discernment, as you keep asking: What has happened? What can we learn from what happened?

- *It stops the community growing stale.* You can keep moving on as you ask: What has the Spirit been doing? What are we being summoned to next?

- *It focuses on discernment.* Evaluation is not a pass-or-fail exam. It is recognizing what the Holy Spirit has been up to in your experience, to help you discern what you are being called to next. It is akin to a concerned tutor rather than a severe judge.

- *It enables outside bodies to monitor progress.* Whether it is the parent church, the denomination or a grant-making agency, *A serving-first journey*, for example, offers milestones against which to measure progress. It allows for shared discernment about sensible next steps in the light of the journey so far.

- *It offers a model of evaluation to the wider church.* Any congregation can prayerfully imagine how it might grow in the four sets of interlocking relationships that comprise church, and look back to see how God has answered its prayers. Evaluation should be for existing, as well as new, expressions of church.

BIBLIOGRAPHY

Useful websites

http://www.acpi.org.uk

http://www.arthurrankcentre.org.uk/library-of-good-practice/item/6689-fresh-expressions-of-church-%E2%80%93-rural-examples-and-links

http://churchplantingcanada.ca

http://edstetzer.com

http://www.emergentkiwi.org.nz/

http://www.encountersontheedge.org.uk

http://www.exponential.org/

http://www.freshexpressions.ca/

http://www.freshexpressions.org.uk

http://freshexpressionsus.org/

http://inspiremovement.org/network/

http://jonnybaker.blogs.com/jonnybaker/worship_tricks/wtindex.html

http://onethousandandone.org

http://www.proost.co.uk/

http://www.urbanexpression.org.uk/

http://www.venturefx.org.uk/

http://vergenetwork.org/

http://www.youtube.com/user/freshexpressions

Selected reading

Addison, Steve, *Movements That Change the World. Five Keys to Spreading the Gospel*, Downers Grove: IVP, 2011.

Allen, Roland, *Missionary Methods – St Paul's or Ours?*, Cambridge: Lutterworth Press, 2006.

Atkins, Martyn, *Resourcing Renewal: Shaping Churches for the Emerging Future*, Peterborough: Inspire, 2007.

Baker, Jonny, *Curating Worship*, London: SPCK, 2010.

Bevans, Stephen B., *Models of Contextual Theology*, revised edition, Maryknoll: Orbis, 2002.

Breen, Mike and Alex Absalom, *Launching Missional Communities: A Field Guide*, 3DM, Kindle version, 2010.

Cole, Neil, *Organic Church: Growing Faith Where Life Happens*, San Francisco: Jossey-Bass, 2005.

Cray, Graham, Ian Mobsby, and Aaron Kennedy (eds), *Fresh Expressions and the Kingdom of God*, Norwich: Canterbury Press, 2012.

Cray, Graham, Ian Mobsby and Aaron Kennedy (eds), *New Monasticism as Fresh Expression of Church*, Norwich: Canterbury Press, 2010.

Croft, Steven (ed.), *Mission-shaped Questions: Defining Issues for Today's Church*, London: Church House Publishing, 2008.

Donovan, Vincent J., *Christianity Rediscovered: An Epistle from the Masai*, London: SCM, 2001.

Flett, John G., *The Witness of God: The Trinity, Missio Dei, Karl Barth, and the Nature of Christian Community*, Grand Rapids: Eerdmans, 2010.

Frost, Michael and Alan Hirsch, *The Shaping of Things to Come: Innovation and Mission for the 21st-Century Church*, Peabody: Hendrickson, 2003.

Gaze, Sally, *Mission-shaped and Rural: Growing Churches in the Countryside*, London: Church House Publishing, 2006, 978-071514084-0.

Glasson, Barbara, *Mixed-up Blessing: A New Encounter with Being Church*, Peterborough: Inspire, 2006.

Goodhew, David, Andrew Roberts and Michael Volland, *Fresh! Study Guide to Fresh Expressions and Pioneer Ministry*, London: SCM, 2012.

Halter, Hugh and Matt Smay, *The Tangible Kingdom: Creating Incarnational Community*, San Francisco: Jossey-Baker, 2008.

Hirsch, Alan, *The Forgotten Ways: Reactivating the Missional Church*, Grand Rapids: Brazos, 2006.

Hopkins, Bob and Freddy Hedley, *Coaching for Missional Leadership: Growing and Supporting Pioneers in Church Planting and Fresh Expressions*, Sheffield: ACPI Books, 2008.

Howe, Mark, *Online Church? First Steps Towards Virtual Incarnation*, Cambridge: Grove, 2007.

Jackson, Bob, *Hope for the Church*, London: Church House Publishing, 2002.

Lings, George and Stuart Murray, *Church Planting: Past, Present and Future*, Cambridge: Grove Books, 2003.

Lomax, Tim and Michael Moynagh, *Liquid Worship*, Cambridge: Grove Books, 2004.

Male, David, *Church Unplugged: Remodelling Church Without Losing Your Soul*, Milton Keynes: Authentic Media, 2008.

Male, David (ed.), *Pioneers 4 Life. Explorations in Theology and Wisdom for Pioneering Leaders*, Abingdon: Bible Reading Fellowship, 2011.

Mission-shaped Church. Church Planting and Fresh Expressions of Church in a Changing Context, London: Church House Publishing, 2004.

Moore, Lucy, *Messy Church: Fresh Ideas for Building a Christ-centred Community*, Oxford: Bible Reading Fellowship, 2006.

Morisy, Ann, *Journeying Out: A New Approach to Christian Mission*, London: Morehouse, 2004.

Moynagh, Michael, *Church for Every Context*, London: SCM, 2012.

Murray, Stuart, *Post-Christendom: Church and Mission in a Strange New World*, Carlisle: Paternoster, 2004.

Murray, Stuart, *Church After Christendom*, Carlisle: Paternoster, 2004.

Nelstrop, Louise and Martyn Percy (eds), *Evaluating Fresh Expressions: Explorations in Emerging Church*, Norwich: Canterbury, 2008.

Potter, Phil, *The Challenge of Change*, Abingdon: Bible Reading Fellowship, 2009.

Stetzer, Ed, *Planting Missional Churches*, Nashville: B & H Publishing, 2006.

Stetzer, Ed and Warren Bird, *Viral Churches. Helping Church Planters Become Movement Makers*, San Francisco: Jossey-Bass, 2010.

Stone, Matt, *Fresh Expressions of Church. Fishing Nets or Safety Nets?*, Cambridge: Grove Books, 2010.

Volland, Michael, *Through the Pilgrim Door: Pioneering a Fresh Expression of Church*, Eastbourne: Survivor Books, 2009.

Ward, Pete, *Liquid Church*, Carlisle: Paternoster, 2002.

INDEX